Coaching Lacrosse For Dummies®

Making Practice Fun

- Give every youngster lots of repetitions.
- Keep the kids active; don't force them to stand in lines.
- Involve the parents in drills sometimes to rev up the excitement and give practice a different look.
- Be enthusiastic and energetic; your attitude rubs off on the kids.
- Sprinkle your practices with new drills throughout the season to keep the kids' interest — and keep pace with their development.
- Take the time to plan your practices.
- If drills turn out to be boring or ineffective, discard them and switch to something else.
- Give the kids the chance to select their favorite drills to use during practice at different times throughout the season.
- Solicit feedback and ideas from older kids on drills you should use.
- Stop practice briefly to point out when players do things well — not just when they make mistakes.
- Applaud the slightest improvements to maintain your kids' interest.
- Conclude practice with the most popular drill to end the session on a high note.

Building Players' Confidence

- When providing feedback, use the "sandwich" method: Place a corrective remark between two encouraging comments.
- Reinforce the fact that making mistakes is part of learning. Even experienced lacrosse players make mistakes.
- Give kids high fives and pats on the back — for good plays, doing their best, and displaying good sportsmanship — so that they know that their efforts are appreciated.
- Set realistic goals so that players can gain a real sense of satisfaction upon reaching them.
- Maintain a positive tone of voice and positive body language during practices and games.

Keeping Players Motivated

- Continually encourage players to hustle and always put forth their best efforts.
- Stay in control of your emotions, and refrain from yelling instructions all the time.
- Allow kids the freedom to make mistakes, and coach effort over skills.
- Always exude confidence in your players' abilities.
- When correcting errors, use words that inspire confidence and reinforce positive thoughts. Instead of saying "Don't turn the ball over," say "Control the ball and make strong passes, just like you did so well in practice this week."

Pregame Responsibilities

- Arrive early to inspect the field for any hazards (broken glass, rocks, loose turf) that could pose injury risks to players.
- Set the tone for good sportsmanship by meeting with the opposing coach and officials.
- Make sure each player has all the necessary safety equipment.
- Have the kids warmed up properly before the game begins, using a series of light drills that cover all the main lacrosse skills.

For Dummies: Bestselling Book Series for Beginners

Coaching Lacrosse For Dummies®

Pregame Talk

- ✔ Speak in a calm, relaxed manner, with a smile on your face.
- ✔ Be brief.
- ✔ Conduct the talk away from any potential distractions.
- ✔ Stress the importance of having fun and displaying good sportsmanship at all times during the game.
- ✔ Avoid using pressure phrases like "Let's score ten goals today." Kids *can* give you their best effort, but they *can't* control the outcome of games.
- ✔ Build confidence by letting the players know that you're looking forward to watching them perform.

Halftime Talk

- ✔ Highlight the positives of the first half, regardless of the score, and stay upbeat. Don't dwell on any mistakes.
- ✔ Zero in on a couple of main points that you want to get across.
- ✔ Pile on the praise for the team's hard work in the first half.
- ✔ At the more advanced levels, solicit feedback and suggestions on strategy from your players.
- ✔ Encourage water consumption so that the players can rehydrate.

Postgame Talk

- ✔ Keep the focus on fun and what the kids enjoyed most about the game.
- ✔ Never let the scoreboard influence what you say or how you say it.
- ✔ Recognize the good sportsmanship your players displayed.
- ✔ Accentuate the positive.
- ✔ Conclude on a high note with a team cheer, and send the players home with a smile.

Positions in Boys' and Girls' Lacrosse

Boys' Team (10 Players)

Goalie

Three defensemen

Three midfielders

Three attackers

Girls' Team (12 Players)

Goalie

Five attackers: first home, second home, third home, and two attack wings

Six defenders: point, cover point, third player, center, and two defensive wings

For Dummies: Bestselling Book Series for Beginners

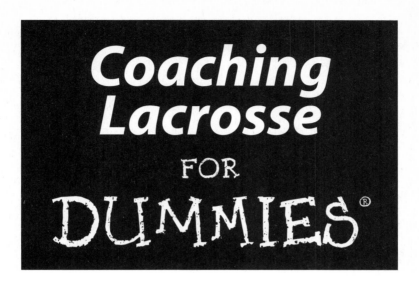

Coaching Lacrosse FOR DUMMIES®

by National Alliance For Youth Sports
with Greg Bach

Wiley Publishing, Inc.

Coaching Lacrosse For Dummies®

Published by
Wiley Publishing, Inc.
111 River St.
Hoboken, NJ 07030-5774
www.wiley.com

Copyright © 2008 by Wiley Publishing, Inc., Indianapolis, Indiana

Published by Wiley Publishing, Inc., Indianapolis, Indiana

Published simultaneously in Canada

For general information on our other products and services, please contact our Customer Care Department within the U.S. at 800-762-2974, outside the U.S. at 317-572-3993, or fax 317-572-4002.

For technical support, please visit www.wiley.com/techsupport.

Wiley also publishes its books in a variety of electronic formats. Some content that appears in print may not be available in electronic books.

Library of Congress Control Number: 2007943298

ISBN: 978-0-470-22699-5

Manufactured in the United States of America

10 9 8 7 6 5 4 3 2 1

WILEY

About the Authors

The National Alliance For Youth Sports has been America's leading advocate for positive and safe sports for children for more than 25 years. It serves volunteer coaches, parents with children involved in organized sports, game officials, youth sports administrators, league directors, and the youngsters who participate in organized sports. The Alliance's programs are utilized in more than 3,000 communities nationwide by parks and recreation departments, Boys & Girls Clubs, Police Athletic Leagues, YMCAs/YWCAs, and various independent youth service groups, as well as on military installations worldwide. For more information on the Alliance's programs, which are listed below, visit www.nays.org.

National Youth Sports Coaches Association — More than two million volunteer coaches have been trained through NYSCA, which provides training, support, and continuing education.

Parents Association for Youth Sports — Parents gain a clear understanding of their roles and responsibilities in youth sports through this sportsmanship training program, which is utilized in more than 500 communities nationwide.

Academy for Youth Sports Administrators — More than 1,500 administrators worldwide have gone through the Academy, which is a 20-hour certification program that raises the professionalism of those delivering youth sport services. A professional faculty presents the information, and participants earn Continuing Education Units (CEUs).

National Youth Sports Administrators Association — The program provides training, information, and resources for volunteer administrators responsible for the planning and implementation of out-of-school sports programs.

National Youth Sports Officials Association — Officials who go through this certification program gain valuable knowledge on skills, fundamentals, and the characteristics that every good official must possess.

Start Smart Sports Development Program — This proven instructional program prepares children for the world of organized sports without the threat of competition or the fear of getting hurt through an innovative approach that promotes parent-child bonding.

Hook A Kid On Golf — Thousands of children of all ages and skill levels tee it up every year in the nation's most comprehensive junior golf development program, which features an array of instructional clinics and tournaments to choose from.

Game On! Youth Sports — This worldwide effort introduces children to actual game experience by giving them the freedom to create and play on their own.

Greg Bach is the communications director for the National Alliance For Youth Sports (NAYS), a position he has held since 1993. Before joining NAYS, he worked as the sports editor of the *Huron Daily Tribune* in Bad Axe, Michigan, where he captured numerous writing awards from the Associated Press, Michigan Press Association, and the Hearst Corporation. He has a journalism degree from Michigan State University, which he earned in 1989, and is a devoted follower of his beloved Spartans in all sports. He's also the author of *Coaching Soccer For Dummies, Coaching Football For Dummies, Coaching Basketball For Dummies,* and *Coaching Baseball For Dummies.*

Dedication

This one's for Jeff and Jodie. Even though they cheer for the wrong team they're still the best brother and sister-in-law around. — Greg Bach

This book is dedicated to all the volunteer lacrosse coaches who give up countless hours of their free time to work with children and ensure that they have positive, safe, and rewarding experiences. We applaud their efforts and commend them for making a difference in the lives of youngsters everywhere. — National Alliance For Youth Sports

Authors' Acknowledgments

A successful youth lacrosse program doesn't just happen. It takes a lot of work and a real commitment from not only dedicated volunteer coaches, but also parents who understand their roles and responsibilities, and league directors and administrators who ensure that every child who steps on the field in their community has a safe, fun, and rewarding experience. Lacrosse plays an important role in the lives of many children. It provides an opportunity to learn the skills of the game and the chance to develop emotionally and physically as individuals. The National Alliance For Youth Sports extends a heartfelt thank you to everyone who makes a positive difference through lacrosse in the life of a child.

First, a big thank you to Stacy Kennedy, whose efforts behind the scenes in working with the National Alliance For Youth Sports has resulted in this, the fifth book in a series for youth coaches; Kathy Simpson and Tracy Brown Collins made a huge difference in the quality of every page of this book; and the wonderful illustrations put together by Joni Burns, Shane Johnson, Shelley Norris, and Rashell Smith to supplement many of the techniques and drills covered; and John Clarke, who was a terrific asset with all of his in-depth knowledge about every aspect of the sport.

Publisher's Acknowledgments

We're proud of this book; please send us your comments through our Dummies online registration form located at www.dummies.com/register/.

Some of the people who helped bring this book to market include the following:

Acquisitions, Editorial, and Media Development

Project Editors: Kathy Simpson and Tracy Brown Collins

Acquisitions Editor: Stacy Kennedy

Copy Editor: Kathy Simpson

Technical Editor: John Clarke

Editorial Manager: Michelle Hacker

Editorial Supervisor and Reprint Editor: Carmen Krikorian

Editorial Assistants: David Lutton and Leeann Harney

Cover Photos: Ed Bock/CORBIS

Cartoons: Rich Tennant (www.the5thwave.com)

Composition Services

Project Coordinator: Katie Key

Layout and Graphics: Reuben W. Davis, Melissa K. Jester, Shane Johnson, Stephanie D. Jumper, Ronald Terry, Christine Williams

Proofreaders: Caitie Kelly, Toni Settle

Indexer: Broccoli Information Management

Publishing and Editorial for Consumer Dummies

Diane Graves Steele, Vice President and Publisher, Consumer Dummies

Joyce Pepple, Acquisitions Director, Consumer Dummies

Kristin A. Cocks, Product Development Director, Consumer Dummies

Kathleen Nebenhaus, Vice President and Executive Publisher, Consumer Dummies, Lifestyles, Pets, Education Publishing for Technology Dummies

Composition Services

Gerry Fahey, Vice President of Production Services

Debbie Stailey, Director of Composition Services

Contents at a Glance

Drills at a Glance

Table of Contents

Part III: Basic Training: Teaching Lacrosse Skills 159

Introduction

Welcome to *Coaching Lacrosse For Dummies,* a book dedicated to helping all the wonderful volunteer coaches who sign up to introduce kids to this magnificent sport. Lacrosse is the ultimate team game — 10 players working as one in boys' lacrosse, and 12 players attacking and defending as a unit in girls' lacrosse. The action-packed nature of the game attracts children of all ages and abilities who want to take shots, deliver passes, and defend opponents. Lacrosse features a unique blend of skills and has mass appeal because anyone — regardless of size, speed, or strength — can find a position on the field to excel in.

This book is packed with valuable information on all aspects of the game and is a useful guide in your quest to ensure that the youngsters on your team have a fun, safe, and rewarding experience. You and your kids will remember this season for years to come!

About This Book

We wrote this book to assist first-time volunteer youth lacrosse coaches who are looking for some guidance before they take the field, as well as for more-experienced coaches who want additional insight into different aspects of the game, such as upgrading offensive attacks or defensive strategies.

If you're new to coaching youth lacrosse or just learning about the game in general, you probably feel a bit apprehensive about your ability to teach the many components of this complex game. Don't worry; this feeling is natural. The book you're holding provides the essential information you need to do a great job and be a success with your players. Each chapter is packed with information you can use to make a difference in your players' development — from attacking on offense to denying scoring opportunities on defense to just having fun. The more chapters you read, the more knowledgeable and confident you'll become, which will help you have a bigger impact on your team.

For those of you who have already been through a season or two, and who understand practice planning and basic game-day responsibilities, we provide plenty of in-depth advice to help you guide your team to the next level (and beyond). In addition to all the basics, we cover drills you can use to raise players' skills operating with the player advantage, winning face-off battles, and dealing with picks. We also discuss advanced strategies you can employ.

Conventions Used in This Book

To help guide you through this book, we use the following conventions:

- *Italic* text for emphasis and to highlight new words or phrases that we define in the text

- **Boldface** text to indicate key words in bulleted lists and the action parts of numbered steps

- Sidebars — the shaded gray boxes that you see in some of the chapters — to present information that's interesting but not critical to your understanding of the chapter or topic

Mixed genders — *he* and *she* — are interchanged throughout this book in discussing everything from techniques to drills, because the bulk of the material works for coaches of both boys' and girls' lacrosse. Also, when you encounter *we,* that word refers to the National Alliance For Youth Sports, which is America's leading advocate for positive and safe sports for kids.

What You're Not to Read

If you ask us, every single page of this book is filled with valuable information that you don't want to miss. But we have to share a little secret with you: You really don't have to read every single word. Take the sidebars you come across from time to time: These boxes feature interesting information that you can skip if you are pressed for time or have a lacrosse practice to get to.

Foolish Assumptions

Following are some things that we assume about you, our reader:

- You know that players in lacrosse use sticks that have pockets and netting on the end to hold the ball, and that these sticks are used to carry the ball, pass it to teammates, or take shots in an attempt to score goals against the opponent.

- You're a first-time lacrosse coach or someone who is fairly new to the sport, and you're looking for information on how to manage a youth team.

- You have a son or daughter who wants to play lacrosse this season, but you're not sure how to go about teaching him or her the game.

- You aren't interested in coaching lacrosse in the high-school or collegiate ranks any time soon.

✔ You want to know how to interact with the kids and their parents, what to do at the first practice of the season, and how to figure out who plays where.

If any of these descriptions hits the mark, you've come to the right place.

How This Book Is Organized

This book is divided into parts, and each part pertains to a specific aspect of coaching a youth lacrosse team. The following sections give you a quick rundown.

Part 1: Gearing Up to Coach Lacrosse

The preparations you make before you ever get near the lacrosse field make a big difference on what happens when you're on it with your team. This part presents everything you need to know to get the season off to a fun-filled start and keep the smiles going all season long. You discover how to create a coaching philosophy that ties into the kids' needs and how to run a successful preseason parents' meeting. You also discover all the key rules and terms that you and your players need to know so that everyone has a well-rounded understanding of lacrosse.

Part II: Fielding a Lacrosse Team

Coaching a youth lacrosse team is richly rewarding for many reasons: interacting with your players at practice, helping them develop an array of offensive and defensive skills, and seeing the excitement in their eyes as they take the field on game day, among others. But before you take the field to run those practices and coach those games, you need to answer some questions, such as the following:

✔ How do I determine who plays where?

✔ How do I plan fun, safe practices that match my players' skill levels?

✔ How can I help all the kids — from the uncoordinated to the super-talented — learn and develop skills?

✔ What do I say to my players before a game to get them ready?

✔ What is the best approach for motivating kids during games, especially when they are really struggling?

✔ How can I be sure I'm getting the most out of my time with the players at practice?

✔ What can I do to teach my players how to be good sports at all times, whether they've won or lost the game?

You find the answers to these questions — and many others that are sure to be swirling around in your head — in Part II.

Part III: Basic Training: Teaching Lacrosse Skills

Showing kids how to cradle, pass, catch, shoot, and defend — the basic elements of lacrosse — is a huge slice of the coaching pie. This part presents these important fundamental skills. The better your players can perform these skills, the more satisfying their playing experience will be. We cover all the basics you need to know when your team is on the attack, as well as the skills that come in handy when your team doesn't have the ball and is trying to prevent the opposition from scoring.

Part IV: Net Gains: Advanced Lacrosse Coaching

As your players get a firmer grasp on the basics of the game, you have to make adjustments in your coaching to keep pace. This section has you covered, beginning with evaluating your players' development, setting goals, and exploring different ways to help your players reach those goals. We also introduce a wide array of drills that you can slip into your practices to help players continue progressing in the sport, and we offer some advanced strategies for excelling both offensively and defensively.

Part V: The Extra Points

We hope that you won't have to spend any time this season dealing with injuries or discipline problems with your players — or their parents — but if any issues arise, this part offers some valuable input for handling them. We address how to help keep your players healthy and reduce the chances of injuries; we also include some tips on pregame and postgame nutrition that you can share with your team. If you encounter any problems with parents, coaches, or your own players, we've got you covered on the best ways to deal with them, and if you have any aspirations to coach a travel lacrosse team, you get the scoop on how to make the transition to this more-advanced level of play.

Part VI: The Part of Tens

A fixture of all *For Dummies* books is the Part of Tens. Here, we present ten qualities of all good lacrosse players, ten ways to prepare your team for a game, and ten tips to help your goaltenders excel.

Icons Used in This Book

 This icon signals valuable tips that can save you time, alleviate frustration, and enhance your coaching skills. If time permits you only to scan a chapter, you should take a moment to read these tips when you come across them. You — and your players — will be glad you did.

 Coaching a youth lacrosse team requires a large time commitment on your part, and having the most important facts and reminders in easy-to-find places is helpful. This icon alerts you to key information that's worth revisiting after you close this book and take the field with your team.

 Pay close attention any time you come across this icon, which puts the spotlight on dangerous or risky situations that you must be aware of to help protect your players.

 This icon alerts you to key information related specifically to coaching a boys' lacrosse team.

 If you're coaching a girls' lacrosse team, pay close attention any time you encounter this icon, because the information will be of particular relevance to your team.

Where to Go from Here

This book has many great aspects — if we do say so ourselves! — and one of the best is that you can jump to any chapter to gain the specific insight you're looking for. You aren't bound by a cover-to-cover rule here. Each chapter is divided into easy-to-navigate sections, and each section contains all the information you need to know about a specific topic in coaching lacrosse.

If you are overseeing a youth lacrosse team for the first time, you probably have a lengthy list of questions about topics ranging from running practices to how to be an effective coach on game day. If you're new to the sport, your best bet may be to settle in with the chapters in Part I and build from there. If you've already met your players, and you want to find out how to evaluate them and hold fun, action-packed practices, Part II is what you need. If you want specific drills for your practices, Chapters 7 and 14 meet your needs.

Before you proceed any further, note that you can find answers to your most pressing questions quickly by checking out the table of contents or index — tools that point you in the direction you want to go.

Whatever approach you take, sit back, relax, and soak up the information that will help you coach your team through a safe, enjoyable, and rewarding lacrosse season.

Part I:
Gearing Up to Coach Lacrosse

The 5th Wave   By Rich Tennant

@RICHTENNANT

"The first thing you need to know about about coaching lacrosse is that it takes patience, understanding their limitations, and allowing them to feel like they're participating. And that's just the parents..."

In this part . . .

Getting your season headed in the right direction really begins with the preparation you put in before conducting that first practice of the season. Defining your coaching philosophy, understanding the rules of the game and any modifications your league has made, and running a productive preseason parents' meeting all affect how enjoyable the season is for everyone involved. You can find all that information — and a lot more — right here.

Chapter 1

Teaching Lacrosse to Children

. . . .

In This Chapter

▶ Preparing to coach lacrosse

▶ Taking the field with your team

▶ Coaching your own child

▶ Dealing with problems

. . . .

Congratulations on stepping forward to coach a youth lacrosse team this season! Few endeavors are more rewarding than working with children and helping them develop skills, as well as grow as individuals. If you happen to be picking up this book because you haven't decided yet whether you want the job, we hope that the information we present here convinces you that coaching can be one of the most rewarding experiences of your life — as long as you do it for the right reasons. Heading into the season, your goals should center on fun, skill development, and safety.

A volunteer lacrosse coach assumes a very important role. The way you approach the season, interact with the kids, and get along with their parents goes a long way toward determining whether your players embrace the sport and play it for years to come or put away their sticks for good.

To get your season headed in the right direction and finish it strong, you simply need some quality information, which begins here and runs throughout the book. In the following pages, you find everything you need to propel your players through a safe, fun-filled season that they'll remember fondly for years to come.

Recognizing Your Behind-the-Scenes Responsibilities

Before you go on a job interview, you research the company to find out everything you can to help you land the position. The same approach applies to coaching lacrosse. Before your players strap on their helmets and take the field, you have to fulfill lots of behind-the-scenes responsibilities to get the season off to a smooth start. So whatever your reasons for volunteering — simply because your daughter is on the team, or because you love lacrosse and want to share your knowledge and enthusiasm with others — be aware that you've accepted an enormous responsibility that you should never take lightly.

Working with your players' parents

One of the most interesting aspects of coaching youth lacrosse — and also one of the most challenging — is working with the players' parents. Most of the parents you'll come into contact with are wonderful, supportive, caring people who naturally want the best for their kids; they may even turn out to be great assets to you as assistant coaches. (Check out Chapter 4 for details on choosing assistants.)

But any time you're dealing with a group of adults in an organized sports setting, of course, some of them can end up being sources of season-long aggravation. If you're not prepared to handle situations involving parents quickly and efficiently, some parents can become distractions and can detract from the kids' enjoyment. They can also have you reaching for the aspirin bottle.

Teaming up with parents

Just as you can dodge an opponent on the lacrosse field, you can sidestep many potential parent problems by gathering all the parents together before you begin working with their kids, laying the ground rules on what you expect in terms of behavior during games, and outlining parental roles and responsibilities. Turn to Chapter 4 for details on how to conduct one of these parent meetings.

Throughout the season, you'll be stressing to your players the importance of teamwork. You really won't do anything different when it comes to the parents. When coaches and parents find ways to work together — the adult form of teamwork — they create a special atmosphere that produces tremendous benefits for everyone, especially the youngsters. Conversely, when coaches and parents clash on everything from playing-time issues to the positioning of players to game-day strategy, they spoil the lacrosse experience for everyone involved. These types of disagreements smother the kids' fun, turning practices and games into activities that they dread instead of look forward to.

Parents play important roles in youth lacrosse programs. Working with them, rather than against them, can have a positive impact on the season.

Keeping parents involved

Keep the following in mind to make your dealings with parents go smoothly:

✔ **Take a proactive approach.** Before that first face-off drill in practice, let parents know what your expectations are — not just for their kids, but for them as well. Explain your coaching methods to them. Detail what you want both players and parents to take away from their experience. Painting a clear picture leaves little room for those dreaded misunderstandings that often develop into major problems.

This season may be some parents' first experience having a child in an organized sports program, so any information you can share to help them navigate this unfamiliar territory will be greatly appreciated.

Telling parents firsthand that you're committed to skill development over winning and that you adhere to the league's equal-playing-time rule helps reduce the chance that a parent will confront you in the middle of the season about how many minutes Junior is receiving on the field on game day. Failing to clarify these issues for parents well in advance opens the door to more problems than you can ever imagine — and you'll get them, too. Chapter 2 helps you develop that all-important coaching philosophy and understand all your league's policies and rules so that you can communicate this information clearly to parents.

✔ **Find different ways to include them.** Parents invest a lot of time in the season by driving their kids to practices and games; they also fork over a lot of money to purchase equipment, uniforms, and even occasional postgame treats for the team. The season will be much more enjoyable for them and their youngsters — and you'll be making a wonderful gesture — if you find ways to include them in the team's season-long journey. Get parents involved at practices, for example, and recruit the right ones to assist on game day. Chapter 4 gives you a variety of tips on boosting parental involvement.

✔ **Keep communication lines open.** Conducting a preseason parents' meeting (covered in Chapter 4) is the first step toward establishing a strong foundation with your players' parents, but you've got to keep communication lines open all season long. Be sure to find time at different junctures during the season to talk to the parents about their children's progress. Parents enjoy hearing about those areas of the game in which their child is really excelling. Also, any time a child encounters some difficulty in picking up a skill you are teaching in practice, suggest something the parents can do to help their child at home — but only if the youngster is interested. You never want to force a player to practice more at home if he or she isn't enthusiastic about it.

You can check in with parents from time to time by having a quick casual chat before or after practice, just to make sure that everything is going well and that their child is having fun playing for you. Including parents in all facets of the season is the right thing to do, the smart thing to do, and one of the most effective ways to ensure that children have a positive experience playing lacrosse.

Regardless of what you do to include parents and make them feel that they're valuable parts of the season, a problem may still arise. No matter what the nature of the issue is, you must remain grounded, calm, and in control of your emotions. In Chapter 18, we cover some of the most common problems that lacrosse coaches are forced to address and offer the best approaches for solving them before they have a chance to affect the season.

Getting a handle on rules and terms

It's no secret that teaching your players offensive and defensive skills is one of your biggest responsibilities as a lacrosse coach, but it's certainly not your only one. You also must go over other aspects of the game that will impact the kids' enjoyment level. The more you know and understand about the game — rules, terms, and (at the advanced levels) strategy — and the better you can explain them to your team, the more enjoyable the experience will be for them and for you. The process isn't as complicated as it may seem, but you need to put in some time and effort to learn the rules, including some of the stranger ones that you may not be familiar with — such as the proper way to execute a check (in some boys' leagues) without being whistled for a penalty or how many players you are allowed to have across the midfield line when your team has the ball and is on the attack.

In Chapter 3, we open the rule book and describe everything from terminology to penalties. Throughout Parts II, III, and IV, we also focus on providing you a detailed rundown of the skills, techniques, and strategies that you need to pass on to your players. We've got you covered if you need a refresher on some of the fundamental skills to teach a beginning team, and we provide more-detailed information if you're coaching an older squad that has been attacking and defending for several seasons.

Often, leagues modify rules to fit players' ages and experience levels, and you need to be aware of all these changes so that you can alert your players. Everything from the size of the field to what types of rules are enforced changes from community to community. Knowing these rules — and being able to share them — makes a tremendous difference in your players' enjoyment of playing lacrosse.

Stepping onto the Field

Seeing kids running up and down the field with smiles on their faces, watching them learn new skills and improve on others, and observing them as they develop a love of lacrosse make all those hours you volunteer worthwhile. During your time with the kids, both in practices and on game day, what you say to them and how you go about saying it have a significant impact on their experience. Based on your interactions with your players, you wield the power to fuel their passion for playing the game or drive them away in disappointment.

Planning and executing practices

Game day is what young lacrosse players look forward to most, but the bulk of their skill development takes place during practices, so you need to design quality practices and use drills that meet all the kids' needs and allow them to see improvement in their play. Well-planned practices pay big dividends in fun and player development, whereas those that are simply thrown together in a couple of minutes squash the team's potential.

To make each practice productive, keep the following tips in mind:

- ✔ **Use your position to shape lives.** Be aware that your impact on your players' lives can extend far beyond showing them how to execute various offensive and defensive skills. Your position allows you to make a significant difference in many other areas, and you should take full advantage of the opportunity. During practices, devote time to discussing the importance of staying away from tobacco, alcohol, and drugs and the ways they can harm the body. Stress the importance of players' doing their best in school so that they can lead productive lives as adults. Talk about getting exercise and eating healthy food to help prevent future health issues, too.

  While the kids are stretching is a great time to talk about topics besides lacrosse that can have a significant impact on their lives.

- ✔ **Make the setting fun.** The most effective practices are conducted in an enjoyable atmosphere in which fun is emphasized and mistakes (such as dropping a pass) aren't viewed as catastrophic. Let the kids know at the first practice of the season that mistakes are part of playing lacrosse and that everyone will make them during the season. Be sure to get across to them that all you ask is that they listen to your instructions and give their all during practices and games. Kids who know that they can make mistakes without being humiliated or yanked out of the game will be much more relaxed on the field and will have much more fun. A relaxed atmosphere also helps the kids pick up skills faster and learn more aspects of the game.

- ✔ **Be creative.** When you're putting together drills, look for clever ways to enhance the fun. Visualize going through the drill, and ask yourself what would make it more interesting. Challenge yourself to run practices that the kids can't wait to get to. You want your players to have so much fun at practice that they hate it when the session comes to a close.

When you're putting together your practice plan, go with those drills that keep the kids on the move and that match their skill level. Drills that force kids to stand in line or spend more time watching than participating kill energy levels, as well as sabotage learning, development, and that all-important fun factor. We provide an array of drills that cover all areas of the game — and that are designed for all skill levels — in Chapters 7 and 14.

Handling game-day duties

Coaching a youth lacrosse team on game day is all about being prepared, adapting to ever-changing situations, and providing a constant source of positive motivation. You have to make a wide range of decisions, often with little time to think about them and while juggling other issues. You have pregame, halftime, and postgame talks to deliver; playing time to monitor; substitutions to make; and strategies to employ. Yes, game day brings a lengthy list of responsibilities, but you don't need to lose any sleep over it. In Chapter 8, you find all you need to help your game day go smoothly so that you won't spend your nights tossing and turning.

Game day provides more than just an opportunity for your players to use the skills they've been working on in practice. It also allows you to get across some other important points, such as working as a team, displaying good sportsmanship toward opponents and officials, abiding by the rules, doing your best at all times — and having fun regardless of the numbers on the scoreboard.

Juggling the Dual Roles of Coach and Parent

If you're a parent, you certainly don't need us to tell you that you already have one of the most challenging jobs around. What we can share with you, though, is that handling the dual role of parenting and coaching your child in lacrosse can present unique challenges, some of which you may not expect. When you and your child step onto the field, new issues can materialize; preparing yourself to handle them can help pave the way to an enormously rewarding and memorable season for both of you.

If you and your child agree that it's a good move for you to coach the team, rely on the following tips to help ensure that the experience is problem free:

✔ **Put parenting first.** Regardless of what happens on the field during a practice or game, you're a parent first and foremost. If the team performed poorly, don't monopolize your child's time at home by dissecting everything that unfolded. Leave the coaching at the field; focus on being a supportive, caring parent.

✔ **Maintain open communication.** Your child must understand that he can come to you with a problem at any time, just as you want any of the other players to do if something is on their minds. Just because you're the coach doesn't mean that certain topics are off limits.

✔ **Ditch the extra repetitions.** Sometimes, your child may have difficulty grasping a particular skill during practice or may struggle during a game. The natural tendency is to work with her at home, giving her some extra repetitions. This territory is dangerous, however, so proceed cautiously. Refrain from pushing the child to practice more. It's OK to ask casually whether she'd like to spend a little extra time working on a certain skill at home. If so, great; if not, let the situation go. Pushing your child to perform extra repetitions can drain her interest in the sport and make her feel inferior to some of her teammates.

✔ **Chuck the comparisons.** Never burden a child with expectations that he should perform as well as his brothers or sisters who are involved in lacrosse or who played it in the past. Let your child develop at his own rate. Comparing kids can result in problems that are difficult to repair, such as crushed confidence, low self esteem, and lack of interest in future participation.

✔ **Pile on the praise.** Kids can have a tough time when their parent is a coach, because they have to adjust to sharing Mom or Dad with a group of other children, so be sure to praise your child's willingness, understanding, and cooperation in this special venture. Coaching your child can be one of the most rewarding experiences you'll ever have, but it isn't always easy.

✔ **Find the proper balance.** Make sure that your behavior falls between providing preferential treatment and overcompensating to avert the perception that you're giving your child special treatment. You want to be careful that you don't give your child extra playing time and attention without even being aware of it. But you also want to exercise great caution that you don't go to unfair lengths to *reduce* your child's playing time or give her *less* attention or instruction during practices because you don't want other parents to think that you're favoring your child.

As a parent, you naturally want your child to excel on the lacrosse field. Just don't allow yourself to view your coaching position as an opportunity to control your child's destiny and help secure a college scholarship for him. Entering the season with those types of thoughts will likely lead you to put unwanted pressure on the child and push him harder than you do the other kids. If you lose sight of what youth lacrosse is all about, you may create problems that affect not just his interest in lacrosse, but also his emotional well being.

Preparing for All Kinds of Obstacles

Being a youth lacrosse coach requires more than just the ability to teach passing techniques and the proper way to scoop up a loose ball. It also takes being prepared and knowing how to handle the many unique challenges that have the potential to appear throughout the season. Following are two of your greatest coaching challenges:

- **Meeting the needs of all the players.** Working with all the different types of kids you'll find on your roster — ranging from the shy and clumsy to the nonstop talkers and the athletically gifted — will keep you on your toes. Sure, the smorgasbord of personalities will test your patience, communication skills, and ability to meet each player's constantly changing needs, but you're up to the task. To help you along, Chapter 13 offers some great advice on refining your coaching strategies as the season unfolds to ensure that each youngster gets the most out of her experience under your guidance.

- **Maintaining a safe environment.** One of your top priorities is keeping the kids as safe as possible every time they take the field for practices and games. Although protecting the players completely and eliminating all types of injuries is impossible, you can take steps that significantly reduce the risk of injuries, as well as their severity. You can accomplish this goal by teaching only proper and safe techniques, being prepared for emergency situations, and knowing how to handle any emergencies that do take place. Chapter 17 provides tips and advice for keeping kids safe.

Any time you take the field for a practice or game, be sure to have a properly stocked first-aid kit on hand. In Chapter 17, we cover what your kit should include.

Chapter 2

Setting the Stage for a Successful Season

In This Chapter

▶ Putting together your coaching philosophy

▶ Knowing your league inside and out

▶ Mapping out practices

▶ Equipping the kids

Coaching a squad of young lacrosse players involves more than showing up with a whistle, a list of drills, and a bag of balls. If you want to be one of those coaches whom kids can't wait to get to the field to play for and learn from — and we know you do! — you have to do a lot of preparation before greeting them at that first practice of the season. You have to examine why you volunteered in the first place, determine your take on distributing playing time, figure out what methods you'll use to motivate players, and decide on your plans to create a relaxed atmosphere that promotes learning and skill development.

The league you're coaching in also dictates a portion of your philosophy, so finding out as much as you can about the league's policies before you step on the field is important. Being involved in a league that promotes values that you want to impart to your team is critical for everyone's enjoyment.

All these ingredients factor into your coaching philosophy. This chapter grabs onto all those areas to help you mold a philosophy that meets the kids' needs and sets the tone for a good season.

Developing a Lacrosse Coaching Philosophy

Coaching a lacrosse team requires thorough knowledge of the rules (see Chapter 3), ability to teach the offensive and defensive fundamentals of the game (see Chapters 9 and 10), and a well-crafted philosophy — something that slips under the radar for many coaches preparing for a season. You're probably wondering what philosophy has to do with attacking and defending. Don't worry — putting together a philosophy that meets the kids' needs is not as difficult as it may sound. Heading into the season with a good plan in place is as important to you as properly fitted equipment is to your players.

A coaching philosophy reflects the standards you set for yourself and your team, and it represents the foundation of your coaching values and beliefs. Entering the season without a coaching philosophy is like hiking in the woods without a compass. Sure, you'll probably manage to get where you want to go, but the experience may not be quite as enjoyable. A well-thought-out coaching philosophy keeps you on the right track as you navigate the season.

In this section, we introduce the various components to consider in developing a philosophy that stresses respect, sportsmanship, skill development, safety, and fun.

Even when you have a well-designed philosophy firmly in place, sticking to it on game days can present all sorts of new challenges. You'll deal with Cameron's mom asking why the team isn't in first place and with Sandy's dad inquiring why his daughter isn't playing goalie all game long, because she's clearly the team's most skilled player in that position. (Explaining your coaching philosophy to parents before the season gets under way helps you steer clear of many of these potential headaches. See Chapter 4 for details.)

Your coaching philosophy says a lot about you — not just as a coach, but also as a person — so take the time to put some real thought into it. You'll be glad you did, and your players will be the beneficiaries. Lead your players in the direction you know is right. Strive to instill in them the values that you want your own kids (if you have any) to exhibit throughout their lives. Accomplish this goal, and regardless of how many games you win this season, you and your team will be winners in the truest sense. That's what coaching youth lacrosse is really all about.

Tailoring your philosophy to age group

The kids you'll coach will be quite different. Some are great attackers; others excel at defense; and some kids struggle to grasp some of the most basic elements of the game, such as scooping up the ball and running with it.

Regardless of the areas of the game that they excel in or struggle with, young-sters possess general characteristics that are influenced by age. Children are continually growing and evolving, and part of your coaching responsibility is to know and understand what to expect — both physically and emotionally — from them at various age levels.

Being fully aware of the general age-related differences we cover in the follow-ing sections can enhance your coaching skills and your effectiveness in relating to your team. It can also ensure that you don't favor the players who are more mature and skilled at the expense of players whose skills are less developed at this point in their young careers.

No matter what the age or skill level of your players, always be supportive and enthusiastic. Pile on the praise, and never stop encouraging them, whether they're playing in a midweek practice drill or the final minutes of a tied game. This approach builds players' confidence and self-esteem. Whether they're 6 or 16, encouragement is a gift that can last for years to come and affect how they approach life away from the lacrosse field.

Ages 6 and younger

Most of the children in this age bracket have probably never played lacrosse before, and this season may very well be their first experience in any type of organized team setting. Your job is simply to introduce them to some of the most basic elements of lacrosse and make the game enjoyable so that they'll be eager to return next season. (Chapters 9 and 10 cover the fundamentals that you can focus on with this age group.)

Most lacrosse programs at this level rarely bother to keep score of games, because competition usually is the farthest thing from these kids' minds. The same can't be said for all parents, some of whom may be a little too concerned about which team is scoring more goals. (For more on dealing with problem parents, check out Chapter 18.) At this level, most kids generally couldn't care less about how their lacrosse skills stack up to their teammates'. They're interested primarily in being with friends, having fun learning, and playing the sport.

When meeting with the opposing coach before games, encourage him to pro-vide positive feedback to your players when the action is near him, and let him know that you'll do the same when the play takes place near you. At this level, you just want kids running around the field, getting a feel for running with the ball and passing and catching it.

Ages 7–9

In this age range, youngsters usually have played a season or two. They may begin expressing interest in learning more about the sport and the skills required to play it. (Head to Chapters 15 and 16 for some advanced techniques you can concentrate on.)

These kids crave feedback from coaches and parents on how they're performing certain skills and how they're progressing with new ones. This age is when they start paying closer attention to their teammates' abilities and comparing their own skills.

Ages 10–12

Most kids in this age bracket have had a few seasons of lacrosse experience. They're back on the field to play for you because they really enjoy the game or have discovered that they're pretty good at it. Your job is to keep the positive momentum going by adding to their foundation of skills so that they can become more well-rounded players and see improvement in their skills. Making sure that practices meet your players' skill level, as well as feature lots of fun, is important. (For more details on crafting quality practices, check out Chapter 6.)

Quite often, sports take on added importance at this juncture in kids' lives, and some of your players really want to do well. As children reach this age bracket, many of them become more competitive; their performance, as well as their team's, takes on more importance. They talk with friends and family members about how their team is doing — especially if their team's win–loss record features more victories than defeats.

Many of these kids begin embracing the challenge of putting their skills against those of others their age. When they're able to help their team prevail, these players feel immense satisfaction, accompanied by a unique feeling of accomplishment that's specific to competing on the lacrosse field.

Ages 13–14

You are entering the challenging world of the teenager! These kids have developed many of the basic skills needed to play lacrosse and now want to improve them. (Chapter 14 introduces more advanced drills for older kids and provides an assortment of challenging drills.)

Be aware that children at this age are adjusting to their ever-changing bodies, as well as trying to figure out who they are. One of the best ways to make a difference with them is to get to know them on a personal level. Ask them who their favorite athletes or teams are, for example. This tip is great for building special coach–player bonds with kids of all ages. See "Keeping communication lines open," later in this chapter.

Ages 15 and older

Securing your players' respect and maintaining it are important for realizing coaching success and minimizing disciplinary problems. Players in this age range have developed a real passion for the sport. Many of them attend lacrosse camps; perhaps they lift weights and run to stay in top condition. In some cases, they may even know more about some areas of the sport than you do.

If you get talked into coaching players in this age range, or step forward to volunteer because the league is experiencing a shortage of coaches, don't lose any sleep over the move. Instead, welcome the chance to enhance your coaching abilities, and embrace the opportunity to coach these kids, who have a deep-rooted love for the game. Be sure to let them know that you value their opinions, suggestions, and input regarding the team. Youngsters' passion for lacrosse is great to see, and coaching kids who care so much about the sport is lots of fun. You'll find that their enthusiasm helps make your job easier.

Emphasizing teamwork

Playing lacrosse requires the entire team to work as a cohesive unit. If even a couple of players aren't on board with the team concept (for more on dealing with ball hogs, flip to Chapter 5), the team chemistry can be spoiled, and everyone's enjoyment of the season will be slightly negated. One of the many unique aspects of lacrosse is that players have opportunities to create plays on their own — such as attackers breaking past a defender and racing downfield. Individual plays are fine, as long as they're carried out within the framework of the team concept and the player uses the advantage to create a scoring opportunity for the team rather than simply to hold on to the ball.

Uncovering the best methods to instill teamwork among your players is one of the most challenging tasks you may encounter as a coach. Focus on getting your players to see the enormous benefits of working as a team (rather than as a bunch of individuals) through the following pointers, and you'll mold a team that opponents hate facing because of its team-oriented style of play:

- ✔ **Point out positive team play.** During practices, try to recognize team effort more often than you single out individual play. If you're conducting a three-on-three drill, for example, and the offensive unit scores a goal, you may have a natural tendency to applaud the player who deposited the ball in the net. But as a coach who emphasizes teamwork, you may be able to trace the success of the play back to the person who made a nice pass that gave the goal scorer a great opportunity. Recognize all the components that went into making a play work, and your players who were involved in the process will feel as much pride and satisfaction as the goal scorer does.

    When you spread praise among all the kids who played a part in scoring a goal, they begin to understand that every one of them fills a very important role on the team.

- ✔ **Promote peer praise.** Sure, kids love hearing your words of praise, but what their teammates say packs just as much punch (and even more at times). Encourage the kids who score goals to acknowledge the teammates who provided them the opportunity to take quality shots. Getting kids into the habit of giving high fives or saying "Great pass" or "Nice play" forges bonds and strengthens team unity — and also makes the kids want to play harder for one another.

✔ **Shoot for sideline support.** On game days, encourage players who aren't on the field to stay involved in the action by cheering and supporting their teammates. Hearing teammates' cheers also provides extra encouragement for the players on the field and can do wonders for a player's tired legs or sagging confidence.

✔ **Give kids chances to make plays on their own.** Yes, lacrosse is a team sport, but you shouldn't stamp out kids' abilities to create plays on their own to benefit the team. During the game, your attackers should be able to make some one-on-one moves to create space for themselves to take a shot or deliver a pass to an open teammate. Individual play becomes a problem only when that player ignores teammates because he wants to try to do everything himself.

✔ **Spread the captain's role around.** Don't rely on two or three players to serve as team captains throughout the season, because captaincy elevates them above the rest of the squad. Instead, give every player the opportunity to lead warm-ups in practice during the season or on game day. This practice infuses the team with the sense that all players are equal parts of the group.

In most youth lacrosse programs, captains usually aren't required until around the age of 14 or on travel teams (see Chapter 19), when the competition becomes more intense and the players are more experienced. At younger age levels, captains aren't necessary during games, but you can use them to your advantage as another way to build kids' self-esteem and to make them feel valued and appreciated — as long as you make sure you give every child the chance to be a captain at some point during the season.

✔ **Recognize hustle plays after the game.** The kids who scored the goals during the game don't need as much additional praise afterward, because their shots generated cheers and applause from the spectators, as well as high fives from their teammates. Use your time following the game to congratulate the player who delivered the cross-field pass that caught the defense off guard and led to the scoring opportunity, or the player who didn't register a goal but hustled all game long and chased down several ground balls that gave your team a few extra offensive possessions. Recognizing these plays and the kids who made them reinforces the fact that wins, losses, and even goals are never the work of one player, but of the entire team.

Motivating players

Regardless of age, ability, or experience playing lacrosse, each player arrives at the field with vastly different motivations for playing the game. Some kids are there to try something new; some are there because they love the game; some come because Mom and Dad think that lacrosse is the perfect sport for them. A few of the kids are strongly motivated — the type who push themselves to succeed and are awfully hard on themselves when they don't fulfill their own lofty expectations. Others rely on your words of encouragement to improve and excel.

You'll discover that some of your players respond in a positive manner to your challenges, such as seeing whether they can make five accurate passes in a row to a partner during a passing drill. For others, challenge-oriented tasks may turn out to be too much pressure to deal with and may actually detract from their motivation to participate. Each youngster you come into contact with is remarkably different from the others, and you have to discover for yourself what works for a child to get the best out of her as both a lacrosse player and a person.

Here are a few general tips you can employ to help ignite passion in your players and motivate them to strive to become the best they can be:

- ✔ **Enthusiasm is contagious.** When you have a sincere passion for lacrosse and want to share this great game and all its wonderful components with children, your genuine excitement and enthusiasm will rub off on the team, and they'll respond accordingly.

- ✔ **Set goals that kids can get their hands on.** Setting unrealistic goals for kids — such as winning every game or scoring a specific number of goals each game — is unrealistic, unfair, and unlikely to produce the results you are aiming to achieve. Keep in mind that your players are children, some of whom may never have played lacrosse before. Keep your expectations reasonable for the kids you're coaching, and set goals that are within their reach. You stimulate and encourage them to keep working when the goals are within sight.

  If a child senses that your expectations are impossibly far-fetched, he wonders what's the point of even trying, and his play on the field suffers. This problem negatively affects the entire team.

  You want to teach winning, but be sure to define a winner as someone who always gives her best effort, regardless of the score in the game.

- ✔ **Make a big deal out of the positives.** Some coaches tend to raise their voices or make a big scene when the team makes a mistake or performs a skill the wrong way. Take the reverse approach instead. Stop practice for a moment to point out when the team does something really well, such as executing a fast break or denying one. Or, if a player who has been struggling with a specific skill performs it the right way you can use this technique to boost his confidence and self-esteem. Being positive is simply one of the best motivational tools around.

  Think about it: If your boss tells you in front of your co-workers that you did a great job on a presentation, you're going to give even more effort on your next presentation. The same goes for kids on the lacrosse field. If you halt practice for even 20 seconds to praise good performance, the mini break can make a youngster's day. Also, the benefits will carry over beyond that practice. Just watch — he'll play that position with pride and continue giving you his best effort to try to gain that recognition again.

Ditch the threats and any motivation-through-fear tactics, because they have no place in youth lacrosse. Making kids run laps for failing to perform at an expected level has no place in the game. This type of coaching approach handcuffs a youngster's ability to perform, because she's afraid of making another mistake that's going to translate into additional punishment. Children have to feel free to make mistakes to improve. Also, relying on these tactics will likely chase kids away from participating in the future. Children are there to develop and to learn from their mistakes, not to be humiliated or punished for them.

Creating a positive atmosphere

The more relaxed and comfortable kids are playing for you, the more satisfying the experience will be for them — and the better the chance that they'll be effective on the field. Here are a couple of ways you can generate an atmosphere that promotes team spirit, encourages participation, and rewards the ideal of doing your best at all times.

- ✔ **Create a team cheer.** Work with the kids to come up with a clever team cheer to use before games. This cheer should remind them that they're taking the field as a team and must work together to play at their highest level.

- ✔ **Cheer mistakes.** Even making a mistake or failing to perform a particular skill the way you demonstrated it is part of playing and learning how to play lacrosse, and kids need constant reminders of that fact. Praising a player's effort for doing his best, rather than criticizing mistakes, frees the child to continue putting forth maximum effort until he gets a handle on the particular skill. Taking this approach opens the door to all sorts of learning; players aren't going to fear making a mistake when they know you won't make negative comments.

Keeping communication lines open

Coaching lacrosse is more than just teaching kids how to cradle or how to execute a stick check. You are in a special position to affect other areas of their lives — but only if your players feel comfortable enough talking to you about subjects unrelated to the game. You want to establish from the beginning that they can come to you with questions, problems, or concerns at any point.

Besides being their coach, you can be their friend. While they're stretching, for example, ask them how they're doing in school, what their favorite subjects are, or who their favorite teacher is. Find out whether they have any brothers or sisters, the names of their pets, and what hobbies they enjoy. Getting to know kids on a more personal level lets them know you care about them as individuals and makes it much easier for them to open up to you if they ever need to — which is more important than any offensive or defensive technique you can teach them.

Making all the kids count

Every player who grabs a lacrosse stick or straps on a helmet should feel valued and appreciated. To make this feeling happen, you must pay close attention to all your players, regardless of how talented they are. Sure, paying attention to everyone sounds easy, but that's not always the case. After all, becoming enamored with the most athletically gifted kids can lead you to shower them with all the attention, accolades, and praise.

Spreading the encouraging words around equally takes real focus and effort. Making sure that each child — no matter how big or small her actual contributions are during games and practices — feels valued and appreciated for her efforts is the cornerstone of good coaching. Appreciation is what helps keep kids interested in lacrosse and eager to keep returning to the field.

Providing immediate feedback and continually recognizing all players for their various contributions are the most effective ways to boost your players' self-confidence and fuel their interest in giving their best efforts all season long. Consider these points:

- ✔ **Acknowledge all on-the-field contributions.** Although the kids who score the goals tend to receive the most praise, don't overlook the contributions of the other players. On a goal-scoring play, for example, recognize the defender who made the steal that led to the goal-generating possession; also recognize the kids who made the passes that set up the player who scored. Getting into this habit goes a long way toward making each child feel truly appreciated and part of the team.

- ✔ **Applaud attitudes (just the good ones!).** Some players aren't the best attackers, or they struggle to stop opponents on defense. Yet even the less-skilled kids can be recognized for their contributions, however big or small. You can applaud his hustle in running down the field to get back into defensive position, the effort she put forth to battle for a loose ball, or the good sportsmanship he displayed in congratulating an opponent for a well-played game.

> ✔ **Hand out hardware.** Many coaches enjoy handing out awards to their players at the end of the season. If you elect to do so, make sure that you come up with something for every player instead of taking the old Most Valuable Player route. Awards you can distribute include Hardest Worker in Practice, Best Display of Sportsmanship, and Most Likely to Win a Battle for a Ground Ball. (See Chapter 4 for suggestions on how to reward your players at the end of the season.)

Spotlighting fun and skill development

Don't view your team's win–loss record as a measure of how good a coach you are. The real tally of your impact is the smiles on the kids' faces, the skills they learn, and the improvements they make along the way. At the more advanced levels of play, winning takes on a more prominent role, and that concept shouldn't be swept aside, because it's part of playing lacrosse. But fun and fair play shouldn't take a back seat while you do your best to achieve victories.

Children are highly impressionable. If they get a sense that winning is all that really matters to you, fun and developing skills will become secondary in their minds, and getting everything back on track becomes difficult. The younger and less experienced your players are, the less you should focus on wins and losses, and the more you should concentrate on teaching skills and ensuring that everyone has fun playing and learning.

Children's short attention spans can make coaching difficult at times but can also work to your advantage. Many youngsters just beginning in the sport usually forget the score of the last game quickly and direct their attention to something else. So even if the team happened to lose a game by several goals, praise your players for their efforts.

Never let scoreboards or opposing teams define how much fun you have on the lacrosse field or impede your team's progress in learning the game. Just because your players outscored their opponents doesn't necessarily mean that they performed to the best of their abilities. A squad can put forth a lackluster effort and still come out ahead because the opposing team played poorly or simply didn't have as many talented players. Conversely, your team can play extremely well and still lose the contest. Whatever the case, push the score to the side and take a close look at how your players performed, and make the necessary adjustments on areas of the game you need to work on at your next practice.

Modeling good sportsmanship

Teaching kids how to hold the stick to catch a pass or take a shot is important for their development as offensive players. Teaching them to being good sports — win or lose — is important for their personal growth. Good sportsmanship is one of the healthiest and most important ideals you can instill in your players.

Here are a few ways you can help make your squad one of the best-liked and most-respected teams in the league:

- ✔ **Talk about sportsmanship all the time.** The more time you spend talking about being good sports, the better chance your message has of sinking in. Reinforcing the importance of sportsmanship every chance you get goes a long way toward building model players.

- ✔ **Set a positive tone on game day.** Greeting the opposing coach and officials with a friendly handshake before the game helps set the tone for a fun day of lacrosse. Remember, being a good sport isn't a sign of weakness or an indication that you don't care about winning the game. It shows that you're a caring coach who respects the game.

- ✔ **Display good behavior at all times.** If you aren't a model of good sportsmanship, you can't expect your players to be good sports themselves. Players are going to take their cue from you, so if you rant and rave to an official about a call, expecting your team to show respect toward them is hardly fair. Good coaching behavior means not yelling at officials or questioning calls that you're sure should have gone your team's way.

- ✔ **Recognize good sportsmanship.** Continually recognizing displays of good sportsmanship reinforces to players that how they behave during and after games really is important.

- ✔ **Always shake hands with opponents after the game.** Regardless of the game's outcome, you always want your players lining up to shake hands with the opposing team's players and coaches. If your team won, your players should be acknowledging that their opponents played a good game, and if they lost, they should congratulate the opponents on their victory. Your players will make an especially classy move if they also shake the referee's hand after the contest.

During the season, you may encounter a win-at-all-costs coach who prowls the sidelines yelling and berating his team. Or you may see an out-of-control parent who spends the entire game shouting instructions at his child or argues every call that doesn't go his way. Chapter 18 presents tips for handling this type of inappropriate behavior, which has no place in youth lacrosse.

Understanding the League You're Coaching In

Youth lacrosse programs are as different as all the children who show up at fields around the country to shoot, pass, and catch the ball. You can find regulation leagues that stick to the official rules of the game (see Chapter 3 for a rundown of basic rules), as well as leagues that tweak the number of players on the field and modify the rule book to fit the community's needs.

In the following sections, I discuss some of the common differences between boys' and girls' lacrosse, the importance of knowing your league's rules, and the differences between recreational and competitive programs.

Coaching girls' leagues vs. boys' leagues

The most noticeable difference between boys' and girls' lacrosse is the amount of contact that is allowed, so you'll have to adjust your coaching and some of the skills you teach accordingly.

Body checking is allowed at certain levels of play in boys' lacrosse — and not allowed at all for girls. Body checking is permitted when the opponent has the ball or is within 5 yards of the ball. All contact must occur from the front or side, as well as below the shoulders and above the waist.

During your practices for a boys' team you'll want to incorporate drills that focus on executing both body and stick checks when defending an attacking player. Since different types of contact are allowed when defending, your players can take a more aggressive approach to deny passes and good scoring opportunities. Offensively, your players will also need to know how to best protect the ball when the defender delivers a body check or makes contact with their sticks in an effort to knock the ball loose.

If you're coaching a girls' team, teaching them the importance of playing good defense will involve an emphasis on good footwork and maintaining proper position at all times. Since body contact isn't allowed, your defenders will need to have a good grasp of how to stay in front of the players they're guarding. Also, being able to read plays that are developing and recognizing when passes are being made, as well as being able to step into passing lanes to deflect or intercept an opponent's pass, are key elements.

Knowing your league's rules

A lacrosse rule book isn't exactly going to have you turning pages in anticipation, like a best-selling novel, but it should be bedside reading for you — and we don't mean as a sleep aid! To be successful as a lacrosse coach, you have to know the standard rules of the game, as well as any that have been modified by your league. You also must be able to teach the rules to your players; otherwise, you're setting them up for a frustrating experience.

Rather than plunging in and attempting to memorize all the rules in a single sitting, review a few pages every night before the season's start until you're comfortable with them. (For a quick primer on the rules of lacrosse — and some modifications that youth leagues often make — check out Chapter 3.)

Don't assume that older kids have a firm grasp on all the rules simply because they've played the sport for years. If no one took the time to explain certain rules that may be somewhat confusing, players may not have learned them. You can make a difference. Also, more rules are typically enforced at the higher levels of play.

Even if you have extensive knowledge of lacrosse, and maybe even if you were a pretty good high school or college player, do yourself and your team a big favor: Read the league's rule book. Consider it a refresher course before you take the field. Besides, chances are good that some of the league's rules were never applied the same way when you played.

Playing for fun or first place

Two distinct classifications exist in youth lacrosse: recreational and competitive programs. Each type requires a vastly different approach to coaching. Before agreeing to volunteer, you should check with the recreation director to learn more about the league and make sure that it's the right fit for you.

Recreational leagues

If you're coaching lacrosse for the first time this season, chances are good that you're involved in a recreational league. These programs focus on teaching kids the basic skills of the game. Generally, a recreational program has rules in place regarding equal playing time, which makes your job easier, because all the kids get a fair chance to play a variety of positions.

Often, for kids ages 10 and younger, the league scales teams down and has them play games on smaller fields to allow each child plenty of chances to run, catch, and shoot the ball. Recreational leagues also feature rules that have been altered to meet the players' ages and experience levels. Some recreational programs allow the coaches of the youngest kids to be on the field with them during games, for example.

Competitive leagues

Children whose thirst for competition can't be quenched in their local recreational programs can turn to the avalanche of competitive programs. These leagues are typically referred to as *travel teams,* which Chapter 19 discusses in greater detail.

This type of program is for youngsters who have demonstrated higher skill levels than many other kids their age. These elite programs give kids the chance to compete against others of similar ability in their state or region. Usually, kids involved in these programs have their eye on long-term advancement in the sport, such as playing at the collegiate level. (Or, as is often the case, their parents are thinking about college scholarships and have pushed the children into this highly competitive environment.)

If you're coaching in a highly competitive league that you don't believe you're adequately prepared for, notify the league director immediately. Let her know that in the best interests of the kids, you prefer to coach a less experienced team in a less competitive league. Do what you're suited for at this time in your volunteer coaching career. Down the road, if you choose to go the travel-team coaching route, you'll be well prepared to do so after a couple of seasons of recreational coaching.

Getting on Schedule

A youth lacrosse coach's handy companion for the season is his schedule, which lets him know the dates and times for both practices and games. When you sign up to coach a team, you typically receive a schedule for the season. In some leagues, arranging practices is up to you; other leagues take care of scheduling practices for you, assigning specific times and fields to your players (every Tuesday from 6:30 to 7:30 p.m. on Field B, for example).

You also need to be aware of your league's policies for handling make-up games. Read on to get the scoop on these areas.

Scheduling team practices

Your players' age group generally dictates how much time you'll get to spend conducting practices for them during the season. Most beginner leagues, for example, generally have just one practice during the week and a game on the weekend. Many leagues restrict the number of practices a coach can hold during the season, so be aware of this rule before you put together your practice plans.

Quite often, leagues set the practice schedule for the entire season based on the number of fields that are available and what other programs are going on, which eliminates a lot of scheduling headaches on your part.

The time you spend with your team during practice sessions is critical. Practice isn't a social hour. Neither is it a matter of lining some kids up on offense and others on defense, and having them scrimmage for an hour while you watch from the sidelines. You have to plan these sessions carefully and be actively involved in them at all times. Chapter 6 features some in-depth tips on running great practices.

Dealing with make-up games

Some days, Mother Nature just isn't going to be a lacrosse fan, and she's going to create havoc with your practice schedule or disrupt game day. Because lacrosse can be played in the rain — and because most kids love playing in these conditions and getting their uniforms muddy — you can still get in quality practices or even play games, if your league allows. But some programs don't allow practices or games while it's raining. In these cases, games are canceled or postponed. Being aware of the league policy regarding cancellations alleviates a lot of confusion among parents and team members when bad weather arrives.

To make sure that everyone's notified about weather-related delays or cancellations, ask parents to organize a telephone tree. See Chapter 4 for details.

Exercise great caution with approaching storms. Waiting for the first sign of lightning before canceling practice or stopping a game is flirting with serious trouble. Storms should never be taken lightly, and attempting to squeeze in a few extra minutes of practice or finish a game before the storm hits simply isn't worth risking the lives of your players. If conditions become dangerous during a game, don't wait for an official to make the call. Get your kids off the field immediately.

Getting in Gear: Lacrosse Equipment

The physical nature of lacrosse requires players to wear a wide assortment of protective gear. To do its job, the equipment must be in good condition, meet appropriate safety standards, and fit the youngsters properly. The following sections examine the different types of equipment used in boys' and girls' lacrosse (see Figure 2-1 and Figure 2-2).

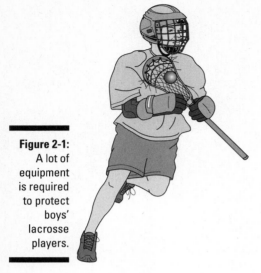

Figure 2-1:
A lot of equipment is required to protect boys' lacrosse players.

Figure 2-2:
Girls' lacrosse players typically wear different gear.

What all players use

The following list is what equipment players typically use when they take the field:

✔ **Stick:** Sticks come in a variety of lengths and styles. Check with your league director to determine whether any specific styles are required.

✔ **Mouth guard:** This guard protects valuable teeth (and helps save parents from taking their children on unwanted trips to the dentist for repairs).

✔ **Shoes:** Check with the league director regarding the types of cleats that are allowed, and let parents know so they can purchase the correct shoes for their child.

✔ **Gloves:** Gloves help players hold on to the stick, and also protect their fingers and hands from the ball or other sticks. Some girls' leagues don't require players to wear gloves.

What boys use

Here is a rundown of the equipment that boys wear:

✔ **Lacrosse helmet with face guard:** The helmet and guard protect a player's head and eyes. All helmets and face masks should be approved by the National Operating Committee on Standards for Athletic Equipment (NOCSAE).

✔ **Shoulder pads:** As the name implies, these pads protect the shoulders.

✔ **Elbow pads:** These pads protect the elbows when players fall or get knocked down.

✔ **Rib pads:** Rib pads usually are optional at the younger levels of play but are recommended to help protect kids' ribs from being whacked.

✔ **Cup and holder:** These pieces are appropriate for older players and cost about $10.

What girls wear

Here is a look at the equipment that girls wear:

✔ **Lacrosse goggles:** Goggles protect the eyes. They feature an eye shield and a band that wraps around the back of the player's head to hold them in place.

✔ **Sports bras/support bras:** These items are appropriate for older players.

Because goalies have to face a ball that's being shot at them, they wear some different protective equipment, in addition to some of the pieces detailed above, to help them play their positions safely:

What boys' and girls' goalies wear

The kids defending the goal require extra protection, which includes the following:

- ✔ **Chest protector:** This garment protects the player's upper body.
- ✔ **Shin guards:** These items are worn to protect the shins.
- ✔ **Knee pads:** Knee pads come in handy, because goalies often must drop to the ground to block shots.
- ✔ **Goalie stick:** These sticks are larger than the other players' sticks, which helps the goalie block the opposition's shots.
- ✔ **Helmet:** In both boys' and girls' lacrosse players wear helmets with a throat protector.

What the league provides

Youth lacrosse leagues across the country are run quite differently, from the rules they enforce to the equipment they provide for the kids. Some leagues furnish helmets and sticks; others rely on parents to purchase equipment. In some leagues, each player gets his own jersey with his name on it; other leagues loan out plain jerseys for the season, and parents are responsible for keeping the shirts in good condition and turning them in at the conclusion of the season.

If parents have to purchase jerseys, they usually buy them through the league to ensure that each child on the team has the same type and color. The uniform cost may be included in the registration fee.

What parents must provide

Make sure that parents understand that they're responsible for purchasing certain items before your first practice. You don't want kids showing up without mouth guards, for example — and being forced to watch from the sidelines — because their parents thought you'd be handing them out.

Parents typically have to provide the following items:

- ✔ **Water bottle:** Every player should bring a water bottle to practices and games, with her name clearly marked on the bottle.
- ✔ **Mouth guard:** Coaches can request that parents purchase the same color to help promote team unity.

Because every lacrosse program is different, always check with your league director to find out what equipment it provides the kids and what the parents need to purchase. Get this information in advance so that you can let the parents know during your preseason parents' meeting (covered in Chapter 4).

Chapter 3

Covering Basic Lacrosse Rules

*L*acrosse is often referred to as the fastest game on two feet, but if you aren't familiar with every aspect of the game, your players' enjoyment of the season will slow to a crawl. Your many coaching responsibilities include knowing all the rules — both the general ones and those that have been specially modified for your league — and explaining them to your squad. Along with being able to identify every area of the playing field, you also must have a crystal-clear understanding of the positions, including the skills required to play them. And your players will have a more satisfying experience if you can share with them some of the many unique terms that comprise this great game. All that valuable information — and much more — awaits you in this chapter.

Playing the Field

The first time you see a lacrosse field, all the lines, circles, and arcs may be rather confusing. No need to worry, though. When you know what these markings are and can identify them easily — which we'll take care of for you in this section — you'll see that each marking serves a specific, easy-to-understand purpose.

Lacrosse fields vary by gender. Figure 3-1 shows a boys' lacrosse field, and Figure 3-2 depicts a girls' lacrosse field. The size of the field your team plays on will also vary, depending on the type of program you are coaching in and on the age and skill level of your players.

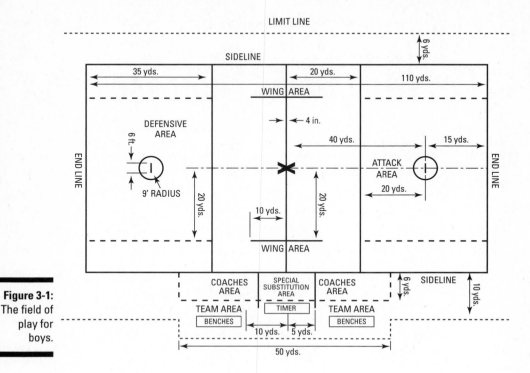

Figure 3-1:
The field of
play for
boys.

The markings on the field

A typical lacrosse field features the following elements:

- **Arc:** The semicircular path between the goal posts.

- **Attack area:** The area defined by the line on the field that runs sideline to sideline 20 yards from the face of the goal on a regulation field. When the offensive team crosses the midfield line, it has 10 seconds to move the ball into its attack goal area.

- **Crease:** A circle around the goal, with a 9-foot radius, that only defensive players may enter.

- **Eight-meter arc:** The arc in front of each goal in girls' lacrosse where a defender must be within at least a stick's length of the player she is covering.

- **End line:** The boundary line at each end of the field.

- **Goal line:** The stripe between the goal posts.

✔ **Goal line extended:** An imaginary line that runs parallel to the end lines and that runs from the goal to the sidelines.

✔ **Midfield line:** The line that runs from sideline to sideline in the middle of the field.

✔ **Penalty box:** The area where players in boys' lacrosse must stand for a specified time when they are whistled for a personal foul. Penalties usually are for 1 minute.

✔ **Restraining line:** A line located 30 yards from each goal line in girls' lacrosse, marking the area in which no more than seven offensive players and eight defensive players (including the goalie) are allowed.

✔ **Sidelines:** The two boundary lines that run the entire length of the field.

✔ **Twelve-meter fan:** A semi-circle in front of the goal that officials use to position players after minor fouls have been committed in girls' lacrosse.

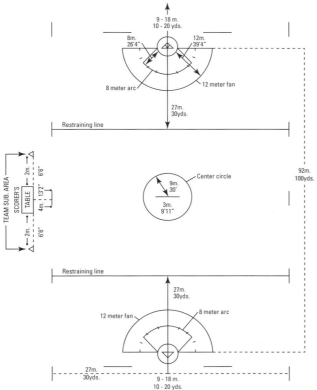

Figure 3-2:
The setup of the field for girls.

Field dimensions

A regulation men's lacrosse field measures 110 yards long and 60 yards wide. In youth lacrosse, fields are scaled down considerably to account for the smaller bodies (see the "Modifications for various age and experience levels" section, later in this chapter). Often, one regulation lacrosse field can accommodate several youth games at one time.

Field sizes vary greatly from community to community and are often dictated by how much space is available and the number of participants involved in the league. Be sure to check with your league director to find out what size field your team will play on.

Knowing the Rules of the Game

Lacrosse is a complex game involving an array of rules. Some rules are a breeze to understand; others may baffle you initially. If you're unfamiliar with all the rules of lacrosse, you can easily become overwhelmed trying to master them all right away — and become agitated in the process.

Don't try to memorize the rule book in one evening, because that isn't realistic. Instead, focus each night on learning just a few rules and how they're applied, and build your base of knowledge from there. It wouldn't be fair to expect your players to learn all the rules during the first week of the season, and you don't need to put that kind of pressure on yourself, either.

A college lacrosse game is 60 minutes long, with four 15-minute quarters; sudden-death play is used to break ties at the end of regulation. High school teams and advanced-level youth lacrosse teams typically play 10-minute quarters. At the younger age levels, teams often play a 30-minute game broken into 15-minute halves, or a 40-minute game split into 20-minute halves. Again, check with the league director for the specifics on length of games in your league.

A lacrosse game begins with a face-off in the center circle. The ball is placed between the sticks of the two face-off players in the middle of the field. Play begins when the official blows the whistle, and each player tries to control the ball. Center face-offs are also used at the start of each quarter and after a goal is scored.

When a team has possession of the ball, players attempt to move it down the field by running with it and making passes to teammates who can get into position to score a goal. Generally, the closer a team gets to the opponent's goal, the better its chance of scoring. The defending team covers the opponent, using different types of checks (depending on what is allowed in the league) to impede the attacking team's progress and force turnovers.

When the ball goes out of bounds after a shot on goal, possession is awarded to the team that is closest to the ball at the moment it crosses the boundary line. So an offensive team that misses scoring a goal with a shot that goes out of bounds can retain possession and generate another scoring chance. When the ball is passed or carried out of bounds, however, possession goes to the opposing team.

Rules for girls' leagues

Following are some of the most significant rules to know if you're overseeing a girls' team:

- **Face-offs:** Games start at the center of the field with a *draw*. The centers for each team square off in the middle of the field; they hold their sticks at waist level and parallel to the ground, with the backs of the pockets on their sticks touching each other. The referee places the ball between the two pockets, and when he blows the whistle, the two centers try to gain control of the ball.

   During a face-off (which is also conducted after each goal and to start the second half), only the centers are allowed in the circle. Also, while the face-off is taking place, only four players — not counting the center — are allowed within the restraining lines.

- **Players on the field:** When a team has possession of the ball and is on the attack, it may have a maximum seven players inside the restraining line at the opponent's end of the field. When the team is playing defense, it can have only eight players (including the goalie) within the restraining line at its end of the field.

- **Penalties:** The referee blows a whistle whenever a ball goes out of bounds or a foul is committed. Players must stop and remain where they are when the whistle is blown.

- **Throws:** Whenever a ball goes out of bounds, the player nearest to the ball gains possession of it — unless the referee rules that the ball was thrown out of bounds intentionally, in which case the opposing team is awarded possession. If two players are ruled to be an equal distance from the ball, a *throw* occurs. A throw works this way: The two players stand 1 meter apart; the referee tosses the ball into the air; and the two players vie for possession of it. Teammates of the two players contesting the throw must be at least 4 meters away from them.

- **Checking:** All types of body checking and rough play are prohibited in girls' lacrosse. Defenders aren't allowed to reach across a player's body to check; they can make only stick-to-stick contact.

   Have your players imagine an invisible sphere around every player's head, and let them know to keep their sticks away from this sphere.

✔ **No hands:** The goalie is the only player who is allowed to touch the ball with her hands, and only while she is standing within the crease. If she chooses to leave the crease (to go after a loose ball, for example), a teammate can take over in the crease for her.

Major fouls in girls' lacrosse

In girls' lacrosse, fouls are classified as *major* and *minor*. The majority of major fouls concern playing the game too roughly and making contact with the body while checking. Here's a breakdown of the major fouls:

✔ **Blocking:** A defender moves into the path of the ball carrier without giving her any chance to stop or change direction.

✔ **Charging:** A player uses her body to run into an opposing player, or pushes or backs into another player.

✔ **Dangerous shot:** A shot that goes toward another player on the field.

✔ **Misconduct:** A player purposely endangers the safety of others by playing too roughly and not adhering to the rules.

✔ **Slashing:** A player on defense swings her stick at an opponent's stick or body in a reckless manner. She doesn't have to make contact with the other player for this foul to be called.

✔ **Three seconds:** Defenders can't stay in the 8-meter arc for more than 3 seconds unless they are guarding an opponent closely.

When your player is fouled within the 8-meter arc, the referee awards her what is known as a *free position*. This means that the player who was fouled is awarded possession of the ball, and the defender who was whistled for the foul must stand at least 4 meters behind her. All other players also must be at least 4 meters away from the player with the ball. When the referee blows her whistle to resume play, the ball handler may shoot, pass, or attack the goal.

When a defender commits a major foul in the 8-meter arc area, if the attacking team is still able to control the ball, the referee won't stop play. Instead, the referee throws his flag to indicate that a foul has occurred, but play continues until the defense gains possession. Then the free position is awarded to the team whose player was fouled. If a foul occurs that injures a player or puts someone at risk of injury, of course, play is stopped immediately.

Minor fouls in girls' lacrosse

Here are some of the most common types of minor fouls:

✔ **Goal-circle foul:** Any part of a player's body or stick (excluding the goalie) enters the goal circle.

✔ **Warding off:** A player removes her hand from the stick to make contact with an opponent's body or stick in such a way that she gains an advantage.

- ✔ **Touching the ball with the hands:** A player other than the goalie touches the ball with her hands. Even the goalie is allowed to touch the ball with her hands only when she is standing in the crease.

- ✔ **Body ball:** Whenever a player's body makes contact with the ball and she gains a clear advantage from it.

When the opponent commits a minor foul against one of your players when she is within the 8-meter arc, she is awarded an indirect free position. The referee gives her the ball; the defender must stand at least 4 meters away; and when the referee blows the whistle to signal the resumption of play, the youngster must pass the ball to a teammate before her team can take a shot on goal.

Rules for boys' leagues

If you're coaching a boys' team, you should have a good handle on these rules:

- ✔ **Face-offs:** Each of the two players taking the face-off stands on the same side of the center line as the goal his team is protecting. The players must have both hands on their sticks, which must touch the ground. The back pockets of their sticks touch each other. The referee places the ball between the two sticks and blows his whistle to signal the start of play, and the players try to win control of the ball. (For some face-off techniques your players can employ, check out Chapter 11.) Players in the wing area may vie for the ball; the others must wait until one player has gained possession of the ball.

- ✔ **Checking:** At advanced levels of play, body checks against the ball carrier are allowed. The contact must be delivered to the ball carrier's front or side, and it must be confined to the area above his waist and below his shoulders.

- ✔ **Positions of the players on the field:** Each team must keep at least four players (including the goalie) in its defensive half of the field and three players in its offensive half. The three midfielders are allowed to roam the entire field.

- ✔ **Serving penalties:** Whenever a player is serving time in the penalty box, he must remain there until he is released by the timekeeper. He can return to the field if the opponent scores a goal or his team gains possession of the ball in its attack goal area.

- ✔ **Four seconds:** When a goalie makes a stop and has control of the ball, he has 4 seconds to deliver a pass or move out of the crease with the ball. During this 4-second period, no one may make contact with him. When the goalie steps out of the crease with the ball, he can't return there until he surrenders possession.

Personal fouls in boys' lacrosse

In boys' lacrosse, fouls are classified as *personal* and *technical*. Figure 3-3 shows the referee's signals for some of the more common types of fouls.

Following are the types of personal fouls:

- **Cross-checking:** A player uses the handle of his stick to make contact with an opposing player.

- **Illegal body checking:** A player delivers a body check to an opponent who doesn't have possession of the ball or isn't within 5 yards of it; he makes unnecessary contact with the opponent after that player passes or takes a shot; or he delivers the check from behind the opponent, below his waist, or above his shoulders.

- **Illegal gloves:** A player uses gloves that don't meet the league's specifications for safety, or which the player alters in some way.

Illegal body check   Slashing   Crosse checking

Tripping   Holding   Warding off   Stalling

Figure 3-3:
The
referee's
signals for
fouls.

Offsides   Crease violation   Play on

✔ **Illegal stick:** A player uses a stick that doesn't meet the league's specifications. The pocket may be too deep, for example, giving the player an unfair advantage when he is cradling the ball.

✔ **Slashing:** A player's stick contacts an opponent on any area of his body other than the gloved hand that is holding the stick.

✔ **Tripping:** A player obstructs an opponent below the waist, using his stick, arms, or legs.

✔ **Unnecessary roughness:** A player uses excessive force to contact a player with his body or stick.

✔ **Unsportsmanlike conduct:** The referee determines that a player or coach has committed an unsportsmanlike act, such as swearing, using an obscene gesture, or taunting.

When a player commits a personal foul, he must leave the game for 1 minute, serving his time in the penalty box. This penalty leaves his team short a player and gives the opposition a good opportunity to generate a goal.

Technical fouls in boys' lacrosse

Technical fouls aren't quite as costly to the offending team and are enforced much differently from personal fouls. When a technical foul is committed, the referee gives a 30-second penalty to the player who committed the foul if his team is in possession of the ball, or possession of the ball to the team that was fouled if it didn't have possession at the time of the infraction. If neither team had possession of the ball when the technical foul was whistled, the referee awards the ball to the team whose player was fouled at the spot of the infraction. In this situation, no penalty time is served by the opposition.

Following are the types of technical fouls:

✔ **Holding:** A player disrupts an opponent's movement by grabbing him or his stick.

✔ **Illegal procedure:** Any unnecessary delay occurs, such as not substituting players correctly or having players standing in the crease area, which is off limits to everyone except the goalie.

✔ **Illegal screen:** An offensive player makes contact with a defender while trying to block him from defending the player he is trying to cover.

✔ **Interference:** A player impedes the movements of the opponent when he doesn't have possession of the ball and isn't within 5 yards of a loose ball.

✔ **Offside:** A team fails to have at least three players on its offensive side of the midfield line and at least four players on its defensive side of the midfield line.

✔ **Pushing:** A player shoves an opponent from behind.

✔ **Stalling:** The team with the ball intentionally tries to run time off the clock by holding on to it instead of running its normal offensive attack. The referee also calls a stalling foul when players trap the ball on the field with their sticks longer than necessary.

When an attacking player is fouled in the opponent's half of the field, the referee usually won't blow his whistle to stop play. Instead, he throws a flag in recognition of the foul that was committed but allows the attacking team to continue its drive. As soon as the offensive team takes a shot on goal, loses possession of the ball, or fails to move the ball forward, the referee stops, and the player who committed the penalty heads to the penalty box to serve his time. If the team scores a goal on the shot, however, the penalty is erased.

Special rules

Lacrosse can be modified easily to fit the age, experience, and skill level of the players participating. At the beginning levels of youth lacrosse, coaching is all about teaching kids the basics of the game, not adhering to the rule book that's used in the upper ranks of organized lacrosse. In the sections that follow, we outline adjustments to the rules and field that are common in youth leagues.

Fewer kids on the field at younger age levels

Although a regulation lacrosse game features 10 players per team in boys' games and 12 players for each team in girls' games, the younger the children are, the fewer you have on the field at any given time. The idea at the youngest age levels is to introduce kids to the game by giving them lots of touches of the ball — a situation that can happen only when just a few players are on the field. Imagine having a full squad of beginning 6-year-olds on the field at the same time! Each child would be lucky to touch the ball a couple of times during the game, which wouldn't be much fun.

Modifications for various age and experience levels

Following are some of the ways lacrosse is modified in programs around the country to meet children's needs:

✔ **Reduced field size:** Typically in youth lacrosse, the younger the players are, the smaller the field that they play on. If you put beginning players on a large field, they'd have to expend too much energy to run up and down it, and they'd get few opportunities to get their sticks on the ball. Even when they did manage to scoop up the ball, chances are that they'd be too tired to do anything with it.

Depending on how much field space a recreation agency has, the size of a youth lacrosse field varies from community to community. Keeping beginning-level players confined in a small playing area allows them lots of touches of the ball. As players get older, stronger, and faster, they can expect to play on larger fields.

✔ **No-goalie games:** At the beginning levels of youth lacrosse, it's not uncommon to have no goalies manning the nets. Because the kids haven't yet developed many of the skills that are required to play the game, sticking a child in front of the net doesn't make a lot of sense; after all, chances are good that he'll see more grasshoppers than shots on goal. At the early stages of youth lacrosse, you simply want to introduce the kids to running with the ball, as well as passing it and shooting it in the general direction they are aiming at. Trying to fake out a goaltender and get shots past him come later in the skill-development process.

✔ **Fewer rules in place:** Usually, the younger the players, the fewer rules are followed. The offside rule, for example, typically isn't enforced in a beginner league, because the kids aren't ready to grasp this aspect of the game.

Sometimes, leagues instruct their officials not to call certain penalties, but to let a child know what she did wrong so she can begin developing sound habits. This tactic allows the child to learn about the infraction and keeps the game moving along.

✔ **On-the-field coaching:** Some youth leagues allow coaches to be on the field of play during games so that they can provide easy-to-understand instruction to the kids. Remember, at this level, lacrosse isn't about scoring more goals than the other team. Many youth leagues don't even keep score at the youngest levels.

✔ **Modified stick-checking:** In girls' lacrosse, many leagues have specific policies regarding the use of sticks while checking. In a beginning-level program, stick checking may be allowed only when an offensive player's stick is at waist level or below; in a slightly more-advanced league, stick checks may be allowed only against offensive players whose sticks are at chest level or below. These rules ensure that players who are just getting accustomed to using lacrosse sticks don't risk injuring anyone by swinging their sticks wildly.

Speaking Lacrosse Lingo

Lacrosse has a unique language. The following list presents some of the most common terms and phrases that shape the sport:

Attackers: The three offensive players who maneuver around the opposing team's goal area.

Backup: A defender who is in position to assist a teammate who's defending the ball carrier.

Body check: Defensive contact with an opponent from the front, between his shoulders and waist, when the opponent has the ball or is within 5 yards of a loose ball.

Bull dodge: A technique for getting past a defender by using strength and speed.

Butt: The lower end of the handle of the stick.

Catching: Receiving a pass from a teammate.

Checking: An aggressive defensive technique in which a player relies on her stick (or, in some boys' leagues, his body) to knock the ball out of the opposing player's possession.

Check-up: A goalie's call to one of her defenders to find the player the defender is responsible for covering.

Clamp: A technique used in a face-off wherein the player pushes the back of his stick on top of the ball quickly.

Clearing: Running with the ball, or passing the ball, from the defensive half of the field to the attack goal area.

Cradle: The technique that a player uses to carry the ball in her stick.

Crosse: Another word for the stick that lacrosse players use.

Cutting: An offensive maneuver involving quick movements, usually toward the opponent's goal, in an effort to get into position to receive a pass.

Dodging: An offensive maneuver by the ball carrier, used to elude a defender.

Extra-player offense: An advantage that occurs when the opposing team has committed a penalty and one of its players must come off the field.

Face dodge: An offensive maneuver by the ball carrier, who brings his stick across the front of his face while attempting to get past a defender.

Face-off: The technique used to put the ball in play at the start of each period of play or after a goal has been scored.

Fast break: A situation in which the offensive team outnumbers the opposition by at least one player and capitalizes on its advantage by moving the ball down the field aggressively.

Feeding: Passing to a teammate who is in good scoring position.

Front swing: An offensive maneuver in which the player moves from the goal line extended area to the front of the net.

Goalie, goaltender: The player who plays in front of the net and is responsible for stopping the opponent's shots.

Head: The part of the stick that connects to the handle.

Inbounds play: A designed offensive play used to generate a scoring opportunity after the ball is put into play from the end line.

Isolation: An offensive technique wherein the ball handler's teammates clear out of the area to allow her to go one-on-one against her defender.

Loose ball: A ball that is on the field but in the possession of neither team.

Man-to-man defense: A defensive strategy in which each player is responsible for guarding a specific player on the opposing team.

Midfielders: The players who play in the center of the field and who do the most running, because they play at both the offensive and defensive ends.

One-on-one: A situation in which a defender is matched against an offensive player, or a goalie faces a shot from an unguarded player from close range.

On-the-fly substitution: A substitution that occurs during game action, when a player enters the playing area while the teammate he is replacing comes off the field.

Overhand: A type of pass or shot released over a player's shoulder.

Passing: Delivering the ball to a teammate.

Pick: An offensive technique in which a player moves into a stationary position and blocks a defender so as to free a teammate.

Man-down defense: A situation in which a player who committed a foul must come out of the game to serve her penalty, which puts her team down a player on the field and at a significant disadvantage.

Pocket: The part of the stick with the netting that holds the ball.

Poke check: A type of stick check defenders use, which involves shoving the stick at the opponent.

Rake: A face-off technique in which the player sweeps the ball to the side.

Release: An official's notification that a penalized player who is serving time may reenter the game.

Riding: Attempting to prevent the opponent from clearing the ball.

Scooping: Using the stick to pick up a ground ball.

Shaft: The pole that is connected to the head of the stick.

Shooting: Sending the ball toward the opponent's goal in an attempt to score.

Sidearm: A technique for passing or shooting the ball, in which the player holds the stick parallel to the ground and swings it across his body.

Sliding: A defensive maneuver in which a player moves over to provide support to a teammate who has been beaten by the player she was covering.

Special substitution area: The area where players who are substituting for teammates during game action enter the field.

Stack: An offensive setup in which two players stand next to each other.

Throat: The part of the stick where the head connects with the handle.

Underhand: A type of pass or shot in which the player follows through below waist level.

Unsettled situation: A situation in which the defensive team is out of position, which happens often when the ball is loose on the field or a clear has been unsuccessful.

Warding off: An offensive foul in which the ball carrier uses one arm to hold or push an opponent's stick.

Zone defense: A defensive strategy in which each player is responsible for guarding a certain area of the field rather than a specific opponent.

Take the time to go over with your players all the terms that you'll be using during practices and games; otherwise, your players may misinterpret or misunderstand your instructions.

Taking Up Positions

In lacrosse, the object of the game is the same for both boys and girls: Score as many goals as possible during the allotted time while preventing the opposing team from doing the same thing. But girls' and boys' lacrosse also have differences, including the positions on the field and the skills needed to play them. The following sections take a closer look at these positions and the responsibilities that come with handling them.

Positions in boys' lacrosse

In boys' lacrosse, the basic positions are goalie, defender, midfielder, and attacker (see Figure 3-4). A typical full-scale game features one goalie, three defenders, three midfielders, and three attackers.

The skills that are required to play these positions are as different as the kids under your care who will be manning them for you. Starting from your own goal and working out, the following section outlines each position in boys' lacrosse. (For the scoop on assigning kids to different positions, check out Chapter 5.)

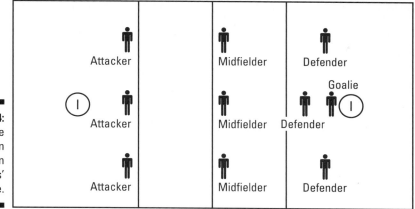

Goalie

This player positions himself between the goal posts, and his top responsibility is to defend your team's goal and stop the ball from going into the net. Good hand–eye coordination and quick reflexes are musts for faring well in this position, because the goalie faces shots from all angles and at varied speeds. Size and speed are nonfactors when it comes to goaltending success, because any player who has the desire to play well here, as well as the courage to face hard-thrown shots without flinching, can excel and be an asset to the team.

Along with defending the net, goalies are counted on to perform many other tasks, including the following:

- **Communicating with the defense:** When the team is defending an attack, the goalie must communicate to his teammates what is unfolding on the field. Because the goalie has the best view of the field — and because some of his teammates will have their backs to the play — he can alert them to certain plays that are being run or tell them where they need to position themselves to stop the attack. He can also warn his teammates when picks are being set so that they can counter those moves. (See Chapter 16 for details on defending picks.)

- **Fueling the offensive attack:** When your goalie has secured the ball, his job isn't done by a long shot. Whenever he stops a shot, he should be looking upfield to see whether a teammate is available to receive a clearing pass that begins an attack, catching the opponent out of position. (For more on training goalies in the art of delivering clearing passes, check out Chapter 16.)

Defenders

These players typically don't receive as much recognition or accolades as the attacker and midfielders, because they aren't directly involved in the plays that produce the goals. But they are just as important as the other positions on the field.

No matter how good your offense is at netting goals, if the team struggles at the defensive end of the field, it probably won't have a lot of success on game days. For more on teaching defensive techniques, head to Chapter 10, and when you're ready to help your players upgrade those defensive skills, check out Chapter 12.

Because a team must keep at least four players (including the goalie) on its defensive half of the field at all times, defenders rarely stray past midfield. Instead, their responsibilities revolve around covering opposing players on the attack. Defenders rely on good footwork to shadow opponents all over the field. They also use a variety of checks, such as poke checks and — if the league allows them — body checks (covered in Chapter 10). Good passing skills also enable defenders to ignite attacks by getting the ball to their midfielders and attackers running down the field.

Midfielders

Lacrosse is a sport of fast-paced transitions, with teams switching back and forth from offense to defense all game long. The midfielders' effectiveness on transitions has a big influence on the team's effectiveness at both the offensive and defensive ends of the field. Since midfielders cover the most territory of any position — they roam all over the field — the quicker they recognize situations the more effective they'll be. For example, when a midfielder anticipates a teammate gaining control of the ball the player can begin moving toward the opponent's goal to try to create a scoring opportunity by outnumbering the opposition and catching it off guard or out of position.

Midfielders typically aren't counted on to provide a lot of scoring punch. The more important qualities for this position are good stick skills for winning duels over loose balls, accurate passing skills, and the stamina to stick with opposing attackers.

Attackers

The responsibility for scoring goals falls squarely on the shoulders of the attackers, who spend games roaming in the opponent's half of the field. Attackers, of course, must rely on the defenders to stop the opposition and the midfielders to feed them the ball, because lacrosse is a team sport, but when they have control of the ball, getting shots on net is largely up to them.

The most productive attackers use a variety of shots to keep the goalie guessing. The sidearm and long bounce shots are among the weapons that attackers should have in their arsenals. (Chapter 9 provides the lowdown on executing these shots.)

Another key asset for attackers is to possess more moves than a disco dancer. When they're closing in on the opponent's goal, and defenders are bumping and stick-checking them, being able to spin free allows for more goal-scoring opportunities. Besides being able to score, attackers must develop a knack for making passes to cutting teammates, often in heavy traffic, to generate scoring chances.

Even though your attackers will likely score the majority of your team's goals, be sure to acknowledge all the efforts that led to the score. Every youngster plays an important role in the team's success, and it's up to you to make each child feel valued and appreciated for his efforts, whatever those may be.

Positions in girls' lacrosse

One of the significant differences in girls' lacrosse is that more players take the field in a regulation game. The following sections discuss the positions in the girls' game (see Figure 3-5) and the responsibilities that go along with them, beginning with the goalie and working out away from the net.

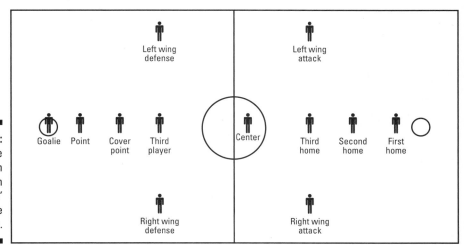

Figure 3-5: The positions on the field in girls' lacrosse games.

Goalie

The primary role of this position is keeping balls out of the net. Besides making saves with her stick, the goalie uses any body part necessary to prevent the opposition from celebrating a goal. She is also expected to communicate with her teammates to let them know where they should be positioned to deny the opponent's attack.

A goalie must be quick on her feet and willing to go after loose balls around the crease area. The more confident your goalie is, the more effective she'll be at turning away the different types of shots she'll be facing. (For some great beginning goalie drills — if we do say so ourselves — to build skills and confidence, head to Chapter 14.)

Point

After the goaltender position, point is the most defensive-oriented position on the field. The player handling this position works closely with the goalie, communicating what the opponent is doing and orchestrating where players need to be on the field to counter the attack.

Your point player must be a good communicator to help prevent defensive breakdowns from occurring. She covers the opponent's first home, so sound checking skills are imperative for keeping that player from getting open shots on net. Because the point player plays so close to the net — and doesn't stray far from this area of the field throughout the game — she's often in position to intercept passes to the middle of the field while defending an attack.

Cover point

This player's main task is to cover the opposition's second home. Good footwork is an asset for excelling in this position, because the player must stick with the opponent to deny passes and shots on goal.

The cover point player is also relied on to make clearing passes, so she must be proficient at catching passes from the goalie and quickly turning upfield to look for teammates who can receive the ball.

Third player

This player's key responsibility is covering the opposing team's third home. Important attributes for doing well in this position are good reflexes, the ability to read the opponent's attack, and the ability to jump into the passing lanes to intercept balls.

Left and right defensive wings

These positions require a substantial amount of running, as the players' primary responsibility is to guard the opponent's left and right attack wings. Besides covering these opponents, the defensive wings move the ball across midfield to help out on the attack when their team has the ball.

Center

This position is a magnet of activity on both offense and defense. Because the position requires strong play both with and without the ball, as well as a variety of other skills, the team's best player usually handles this position.

The center patrols the middle of the field. When her team has control of the ball, she looks to step up into the action, where she can feed the ball to the first, second, and third home players. When her team is on defense, she retreats to her team's defensive half of the field, providing coverage against the opponent's center, disrupting the passing lanes, and looking to intercept balls delivered by the attack wings.

At the beginning levels of lacrosse, you should do your best to ensure that the girls get the chance to play as many positions as possible. That way, they can fully experience what the sport is about. Only at the advanced levels of lacrosse should you be concerned about players handling a specific position on the field.

Left and right attack wings

These positions require covering a lot of territory. The players carry out supportive roles at the offensive end of the field — most notably, feeding the ball to the players manning the first, second, and third home positions. They also must hustle back on defense to help out the left and right defensive wings.

When your team turns the ball over in the opponent's end of the field, your attack wings have to hustle back to lend defensive support. If they're unable to get back in time, the opponent has a scoring opportunity.

Third home

A team's offensive prowess is enhanced whenever its third home player is an efficient passer. She can feed the ball to the first and second home players, as well as the right and left attack wings. She also takes shots on goal when scoring opportunities arise and creates openings for herself to shoot or pass.

Second home

This position is similar to the point guard position in basketball, because the second home orchestrates the offense and makes the passes that help the offense run smoothly and effectively. In lacrosse, this player should be an excellent ball handler, because she'll likely have the ball on her stick more than most of the other players. It's also helpful if she's comfortable maneuvering behind the opponent's goal and delivering passes from there to teammates cutting to the net.

Collecting assists isn't her only responsibility, though. The offense will be more difficult to defend if the second home player is a threat to score goals, too. When this player can mix up shooting and passing, she keeps the opponent off balance.

First home

This position represents the most offensive play on the lacrosse field. The first home's main responsibilities are to score goals and to deliver accurate passes to teammates who are in scoring position.

To excel in this position, a youngster must be quick, with good footwork that helps her maneuver around defenders; she must have sound ball-control skills, so she can maintain possession while negotiating the defensive congestion she'll regularly encounter around the net; and she must be able to recognize opportunities to exploit the defense with accurate passes. The more types of shots she's comfortable executing while defenders are harassing her from all angles, the more potent your team will be every time it ventures toward the opponent's goal.

Chapter 4

Parental Guidance: Meeting Your Players' Parents

Good communication skills are important for air traffic controllers, public speakers, and volunteer lacrosse coaches too. The better your communication skills are, the bigger impact you'll have on your players, and the greater chance you'll forge a positive relationship with all their parents. Your ability to interact with parents and encourage them to work with you rather than against you determines — to a large extent — whether you have a smooth season or bump into obstacles at every turn.

In this chapter, we help you plan the preseason parents' meeting, which is imperative for getting the season headed in the right direction. We cover the items you need to share with parents, ranging from your coaching philosophy to your policy on spectator behavior and including piles of paperwork. We also discuss enlisting parents to do all sorts of jobs that can ease your workload and keep your focus where it needs to be: on the kids. It's time to meet those parents!

Planning the Preseason Parents' Meeting

Holding a preseason parents' meeting before you step on the field with your team is as important to you as a full tank of gas is to a race-car driver at the start of a race. Without the fuel, the driver has no chance of being successful, and the same holds true for you if you skip this meeting. It's one of the most important hours you'll spend this season.

The preseason parents' meeting serves multiple purposes:

- ✔ It's a chance for parents to get to know who their children will be spending time with this season.
- ✔ It's an opportunity for you to let parents know how you'll be managing the team and handling all the issues that pop up during the course of a season.
- ✔ It opens critical lines of communication and sends the all-important message that you'll be working with parents to help ensure that their children have a rewarding season.

Making a good first impression

First impressions leave lasting imprints on parents. Because this meeting is so significant, approach it with the same effort and enthusiasm you would apply to an interview for a job you covet. Explaining your thoughts clearly on the topics you'll be covering demonstrates how deeply you care about the upcoming season and reinforces your commitment to each child on the team. Parents will appreciate your initiative and feel much more at ease turning their children over to you this season.

The more comfortable parents are with you, the stronger your relationship is going to be with both them and their children.

Covering the important points

Here are some additional points to keep in mind regarding the meeting:

- ✔ **Touch base with all the parents as soon as possible.** Most parents juggle chaotic schedules, so getting everyone together can be a little tricky. As soon as you get your hands on your team roster, contact each child's parents via phone. Introduce yourself as the coach; let them know the date, time, and location you chose for your parents' meeting; and stress the importance of being there. Giving parents as much notice as possible gives them time to rearrange their schedules, if necessary, and increases their likelihood of showing up.

✓ **Find a familiar meeting place.** Your best bet is to meet at the offices of the recreation department that runs the league. If you let the league director know you want to meet with your team members' parents, he or she can make arrangements to reserve a room for you. If meeting at the recreation department isn't an option, local libraries often have meeting rooms available. Be sure you check with the library staff to ensure the room can accommodate how many parents you invited to attend.

✓ **Pick a convenient time.** Choose a time that matches, as closely as possible, the time your team will take the field for practice. This way, you'll know that your meeting fits into most parents' schedules.

✓ **Plan for less than an hour.** The meeting should last at least half an hour, but no more than an hour. Just like your practices should only be an hour in length, there is no reason to drag out a meeting beyond this time frame either.

✓ **Outline your key points.** Jot down the main points you want to cover. A great starting point is to ask yourself what you would want to know if you were handing your child over to a coach you didn't know. You'd want to know what type of coaching experience the coach has, how often the team is going to be practicing, and how positions and playing time will be determined, among many other areas.

✓ **Rehearse your presentation.** What do you tell kids to do to get better at something? Right: practice. The same applies to you concerning public speaking. Proper preparation is the best antidote for speaking nerves. In the days leading up to the meeting, stand in front of a mirror, and practice what you're going to say. If you sense that you're going to be really uncomfortable, rehearse in front of your spouse, a family member, or a friend. No one expects you to be a professional speaker or to sound like a polished politician delivering an address, but the more comfortable you are, the more smoothly your talk will go.

✓ **Take good notes along.** Outline all your main points on a notepad, and bring it to the meeting. Referring to your notes often throughout the meeting isn't a sign of weakness; it indicates that you want to make sure you're covering all the important points for the parents' benefit.

✓ **Talk off the cuff.** Don't write out everything you want to say and read it word for word at the meeting. Just reading a speech will bore parents and make them wonder how much fun their children are going to have with you this season.

✓ **Schedule time to have the parents introduce themselves.** Parents will be seeing quite a bit of one another during the season, so at some point during the meeting, have the parents introduce themselves (and tell the group who their children are, too). Although some parents may already know one another, introductions are good ice-breakers.

> ✔ **Organize your handouts.** Collect all the paperwork you need to give parents, and plan to pass it out at the end of your meeting, prior to conducting your question and answer segment. Holding the paperwork to the end prevents distractions; otherwise, some parents may tune out what you have to say because they're too busy flipping through your handouts. For more info, see "Managing Paperwork Parents Need to Fill Out" later in this chapter.

Allow parents to ask questions at any time during the meeting or, if they prefer, to hold on to their questions till the question-and-answer period at the end.

Despite your efforts, if any parent simply can't make the meeting, arrange to go over everything with him or her later — on the phone or in person — to share what you covered during the meeting. You don't want to head into the season without touching base with all the parents and clearly explaining what's in store for their children. Also make arrangements to get the paperwork to them, either via mail or meeting with them in person.

Explaining Your Coaching Philosophy

Your first task in the meeting — after introducing yourself — is introducing your coaching philosophy. To reduce the chances of misunderstandings throughout the season, let parents know up front how you'll be handling the team. Clearly defining your stance on playing time, good sportsmanship, and other issues represents the foundation of your coaching philosophy (see Chapter 2 for more on developing your philosophy). Giving parents this heads-up provides ample time for them to find a more appropriate league or level of competitiveness for their children if they discover that the current one isn't a good fit.

Emphasizing good sportsmanship for players

The best lacrosse coaches teach kids the fundamentals of the game — skills such as stick handling, shooting, and defense — as well as other aspects that often don't get the attention they deserve, such as good sportsmanship. Parents appreciate knowing that their youngsters are learning what being a good sport means; how the team behaves after both wins and losses is always more important than how team members performed on the field.

Tell parents that you'll be having your team shake hands with the opponents following each game. Note that when your players win, you'll expect them to refrain from excessive celebrating, and when they lose, you'll expect them to congratulate their opponents for playing well.

Modeling good sportsmanship isn't easy, but playing fairly, showing respect toward referees regardless of the call, and accepting the game's results graciously are important traits to teach young players. The habits they pick up from you are the ones they'll carry with them during their future years if playing lacrosse or any other organized sport. You can feel good knowing that you instilled positive traits in your players. (For more on teaching sportsmanship by example, see Chapter 2.)

Maintaining model parent behavior in the stands

When it comes to explaining the type of behavior you expect from parents during games, be very clear and straightforward; leave no room for misinterpretation or misunderstanding. Emphasize the importance of modeling good sportsmanship before, during, and after games. Let the parents know that children don't perform as well — or have as much fun — when they're being screamed at to score a goal or to get back on defense.

Your season will go more smoothly and will be more enjoyable for everyone involved when parents are working with you — not against you — as you teach your players proper behavior. If you can get parents to understand fully the importance of showing good sportsmanship, their youngsters will be more likely to follow in their footsteps. If your message to the team is distorted by unruly parent behavior in the stands, these mixed signals can lead to confusion and problems. Actions — yours as well as those of the parents in the stands — speak much louder than any words.

Stress the following points to parents:

✔ **Bad behavior can get them ejected.** Make it clear that although you never want to have to remove parents from the stands for behaving inappropriately, you won't hesitate to do so if they're being a negative influence. (Many leagues have policies for removing spectators, and you should be aware of what steps you're required to follow.) Don't be condescending in your tone, but hammer home the point that the game is about the kids. You want their memories to be of having fun and developing skills — not of watching out-of-control parents make everyone miserable. (See Chapter 18 for more on dealing with disruptive parents.)

✔ **Audience participation should be positive.** You never want parents yelling at officials, coaches, or players on either team. Spectators' comments should be only positive and encouraging — and never so overbearing that they infringe on your communication with the players.

✔ **Only coaches should coach.** Let parents know that they need to refrain from shouting directions, because hearing multiple sets of instructions confuses kids. Remind parents that you're the coach and that all the coaching needs to come from you.

✔ **Officials are people too.** Especially at the beginning levels of play, the officials may be teenagers who — despite doing their best — may make some mistakes. (Everyone makes mistakes, because we're all human.) Remind parents that yelling at officials is unacceptable, no matter how bad a call seems to be. Explain that having calls go against your team is simply part of the game and that over the course of the season, the calls will certainly balance out.

When the parents don't make a big deal about calls, neither will the kids. By the time the game ends, the players won't give that penalty call another thought — as long as they didn't hear Mom or Dad screaming about it at the top of their lungs.

Determining playing time and positions

Coaching a youth lacrosse team involves making as many decisions as the chief executive officer of a Fortune 500 company — or at least it seems that way. A couple of the most challenging decisions you face are assigning playing time and positions.

A lot of parents sign a child up for lacrosse with a position in mind that they think the child is best suited for. This plan seldom works out the way they envision — particularly when half a dozen dads think their sons should be the goaltender. Explaining your process for positioning kids well in advance of stepping on the field for that first practice of the season alleviates some of these potential headaches. It's also important to run down your philosophy on playing time. At the beginning levels of play game day minutes are divvied up equally among all the players, as long as they regularly attend your practices. Only at the more advanced levels of play is playing time dictated by skill level.

Assigning playing time

Many parents keep track of their child's minutes on the field as closely as they do the figures in their checkbook. Telling parents how you decide how long each player spends on the field can help prevent misunderstandings and frustration. (If questions about playing minutes surface later during the season, flip to Chapter 18 for tips on dealing with these issues.)

For kids, playing lacrosse is all about being on the field, running around and getting lots of opportunities to shoot, pass and catch the ball. Take a look anywhere kids get together to play pickup games; nobody stands on the sidelines, because that's as exciting as being given a big homework assignment for the weekend. Giving kids equal opportunities to play is crucial for their development in the sport. Kids who are forced to sit on the bench for long stretches, or who don't receive the same amount of playing time as their friends, quickly lose interest in the sport.

Whether you're coaching a couple dozen players or barely enough to make a complete team, one of your top priorities on game day (see Chapter 8 for more on this aspect of coaching) is making sure that playing time is divvied up equally among the kids, regardless of how fast they are, how accurately they shoot, or how well they defend — as long as they attend practices regularly. It's not fair to the kids who show up for every practice to have to share playing time with teammates who appear only on game day. Be sure to discuss that policy with parents ahead of time to prevent conflicts during games.

At the older and more advanced stages of lacrosse (usually around the age of 14), where winning games takes on a more prominent role, playing time is distributed based on the player's ability. The same goes for travel teams. (For more details on coaching this more elite level of lacrosse, check out Chapter 19.)

As kids move up the lacrosse ladder and stick around the sport for several seasons — hopefully, in part, because they've had so much fun playing for you and want it to continue — they'll recognize that games take on a more competitive feel and that will be embraced by many. Gradually, they'll also begin comparing their skills to others on their team, as well as their opponents, and develop a sense of where they fit in skill-wise. When letting kids know how playing time is divvied up, emphasize that everyone plays a significant role on the team, regardless if they're a starter or not, and everyone contributes something in their own unique way. (For the scoop on working with all different types of kids, flip to Chapter 5.)

Lining up: Who plays where and why

Choosing playing positions for all the kids — at the advanced levels of play — is like putting together a Rubik's Cube. You've got all these different colors that somehow go together, much like all your different players, and it's up to you to figure out the right combinations.

When you're coaching at the youngest age levels, your mission is simply to give kids a taste of as many positions as possible so that they enjoy a well-rounded experience. Most parents will appreciate your interest in giving kids a chance to try different aspects of the game.

Talking to the parents of more advanced kids

At the more advanced levels, figuring out where kids are best suited to play takes on more importance and impacts how much success a team enjoys. You may have four or five kids who desperately want to play goalie, but your job is figuring out which player has the talent and proper attitude to handle the position, as well as determining what other positions those players who were eyeing that spot can fill to best help the team excel. Remember, at the older and more advanced levels of play the game day minutes are given to the most-skilled athletes, so it's important that parents are aware of this. In Chapter 5, we go into detail on evaluating players and assigning positions.

If you slide a youngster into an offensive position during the first practice of the season, for example, and never allow him even a glimpse of what playing defense is like, you're not giving him a true taste of the sport. Who knows? He may end up walking away from the game after the season because he didn't enjoy playing the position you gave him; he might have loved playing a defensive position instead and would've stayed involved in lacrosse for years to come. Parents who are disappointed that their child isn't getting to play a specific position full time may be pleasantly surprised to see him excel in a different position.

Other parents who had their hearts set on their child's playing a particular position all season may not be thrilled that she'll be moved around on the field. Those parents may opt to sign the child up elsewhere, thanks to your advance notice of how the season is going to run, which prevents potential headaches for everyone.

Managing Paperwork Parents Need to Fill Out

Most youth lacrosse programs around the country require parents to sign a series of forms. These forms are usually filled out during registration, but sometimes the responsibility of securing parents' John Hancocks on all the paperwork falls to you. Although the content and style of paperwork varies from league to league, the purpose is generally the same. This section gives you a rundown of the forms you may see.

Beyond the league paperwork, you can make your job easier (and keep your sanity in the process) by distributing your own packets of information to parents. These packets can include

✔ Team rosters and contact information for everyone, including yourself.

✔ Practice and game schedules.

✔ Basic information on lacrosse (a big help for parents who aren't familiar with the sport).

✔ A rundown of the rules. (To prevent confusion, highlight any rules that the league has modified. Check out Chapter 2 for a look at some rules that are often tweaked by leagues.)

League documents

Most leagues require parents to fill out a variety of forms before the kids can put on their helmets:

✔ **Practice and game schedules:** Leagues typically set the schedule for the season well in advance, so be sure parents get a copy so they can plan accordingly. Also, if the league has assigned your team specific days and times to use the field for practice, make sure to give parents that schedule as well. The more information parents have, the better they can plan for what's coming each week.

✔ **Consent form:** A consent form states that a child may get hurt during practices or games, and says that in the event of an injury, the league isn't responsible. Most programs carry insurance against possible litigation. Be sure you ask about the league's coverage and your own status under the policy, and share with the parents.

The National Youth Sports Coaches Association (a program of the National Alliance for Youth Sports) provides insurance coverage to coaches who complete its training program. The association recommends that all coaches go through training to help ensure that they are knowledgeable in all areas of the sport and can provide a safe and fun experience for every child on their team. For more information visit www.nays.org.

✔ **Medical evaluation form:** This form, signed by the child's physician, states that the youngster is physically healthy and able to participate in the sport. If the child has a condition such as asthma or diabetes, that condition is listed on this sheet. (For more details on what should be in a properly stocked first-aid kit, which is your responsibility, check out Chapter 6.)

Personal packets

You can make a great impression on all the parents by providing information packets. Parents will appreciate and use these handy resources throughout the season:

✔ **Rules guide:** For some parents, the sport of lacrosse is unfamiliar, and chances are that many of them aren't up to speed on all the rules and terminology of the game. You — and they — simply don't have time to go over the game itself in great detail without dragging the meeting into all hours of the night. To help them out, as well as save them hours searching the Internet for information on the game, print up the following:

- A rules primer — a couple of pages on the basics of the game — that they can review to get a better understanding of lacrosse.

- A page noting any special rules in effect in the league. (Maybe the league has instructed officials not to call certain penalties to keep the game moving, for example.)

- A rough sketch of the field, indicating where each player is positioned.

- Definitions of some basic terms that they'll hear often during the season.

- A page describing the referees' hand signals and what they mean (you can copy them from Chapter 3).

✔ **Phone list and contact information:** A sheet with all the kids' names and their parents' telephone numbers and e-mail addresses can be handy for parents. At some point during the season, someone may need to contact another parent to arrange for a child's ride to practice.

Make sure that you include your own contact information for parents who want to get in touch with you later.

✔ **Emergency treatment authorization form:** The child's parent or guardian signs this league form, which lists the names of usually three people, as a rule of thumb, who should be contacted if the child is injured and requires emergency medical treatment. The form usually gives the coach or other league personnel the authority to seek medical treatment for the child if no one can be reached.

Recruiting Parents to Help on the Sidelines

Parents put in a lot of effort and make sacrifices along the way to help ensure that their children have a memorable time playing lacrosse. As a result, most parents are willing to lend a hand to help make the season run smoothly.

Encouraging your players' parents to take an active interest in the season lays out the welcome mat for those who want to help. Parents can assist in many ways that can make a difference in the quality of your team's season.

Attracting assistant coaches

Running a quality lacrosse practice takes a lot of work, so the more bodies you can count on — whether it's friends you're comfortable working with or parents you appoint as assistant coaches — the more efficient your sessions can be, as well as the more beneficial for the kids. When you can put knowledgeable and caring adults in assistant coaching positions, you'll increase your chances of accomplishing more each session. The payoff will be greater skill development for the players — and more fun, too.

In addition to helping during practices, assistant coaches can be valuable resources on game day (for more details, check out Chapter 8), providing additional sets of eyes and ears.

Assistants can help you in many areas, such as the following:

- **Monitoring minutes:** Assistants can monitor your substitution patterns and track each child's playing time to ensure that everyone receives an equal amount. This info comes in handy if a parent ever questions the amount of playing time his or her child is receiving (see Chapter 18 for more on dealing with those types of parents).

- **Assisting with pregame responsibilities:** You have many duties to fulfill on game day before play begins, such as meeting with the officials and the opposing coach. Being able to rely on an assistant to run your warmups and oversee the stretching routine frees you to perform your other duties.

- **Keeping parents in check:** When the game begins, your focus is on the players, to ensure that they're having a fun and safe experience, so if parents make inappropriate comments to the officials (or anyone else), you may not hear them. Assistant coaches can alert you to these issues so that you can address them at the appropriate time to ensure that parents conduct themselves properly. (Refer to "Maintaining model parent behavior in the stands" earlier in this chapter for details on communicating your expectations, and check out Chapter 18 for help on dealing with problem parents.)

- **Scouting the opponent:** At more advanced levels of play (with older kids), you can have your assistants check out the opposition players as they warm up. Maybe they'll spot a tendency in the other team's passing, such as passing to the left a majority of the time, or they may note that certain players aren't as proficient at handling passes. These little bits and pieces of information can help your players enjoy higher levels of success on the field.

Poll the group to see who is interested in helping out on the sidelines, but hold off on naming your assistants at this time. You probably won't know most (if any) of the parents at your preseason meeting, particularly if you're in your first season of coaching. Use the first few practices of the season to get to know the parents and gauge how they interact with the children — their own and others. You may want to set aside some time after the first few practices to interview any interested parents, making sure that their approaches and philosophies match yours. By going this route, you're more likely to select parents who will support your coaching philosophy (see Chapter 2) and emphasize the fun and learning you want to stress.

At more advanced levels of play, you always want to find out in advance who's interested in assisting and set aside times to interview them. Question their experience playing and coaching the game, why they want to be involved, and how they think they can be assets to your team. Through interviews, you want to determine who's going to be helpful and who's going to be a hindrance. Assistants can be of enormous value, but if they overstep their roles, they can create unwanted confusion.

Your assistants are among the most important selections you'll make, because your coaching will only be as good as your worst assistant.

Exercise great care in choosing assistants, because some parents can surprise you the first time they step on the field with you. They may try taking over your practices by imposing their own teaching methods, for example, or they may require so much mentoring that they detract from your time with the kids. What you want to steer clear of at all costs — much like a bad case of food poisoning — is choosing a parent who seems laid-back at your preseason meeting but transforms into a yeller when the games begin. If you somehow make a bad judgment call on a parent, you must solve this touchy problem immediately so that it doesn't linger and cause additional headaches for everyone. (You can find suggestions for dealing with this problem in Chapter 18.)

Signing up parents for support roles

Many parents probably never played lacrosse growing up, and the sport may be unfamiliar to them, so they're not going to be jumping at the chance to provide instruction on the field. Inexperience with lacrosse doesn't mean that they can't help out in other areas, though. Most parents want to be involved to some degree; they just need to know where they can fit in.

Following are some of the jobs you can recruit parents to fill:

✔ **Telephone-tree coordinator:** When Mother Nature drops rain on the field a few hours before a practice or game, parents won't know whether they still need to get their children to the field or whether they get a break for the day from chauffeuring duties. If a game or practice is canceled, it's impossible for you to contact every parent in a timely manner. Enter the telephone-tree coordinator, who maintains a list of all the parents' numbers to ensure that messages are communicated to everyone quickly.

If you need to cancel an event, let your telephone-tree coordinator know that the event is canceled and when it's rescheduled for. The coordinator calls, e-mails, or text messages two parents on the phone list; those two parents do the same for two parents, and so on. In a matter of minutes, everyone has been contacted.

✔ **Team parent:** Handing out chilled beverages or healthy postgame snacks (see Chapter 17) is a nice way to wrap up a practice session or game. Choose a team parent who can put together a schedule assigning parents the games or practices they're responsible for bringing snacks to. This role can also include organizing an end-of-season pizza party or even making arrangements to take the entire team to watch a local high school or college lacrosse game.

✔ **Concession-stand worker:** Some leagues require each team to provide a couple of parents to work the league's concession stand during the season. Check with the league director to find out what dates need filling, and see which of your parents are willing to handle that role.

✔ **Photo coordinator:** Team photos are great keepsakes for the children, who years from now will enjoy seeing pictures of themselves and their teammates all decked out in their uniforms. Some leagues work directly with a local photography company; in other leagues, organizing a photo shoot is left to the discretion of the coach. Either way, having a parent fulfill the photo-coordinator position can be extremely helpful.

Besides working with you to select a convenient time for the team photo, the photo coordinator can arrange for a photographer to come out for a game or two to take action shots of the kids. Just be sure to verify that all the parents are on board with forking over extra cash for these photos.

✔ **Team trainer:** Lacrosse is a contact sport, which means that during the season, children are going to suffer bumps and bruises, scrapes and abrasions, and other minor aches and pains. Ask a parent who's been properly trained in first aid, and who has experience dealing with minor injuries, to help out as team trainer. Although all coaches should be trained in cardiopulmonary resuscitation (CPR) and familiar with basic first aid, having a trainer who's skilled in these important areas is comforting — not only to you, but also to the other parents. (Turn to Chapter 17 for some information on treating common lacrosse injuries.)

- ✔ **Trophy coordinator:** Some leagues present a trophy to the first-place team; others hand out participation trophies or certificates to all the players; and some simply don't have the financial resources to provide anything extra. Depending on the type of league you're coaching in, you may want to consider assigning a trophy coordinator, who can arrange to get small participation trophies or plaques to present to all the children at the end of the season.

- ✔ **Game-day help:** In beginner lacrosse programs, a couple of parents are sometimes needed to help out on game day with tasks such as keeping score or retrieving loose balls that go out of play. If your league needs this sort of help (see Chapter 2 on the importance of knowing the league's rules), be sure to mention it during the parents' meeting. Find out which parents are willing to fill these positions, and write their names down. You don't want to be scrambling around minutes before your game looking for parent volunteers when you could be spending that time getting your team ready.

- ✔ **Travel coordinator:** This position is appropriate only for an older and more-experienced team that competes against teams in other cities. (For more on travel teams, check out Chapter 19.) This person tracks down the most cost-effective and convenient hotels for the team to stay in, and arranges a team bus or coordinates car pools for the road trip itself.

- ✔ **Fund-raising coordinator:** Sometimes, lacrosse teams rely on fund-raisers to offset the cost of uniforms or to purchase new equipment. These events can include everything from selling candy bars to washing cars, and they require a lot of behind-the-scenes work to pull off. The job entails determining what items to sell and the best location for doing so.

 During your meeting, circulate a list of responsibilities that you need filled, and have parents jot down their names next to the duties they're comfortable helping out with. If a large number of parents express interest in a specific role, your best bet may be to have them work together as a committee so that no parent is alienated. Or if no one signs up for a certain role, see whether a parent who signed up for another position would be willing to fill in there instead.

Meeting Players' Special Needs

Taking on the role of a youth lacrosse coach means accepting responsibility for working with kids of vastly different abilities. Some players are fast, and others are slow. Some players are athletically gifted, and others have trouble keeping their eye on the ball while they're running down the field. You may also have a child or two on your team who has special needs, such as a hearing or vision problem or a learning disability. As a coach, you must provide opportunities to all your players and do what you can to make the season fun for everyone. (Head to Chapter 5 for a look at all the different types of kids you may be coaching this season.)

During the parents' meeting, be sure to find out whether any of the children under your care have medical conditions that you need to be aware of and whether any special accommodations need to be made for those conditions. These can range from inhalers to insulin. Of course, make sure you take the time to meet with the parents so that you clearly understand how to use them, if the child needs assistance.

Understandably, parents may not feel comfortable divulging their children's medical information in front of all of the other parents, many of whom they may not have met before. For that reason, you should set aside time at the end of the meeting for one-on-one discussions in private. Also, let parents know that they can contact you later to discuss anything.

Concluding Your Meeting with Q & A

Before wrapping up the meeting, you want to give parents a chance to ask any questions that they may have. It's perfectly okay if a lot of hands go up during the question and answer session; that's a good sign! It shows that the parents are listening to what you're saying and are deeply interested in their kids' well-being.

To ensure open dialogue, let parents know that no topic is off limits. The question-and-answer session also allows parents who were hesitant to interrupt your talk to pose their questions and get answers.

Also let parents know that if they'd feel more comfortable speaking with you in private, you'll be happy to hang around after the meeting to chat with them (refer to "Meeting Players' Special Needs" earlier in this chapter).

If you can't answer any questions posed during your meeting, make a note of them, and let the parents know that you'll get back to them with answers as soon as possible.

Remind parents that if they have any questions or concerns during the season, you'll be eager to speak with them in person, over the phone, or through e-mail. Make sure, however, that they're aware of the times that aren't conducive to productive discussions — such as before and after games and practices, when your focus is on the kids and your other responsibilities.

Part II:
Fielding a Lacrosse Team

The 5th Wave
By Rich Tennant

"This is great! It even comes with a jar of tooth-black for that 'just checked' look."

In this part . . .

Understanding the talent level of your players — and the areas of the game in which they are strong and weak — allows you to create and run fun-filled practices that meet their needs. This part shares lots of tips for planning quality practices that promote skill development, and it provides an array of drills you can use to teach some of the basics. The part also gives you information on handling all the game-day responsibilities you must fulfill to ensure a rewarding day on the lacrosse field.

Chapter 5

Managing Your Team

The more lacrosse skills your players know how to perform — and can execute on game day while opponents are shadowing them and disrupting them all over the field — the more enjoyment they will get out of the game. Your many responsibilities include figuring out which skills your players have a grasp of and which ones need attention, and then ensuring that you meet their training needs. Not to worry — these tasks aren't as daunting as they may seem. This chapter has you covered.

Teaching Basic Lacrosse Skills

Lacrosse requires a broad range of skills. The following sections look at the skills all beginning players need to know to make their first experience with the sport a rewarding one.

Moving with the ball

Players who are unable to move with the ball are about as successful as sky-divers without parachutes. A player's ability to maneuver with the ball makes it more difficult for defenders to stick with him; it also creates passing lanes he can use to deliver the ball to teammates and opens up scoring opportunities.

The technique lacrosse players use to maneuver with the ball — simply moving the stick side to side, up and down, or back and forth — is known as the *cradle*. Using the cradle allows a player to keep the ball in his stick while he's running or fending off a check. (For more on the different types of cradles, see Chapter 9.)

When running with the ball, a player should hold his stick in an upright position (see Figure 5-1), with his dominant hand toward the top of the stick and the other hand at the bottom of the stick. This stance allows him to pass or shoot quickly. Many children tend to carry the ball at waist level while they're running, which takes away a lot of their effectiveness; they waste valuable time in passing to an open teammate if they have to raise their stick before releasing the ball.

Figure 5-1:
Lacrosse players carry the ball in this position to maximize their effectiveness on the run.

Gaining control of the ball

Any time the ball is loose on the field, your team has an opportunity to gain possession. You certainly don't need a mathematics degree to figure out that the more times your players scoop up loose balls, the more opportunities they create for scoring goals. Teach your team the *scoop method* to corral those balls while denying the opposition the chance to go on the attack. Here's how a player should pick up the ball:

1. **She uses her dominant hand to grab the stick at its *throat*, which is where the head and shaft come together.**

   Her opposite hand is at the end of the stick.

2. **Keeping her feet shoulder width apart, she bends her knees while lowering her stick to the ground (see Figure 5-2).**

   The head contacts the field while the shaft is as close to the ground as possible. The handle is slightly below her knee. The lower the opposite hand, the better. Ideally, a young player is scraping her knuckles along the ground.

Figure 5-2:
A player uses the scoop method to grab loose balls.

3. **She drops the hand at the end of the stick almost parallel to the field and uses a quick, scooping motion to slide the pocket under the ball.**

Passing and receiving

For some players, passing the ball can be about as much fun as eating their vegetables. But accurate passes and catches are much-needed elements of a productive offensive unit that is difficult to defend against.

This section begins with the basics of executing a stationary pass and then follows up on the technique for catching those passes. (For more details on passing and catching on the run, flip to Chapter 9.)

Here's how a player passes while standing still:

1. **The passer stands with his feet about shoulder width apart.**

   His stance is similar to that of a player batting in a baseball game, with his front shoulder facing the intended target.

2. **He places his bottom hand on the end of the stick, holding it loosely with his fingers.**

3. **He places his top hand just short of the midpoint of the stick, again holding it loosely with his fingers.**

4. **He moves the stick over his back shoulder (see Figure 5-3).**

5. **His top hand moves the stick back so that the stick points at his target while his weight shifts to his back foot.**

6. **He uses his top hand to bring the stick forward so that it is vertical while taking a step forward with his right foot (see Figure 5-4).**

He snaps the top wrist to get more force behind the pass while stepping toward the target with his opposite foot. The motion is fundamentally the same as throwing a ball, except that you are using both your dominant and opposite hands.

Figure 5-3:
The player moves his stick over his shoulder to deliver an overhand pass.

Figure 5-4:
The player turns his body toward his intended target when passing the ball.

7. **His top arm should be fully extended, with the end of the stick facing the target when the ball is released.**

   His upper body faces the target. In order to pass accurately, it is necessary to swipe the top hand down the shaft. Not all the way to the bottom hand, but enough that it allows your shoulder to rotate forward to face the target. As the top hand rotates forward, the lower hand should be held away from the midsection. This will allow the throw to have a great trajectory and not end up on the ground in front of the player.

When the ball is on the way, here are the steps for catching it:

1. **Just as she would for passing, the player places her bottom hand on the end of the stick and her top hand slightly below the midpoint of the shaft.**

   She holds the stick lightly in her fingers.

2. **She holds the stick in a vertical position about a foot in front of her, keeping it over her shoulder of her top hand with the pocket facing the passer to create a clear target (see Figure 5-5).**

   For a right-handed passer, this target is over his right shoulder.

3. **As the passer delivers the ball, she keeps her stick out in front of her body.**

Figure 5-5:
The proper
stick
position for
receiving
a pass.

4. **When the ball is about to reach the pocket, she pulls the stick back slightly to help cushion the impact and receive the pass (see Figure 5-6).**

   Her stick should be in front of her shoulders when the ball makes contact with the netting.

5. **As the ball makes contact with the pocket, she relaxes her grip on the stick with her top hand.**

   This maneuver helps cushion the impact so that the ball doesn't bounce out of the pocket.

Shooting

Without doubt, what the majority of kids love most about lacrosse is shooting the ball at the net. Scoring a goal off the shot is even more enjoyable. (For details on teaching the more-advanced technique of shooting on the run, check out Chapter 9.)

Here are the basics for executing a long overhand shot:

1. **The shooter positions his feet shoulder width apart and bends his knees.**

   His front foot is pointed at the net, and his weight is on his back foot, which is parallel to the net.

2. **He places his bottom hand on the end of the stick and the top hand just below the midpoint of the stick.**

Figure 5-6: The player gradually pulls her stick back when catching a pass.

At more-advanced levels, you can teach the player to drop his top hand down the stick several inches, which will generate more power on the shot.

3. **The player moves the head of the stick behind the plane of his shoulders. It is similar to throwing a ball (see Figure 5-7).**

4. **He steps forward and shifts his weight to his front foot.**

5. **As he shifts his weight onto his opposite (and front) foot, he brings both hands forward, snapping the top hand over the bottom hand.**

Although shooting with the hands, arms, and shoulders, the center of power is in the hips and legs. By stepping toward the target and shifting his weight forward, he is using his entire body to accelerate his shot (Figure 5-8).

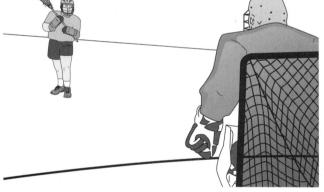

Figure 5-7:
The overhand shot requires the stick to be parallel to the field.

Figure 5-8:
The faster the player brings the stick forward, the more force he generates.

6. **He follows through on the shot, transferring all his weight to his front foot.**

   The head points to the target.

Defending

Playing defense typically isn't one of the first skills that young players practice. Nonetheless, it is one of the most important parts of the game, especially considering that roughly half of every game, your team won't have possession of the ball and will be defending its goal.

One basic element of good defensive play is always being in proper position to move in any direction in the blink of an eye. Teach your players the following basic defensive stance:

1. **She places her feet just beyond shoulder width apart, with her weight on the balls of her feet, keeping her head up and her eyes on the opponent's midsection.**

2. **She flexes her knees and bends her back slightly (see Figure 5-9).**

   This stance puts her in prime position to move in any direction the opposing player goes.

Checking

In some boys' lacrosse leagues, checking is permitted. If your league allows it, read on to see how it can be an effective technique for players to use.

The following are the basics of executing a check:

1. **The defender takes the defensive position described in "Defending," earlier in this chapter.**

2. **With his head up and his eyes on his opponent's midsection, he takes a small step toward the opponent.**

3. **He leans slightly forward and, keeping both hands on his stick, raises his arms to make contact with the opponent (see Figure 5-10).**

   He makes the hit short and hard, without fully extending his arms.

4. **He pulls the stick back and resumes his defensive position.**

Figure 5-9:
This basic
defensive
position
allows a
player to
move in any
direction
quickly.

Figure 5-10:
To deliver a
check, the
player leans
into his
opponent
with his
stick.

Goaltending

Manning this position requires a unique set of skills, many of which are vastly different from any of the others you'll be teaching your players. Whenever the opponent has the ball in the defensive zone, you want your goalie ready to move in any direction to defend a shot. Following is the basic ready stance you should teach (for more information on stopping shots, jump to Chapter 10):

1. **The goalie places her feet shoulder width apart and her knees slightly bent, with her weight on the balls of her feet.**

2. **She keeps her head up and her eyes on the offensive player who's handling the ball.**

3. **He holds the stick above the shoulder of his dominant hand.**

   Because of the quick reflexes required by a goalie, both his hands are in front of his body (Figure 5-11).

4. **To stay in the center of the goal, the goalie will use the end of the shaft to tap the goal posts to locate himself properly.**

   By doing so, he never leaves a large portion of the goal open to his opponents.

Sizing Up the Players

When you receive a job promotion and find yourself in charge of a staff, one of the first things you do is examine the skills of your employees and determine whose talents fit best where. If you don't, you probably won't be too successful in your new position. The same principle applies to coaching lacrosse. To maximize your effectiveness and push your players to reach their potential, you must be proficient in the art of evaluating skills.

Figure 5-11:
A goalie in the basic ready stance.

Most leagues hand a group of kids over to you with no indication of how talented they are or what their strengths or weaknesses may be, so be prepared to begin evaluating your players the first time you get together with them. (For information on evaluating players during competitive travel-team tryouts, check out Chapter 19.)

Evaluating skills

If you don't know what you're looking for, evaluating young lacrosse players can be challenging. After all, lacrosse is a complex sport that requires a wide range of individual skills and the ability to use them in a manner that benefits the team. Being able to assess a player's strengths and weaknesses properly is essential for determining which areas of his game need additional work and what you can do to remedy any difficulties he's having.

Although evaluating players is critical all season long, it takes on added importance during the first few practices of the season. You risk frustrating your developing players if you evaluate them improperly, and they risk injury if you force them into exercises that are too difficult for their skill level. Take the time to evaluate all players properly at the beginning; then help them strengthen the areas of their game that are lacking.

Small-sided scrimmages work really well for evaluating younger players' skills. (If your league plays regulation games, chop the games down to five-on-five, for example.) Because the players get to touch the ball a lot and handle it in a variety of offensive and defensive roles, you can see how they handle all sorts of situations in a short period.

Identifying players' strengths and weaknesses

The better you understand your players' strengths and weaknesses, the more effective practices you'll be able to put together. When you recognize areas of the game that your team doesn't perform quite as well as others, you can attack those areas enthusiastically with specific drills during your practices. But don't neglect the parts of the game that the team is strong in; you still need to run drills in those areas to keep the players sharp. (See Chapter 13 for more details on making midseason adjustments to account for your team's improving skills.)

The following sections give you some pointers to keep in mind while evaluating players.

Don't focus all your attention on players' ability to score goals. A player may be proficient in the shooting department, but shooting skill doesn't necessarily mean that she's a well-developed, all-around player. Perhaps her teammates are great passers who are always able to feed her the ball when she's open, or maybe she has more strength than some of the other kids, which makes her shots more difficult to stop. Also, if her offensive skills are especially well developed, she may have defensive deficiencies.

Mobility

Lacrosse is a game of constant motion, on both offense and defense, and active feet are paramount for productive participation. Players who are flat-footed or who tend to stand still on the field are less likely to take advantage of opportunities to attack when their team regains possession of the ball. Also, they may be a defensive liability when their team turns the ball over and they're suddenly required to defend.

When evaluating a player's movement, take several factors into account to get a true sense of his ability in this area of the game:

- Is he involved in all facets of the game?

- After he delivers a shot on goal, does he stand there and admire his shot, or does he move forward aggressively in case the ball rebounds or the goalie misplays it?

- When he makes a pass to a teammate, does he become a statue immediately afterward, watching to see whether the ball reaches the intended target?

- When he doesn't have the ball, does he look to get open to receive a pass, or does he turn into a spectator and watch his teammates continue the attack?

Response to defensive pressure

How a player responds when a defender closes in on her makes a big difference in her game-day productivity. Look for these traits:

- Can she weave through defenders and get off a pass or shot?

- When she receives a pass, does she look to attack and create opportunities for herself or his teammates, or is she more comfortable getting rid of the ball quickly so that she doesn't have to deal with a defender in her face?

- Boys' lacrosse only: Can he hang on to the ball when he's being checked by the opponent's stick or is otherwise forced to deal with body contact?

Offensive ability

At advanced levels of youth lacrosse, in which players are strong, fast, and skilled, the ability to beat opponents one-on-one is critical for your team's success. Look for these traits in a player:

✔ Does he have the skills to negotiate past a defender and get a quality shot on goal?

✔ Can he make both short and long passes?

✔ Is he effective delivering shots on goal either while stationary or on the move?

✔ Are his shots difficult for the goalie to stop?

Defensive tenacity

One of the best indicators of a well-rounded lacrosse player is her ability to excel both offensively and defensively. A one-dimensional player who's good only moving with the ball — and not very effective defending a player who has it — is a liability that other teams will take advantage of, especially at advanced levels of play. Continually work to make your players tenacious defenders who make it difficult for the opposition to maneuver the ball. (Turn to Chapter 10 for the rundown on defensive fundamentals.) Keep an eye out for these traits:

✔ Does she pursue loose balls with enthusiasm?

✔ When an opponent maneuvers past her does she try to recover quickly and chase down the player?

✔ Does she try to keep opponents out of the middle of the field when they near her team's net?

Mindset

How much impact a player has on the game is influenced, to a great extent, by his mindset. Look for these traits:

✔ Does he give you his best effort at all times?

✔ When a play doesn't turn out the way he expected, does he drop his head, run slower, or act frustrated?

✔ How well does he handle constructive criticism and suggestions for improving his level of play?

Influence on the team

What type of teammate a child is speaks volumes about what type of player she is. Look for these traits:

Transferring practice skills to game play

Some kids perform well during practice but are unable to bring those skills to the field on game day. You may have a truly gifted attacker who happens to be an incredible passer, for example, but when game day arrives, he's unable to get the ball to open teammates and often surrenders the ball to the opposition. His impressive practice skills are gone, just like a rabbit disappearing from a magician's hat.

By watching him carefully, you may discover that problems arise as soon as a defender begins to close in on him. If you work with this player on some one-on-one moves (see Chapter 11 for some techniques you can teach your players) and get him comfortable having a defender in front of him all the time, his skills will improve, and you'll see him emerge as a more effective performer on game day.

✔ Is she a positive influence on the squad?

✔ Does she pump her teammates up with words of encouragement when the team is struggling to score goals?

✔ Is she enthusiastic regardless of the score in the game?

✔ When she isn't in the game, is she vocal in her support of her teammates?

Choosing a Starting Lineup

As a youth lacrosse coach, you'll face more questions throughout the season than a contestant on "Jeopardy!" One of the biggest ones is determining who fills which positions on game day. At beginning levels of lacrosse, positioning players isn't terribly important, because your main goal is introducing kids to the sport and its most basic components. At more-advanced levels of play, choosing positions takes on more prominence, because fitting kids into the right positions affects how the team performs.

Never typecast players based on their physical appearance. Children who are slightly overweight, for example, are often delegated to play goalie because goalies aren't required to run around much. They may not even be considered for attacker positions because they don't look like players who can maneuver with the ball all over the field, sprint or pivot past defenders, and create scoring opportunities for the team. A child who gets typecast in one position early may never fully enjoy the experience of playing lacrosse. You may have a wonderfully skilled player just waiting to emerge, but if you don't give him the chance to play different positions, he'll never know how successful he could have been, and he may miss out on a rewarding, enriching experience.

Assigning positions

As players gain experience in and knowledge about the game, you need to determine the positions that not only fit their particular skills, but also benefit the team.

When positioning your players, take these factors into account:

- ✔ The positions you need to fill
- ✔ The skills needed to play those positions successfully
- ✔ The responsibilities that come with each position
- ✔ The types of kids who are best suited for handling the various positions

When assigning positions, remind each player that you chose her for that position because of her special skills and the ability she demonstrates in practice. As the season progresses, however, you may recognize that a player is better suited for another position. Flip to Chapter 13 for more information on making midseason adjustments to benefit the team.

Any child is capable of playing, enjoying, and excelling at any position on the field, but keep some general characteristics in mind when determining who plays where when you start dealing with older, more-experienced teams. The following sections describe the skills needed to excel in different positions.

Goalies

Goalie is a challenging position to play, simply because of all the different types of shots that come the goalie's way — many at high rates of speed. Often, it is the goalie who is the best athlete on the field. Because stopping all the shots is impossible, you need a youngster in the net who doesn't get down on himself easily. Look for these traits:

- ✔ Mental strength and confidence, and the ability to bounce back after surrendering a goal
- ✔ Excellent hand–eye coordination
- ✔ Quick reflexes
- ✔ Ability to stay focused on the game
- ✔ Good communication skills (important for a goalie, because he can let teammates in front of him know what is unfolding and thereby help eliminate some defensive breakdowns)

Attackers

This position requires players with these traits:

- Strong shooting and passing skills
- Ability to make sharp cuts to get away from defenders
- Proficiency with the stick and with both hands
- Good vision of the field to find open teammates and get them the ball
- In boys' lacrosse leagues in which checking is allowed, enough physical strength to absorb the contact from defenders' checks

Midfielders

Midfielders should have these traits:

- **Stamina:** This position requires the most running on the field, so midfielders must have the stamina to handle their responsibilities.
- **Versatility:** Midfielders must be able to play both offense and defense, and must be able to make the switch from one role to the other quickly.
- **Speed:** Because of the fast-paced nature of lacrosse, teams with strong midfielders who can move down the field quickly get some good scoring chances with an extra-player advantage at the offensive end of the field.
- **Fast reactions:** Midfielders who can react to plays and scamper back on defense when play calls for it can help deny the opposition a good scoring chance.

Defenders

This position is a challenging one because defensemen don't know what the opponent is planning to do. The position requires the following traits:

- Ability to read and react quickly to opponents' moves
- Aggressiveness and agility
- Tenacity to recover and get back into the play when an opponent gets past
- In boys' leagues that allow checking, good footwork so that the player is always in proper position to apply a check

Soothing disappointed players

Regardless of how carefully you choose positions for your players, you're going to have kids who aren't content with where you have lined them up. Now what do you do?

If you are working with beginning-level players, you can ease the disappointment by reminding them that everyone will have the opportunity to play each position at some point in the season. In the meantime, use this situation as an opportunity to begin teaching them the essence of teamwork. Point out that for the team to work as a cohesive unit and enjoy success, everyone will have to make sacrifices throughout the season. Not everyone can be an attacker all the time; some players have to fill defensive positions, which are extremely important.

One approach you can take to help kids get over the disappointment of not playing the positions they wanted is to take a team field trip to a high school, college, or professional lacrosse game in your area. If that isn't an option where you live, gather the team to watch a televised game on ESPN. These contests can be outstanding learning experiences for the entire team. Instruct your team to monitor the athletes who play their positions. Having a young-ster watch how a player at a more elite level of competition plays the same position will give her a better sense of the position's importance to the over-all structure of the team. She may even pick up a few pointers along the way.

Working with All Kinds of Kids

Whether you're coaching a beginning team of 6-year-olds or an experienced team of 14-year-olds, you're embarking on a pretty cool adventure filled with challenges to your creativity and patience — one that will test your ability to communicate with all types of personalities and skill levels.

Youngsters' athletic talents, physical development, and emotional characteris-tics cover a wide spectrum. How you handle all these different types of kids plays a large role in determining how much fun they have playing for you and whether they want to return next season.

Average players

Most of the kids you'll come into contact with are regular, everyday kids — which means that some of them will have short attention spans. Here's a glimpse at what to expect when working with these kids.

The average child

Average children are players who enjoy playing lacrosse, running up and down the field, and being with their friends. They'll never play college lacrosse, but they'll be content to play for you, learn from you, and improve as players under your guidance and instruction. Some of these kids, through their involvement with you this season, will develop a real love and passion for the game and will continue playing it for years to come. Others will be content to try a new sport next season but will have a handle on the basics of lacrosse if they ever choose to return to the sport in the future.

The inattentive child

The younger the child, the shorter his attention span is likely to be. Because lacrosse is an outdoor sport, distractions abound — from planes in the sky to cars honking in the street. You have to compete with all sorts of things that are vying for your players' attention, so you have a greater responsibility to run practices that grab the kids' attention and keep their interest and excitement levels high. If you spend most of practice talking rather than letting the kids run around on the field, you'll drain their interest. (See Chapter 6 for tips on making your practices fun.)

Fearful players

Harboring fears is natural for children, but how you go about helping them overcome those fears makes a big difference. Following are some of the most common fears and what you can do to erase them.

The child who is afraid of getting hurt

Any time kids are involved in a contact sport like lacrosse, some of them are bound to be afraid of taking a check (in boys' leagues), getting knocked to the ground, or even suffering an injury. Who can blame them? Getting whacked with a stick or having a shot ricochet off a body part is about as much fun as getting shots at the doctor's office.

Kids need to know that assorted bumps and bruises are going to occur from time to time, but they can't allow minor injuries to chase them away from playing a sport they otherwise enjoy. Talk to them about skinning a knee on the playground: Although it hurts at the time, it doesn't stop them from playing with their friends. Encourage your players to use the same approach with lacrosse. Help them accept the fact that sometimes, things happen on the field that result in pain or discomfort, but the pain is usually momentary, and they shouldn't let it detract from their fun. (See Chapter 17 for ways to keep your players healthy and minimize any hurt.)

The child who is shy

Shyness is as common in lacrosse as grass-stained uniforms, yet it can be one of the easiest problems to handle, as long as you're patient and gradually work to lure the child out of her protective shell. Be aware that pushing too hard and too early in the season may scare her enough that she actually pulls back and further isolates herself from the team.

Shy children often go to extreme lengths to blend into the background and dodge attention. During practices, they avoid eye contact; they don't ask for help when working on skills; and they quietly move throughout the various drills while doing everything in their power not to draw attention to themselves.

One way to help shy players is to rotate the kids who lead the calisthenics and stretching at the beginning of practice sessions. Select a shy child along with a couple of other players to lead the warm-up. This selection is a small step toward helping the shy youngster become comfortable in front of the team. Because other players are up there with him, he won't feel isolated or gripped with fear that all eyes are on him.

 After a shy child does something well during team exercises, give her a pat on the back. She may not enjoy a verbal acknowledgment from you that draws attention from other team members, but small acts that go unnoticed by everyone else can make a big impact on this child and slowly draw her out.

 Lacrosse is a contact sport, so the possibility always exists that a child may get knocked around or suffer a minor injury, that momentarily takes away a little bit of their enthusiasm for participating. Perhaps the child was whacked with an opponent's stick, or took a hard fall to the ground because he was tripped. Whatever the reason for his reluctance to go back on the field, when you call upon him during a game, never embarrass the youngster or force him back out there against his will. If the child isn't comfortable explaining why he's hesitant to return at the time, be sure to speak with him privately after the game to learn what happened and what you can do to ease those fears before the next game. Of course, share your conversation with his parents, too. They need to know what happened and why their child didn't play his normal amount of minutes.

The child who doesn't want to be there

Youngsters with low or nonexistent self-esteem typically don't fare well in athletic endeavors, so they tend to avoid participation. A child who doesn't want to be there may have written off having fun playing lacrosse for any number of reasons:

- He watched an older sibling play lacrosse and felt that lacrosse players are pressured to excel.
- Even though he doesn't want any part of lacrosse, his parents signed him up anyway.
- He's already played lacrosse for several years, has grown tired of the sport, and simply needs a break.
- He has his eye on another sport.

Talk to the child to find out the reason for his lack of interest. You can address many of his concerns, take care of and comfort him, and restore his interest in playing again. Connecting with the child emotionally and helping him solve his dilemma can do wonders in reestablishing his enthusiasm about lacrosse.

Fearsome players

Some players on your team may present more challenges than you expected, and we're not referring to teaching them how to hold their sticks or defend an attacking player. Some kids display bullying tendencies or hog the ball, and you must deal with them to ensure that the entire team's experience isn't compromised.

You'll also be challenged in a different way if you coach supertalented children. The following sections look at how to handle all these types of kids.

The bullying child

Most of us had the unpleasant experience of dealing with a bully at some point during childhood. Whether they turn up on the school playground, in the neighborhood, or during an organized sports program, bullies have a way of making life miserable for those on their radar.

Bullies can also show up on the lacrosse field, ready to torment, tease, and create trouble. These children thrive on attention and find pleasure in upsetting others, usually because of their own insecurities. The lacrosse field has no room for bullies and their intimidating tactics.

Most kids who are being tormented by a bully don't complain for fear of making the situation even worse. You've got to keep a close eye on interactions among your players — not just during practice, but also before and after practice — because bullies wreak the most havoc when adults aren't able to supervise everything that's going on.

If you're having problems with a child who's bullying others, speak with her away from the team, and let her know that she must change her behavior. Let her know that you admire her tenacity on the field, but that she must use it only during the course of play. If the child is picking on or making fun of her teammates, remind her that she should be encouraging and supporting them instead.

Never allow a player to use his stick as a weapon to intimidate or harm others. Children who use their sticks to bully must face immediate and serious repercussions because a teammate's safety should never be compromised.

The child who hogs the ball

Ball hogs — players who seem allergic to passing and refuse to give the ball up, even to wide-open teammates in prime scoring position — can create real problems, because their behavior directly affects everyone's enjoyment of the game. Ball hogs typically aren't problems at the younger age levels, because most kids haven't developed their skills to the point that they can maintain control of the ball for extended periods. The problem generally occurs when kids begin to develop skills, their talent begins to shine through, and they realize that they're pretty good.

A player can earn the ball-hog label for several reasons, all of which you can help him discard by taking the right approach. The player may be

- ✔ **Unaware:** Quite often, the child isn't aware that he's hanging on to the ball longer than he should be. Relying on practice drills that stress passing, or scrimmages in which the team must complete a set number of passes in a row before taking a shot on goal, is one approach to erasing ball-hog problems.

- ✔ **Dealing with conflicting instructions:** A challenging scenario occurs when the child receives conflicting instructions from Dad or Mom at home. The parent may tell the child that he needs to exert more control and dominate the game, and that he shouldn't relinquish the ball so often. If you suspect that this situation is happening, have a quick meeting with the parents; remind them that you would appreciate their help in reinforcing at home what you are teaching in practice.

- ✔ **Unfamiliar with the sport:** The child may be new to participating in organized team sports or simply unfamiliar with lacrosse. He may require a little time to become accustomed to the team setting and to see how passing the ball fits into the team concept of working to create the best scoring opportunities.

- ✔ **Following your lead:** Ask yourself whether you are guilty of allowing kids to hang on to the ball too long without saying anything about it. Stress the importance of teamwork during practice, and point out to players who show a tendency to hang on to the ball too long that they should have passed it to a teammate.

- ✔ **Ready for a chat about his future in the game:** The player may have aspirations of playing at a higher and more-competitive level of lacrosse. Let him know that when he begins playing at more-competitive levels, the players he'll go up against will have the same skills that he does — and perhaps more skills, which will make his ability to distribute the ball to teammates even more important. Talk to him about being a well-rounded player who can not only handle the ball deftly and score goals, but also thread accurate passes through a maze of defenders.

When you notice a child hanging on to the ball a bit too long, don't embarrass her, because you risk making her suddenly afraid to take any shots or carry the ball for any length of time for fear of being reprimanded again. A ball hog doesn't need to be disciplined; she simply needs coaching and guidance on how to work more effectively within the framework of the team.

Athletically gifted

The athletically gifted player stands out. His teammates know he's the best player, and all the parents recognize his talents too.

When coaching a youngster who's far superior in skill development, be aware that you must provide challenges for him in your drills that allow him to enhance his skills without compromising the rest of the team in the process. This balancing act can be tricky at times; you don't want to isolate the player from his teammates, but you also don't want him to be bored and unchallenged performing a drill that he's already good at (but that the rest of the team is just learning). Rely on your creativity to concoct clever ways to help both the kids who are just learning a skill and the talented players excel at the same time.

If you're working with the team on taking shots on goal, and you're serving as the defender in the drill, you can make minor adjustments to ensure that every player benefits, regardless of skill level. For youngsters who are just learning to deal with an opposing player in front of them, you can remain stationary so that they can take a step around you and have a clear shot on net. For more experienced kids, you can easily increase the difficulty of the drill to challenge them more by stick checking them (in boys' leagues) or taking an extra step in the direction in which they are moving to make getting off a shot more difficult. Using a little ingenuity can make a big difference in meeting all the kids' needs.

It's easy to fall into the habit of piling the praise on those players who continually put a smile on your face with their offensive and defensive skills. Keep yourself in check and refrain from going overboard with the superlatives, because overdoing it can have adverse effects:

 ✔ Some kids may begin feeling unnecessary pressure, which can inhibit their performance and smother their fun with lacrosse. They may feel that with all the attention being thrown in their direction, they have to shoulder more of the responsibility for the team's success and failure. If they don't score a certain number of goals, they may feel personally responsible for a loss.

 ✔ Going overboard with the praise can also alienate other members of the team who may begin to feel as though the talented player is your favorite. If you allow this alienation to happen, the team will harbor resentment toward you and the talented player, and that causes problems with the team spirit and chemistry you're trying to build.

There is certainly nothing wrong with enjoying coaching talented players (though hopefully you derive equal pleasure working with all the kids). In fact, if these players possess good attitudes, and aren't critical or condescending to their teammates, they have the potential to emerge as wonderful team leaders and positive role models. Just remember to maintain a proper perspective and that they are just one piece of the team puzzle. The entire roster is counting on you for your help, support, and guidance as well.

Players who need extra help

A big part of coaching lacrosse is meeting challenges head on and helping youngsters who are encountering difficulties develop their skills and see improvement in their play. The following sections discuss some of these types of kids.

The inexperienced child

Some players get a late start in lacrosse. Your entire team may have been playing for several years except for one child who is giving the game a shot this season. With the relatively short amount of contact you'll have with her this season, helping her get caught up to the skill level of her teammates simply won't be possible unless she's an exceptional athlete. But you can still help her become a contributing member of the team.

Try to gauge whether the youngster is uncomfortable knowing that she's lagging in many skills because of her inexperience. If you sense that she isn't bothered by it, you may want to work with her one-on-one for a few minutes before or after practices if she is interested.

You want to be sure that the inexperienced player fully understands proper techniques before you insert her into drills. Otherwise, she could pose an injury risk to another player or even to herself.

The uncoordinated child

Coordination takes time to develop, so many children are challenged in this area, particularly at beginning levels of play. They're adjusting to their growing bodies, and some of the movements required for playing lacrosse may seem unnatural to them. Uncoordinated children struggle with some of the most basic lacrosse skills, and simply catching a pass or running downfield with the ball can present challenges for them. Regardless, these kids are trying their very best. Be aware that they can become enormously frustrated; feelings of inadequacy can settle in and further compromise their experience.

Helping a child improve his coordination takes practice, but if you stick with it, you can make a positive difference. Here are some points to keep in mind when coaching these players:

- **Camouflage any frustration.** The uncoordinated won't pick up what you're teaching as quickly as a lot of their teammates will, so make sure that you don't reveal frustration in your words or body language. Never give uncoordinated players any reason to think that you're disappointed in them.

- **Be supportive.** Players who are handcuffed by coordination difficulties won't be too enthusiastic about stepping onto the field on game day. They're afraid that they'll struggle, disappoint their teammates, or embarrass themselves. Be constantly supportive of their efforts, because when they see their friends performing at a level they believe they can never reach, they may become disenchanted with lacrosse and reluctant to continue participating.

✔ **Encourage parental assistance.** Get the parents involved. They can help an uncoordinated child simply by passing the ball back and forth to him at home for a few minutes a couple of times a week. That way, the child won't have to worry about teammates watching him. Just be sure to have the parents stress having a good time over how well the child is performing the skill. Also make sure that parents don't overdo the sessions at home.

The child with special needs

All kids have a legal right to participate in lacrosse, including those who have special needs — which may range from hearing loss and vision impairment to medical conditions such as diabetes and epilepsy. Youngsters who have physical conditions that don't give them full use of their arms or legs also fall into this category.

As a volunteer lacrosse coach, you're likely to question your qualifications to work with these kids. But remember — you're a coach, and these kids are looking for your help and guidance just like everyone else on the team.

If you have a child with special needs, set aside some time before the first practice of the season to talk to the family about their hopes and expectations for their child's participation. Keep in mind that this season may be the parents' first foray into organized sports, and they may be nervous and apprehensive about having their child participate. Explore the endless possibilities. Figure out ways that the youngster can be included and can be a valued and contributing member of the team.

If a child has a visual impairment and has difficulty seeing the ball, perhaps playing with a different-colored ball would make a difference without compromising anyone's safety or enjoyment of the game.

If you're coaching a team of older kids, ask them for their thoughts and ideas. They can be great resources for you, and they may just surprise you with their creative suggestions on how to ensure that their teammate is part of the action.

Regardless of the age or skill level of your team, having a child with special needs on the squad can be enormously beneficial for your other players. Youngsters get a firsthand lesson in developing understanding, compassion, and patience for their teammates, as well as in accepting everyone's differences.

Chapter 6

Conducting Fun-Filled Practices

In This Chapter
▶ Making your first practice a hit
▶ Putting together fun and creative practices
▶ Making your practices beneficial
▶ Ending practices on a high note

One of the many secrets of being a successful lacrosse coach is conducting practices that the kids look forward to, week after week, as much as they look forward to sleepovers with their friends and trips to the toy store. As long as you're able to keep the excitement and enthusiasm running high during these sessions, nonstop fun, learning, and skill development follow.

In this chapter, we run down all the elements for pulling off practices that challenge, entertain, and motivate children. We cover how to charge out of the starting blocks strong, setting a positive tone for the season with a great first practice. We discuss how to conduct fun and effective practices each time you get together with the kids, how to squeeze the most out of every minute, and how to help players overcome difficulties in learning new techniques. We also devote a section to the importance of concluding your practices on a positive note.

Beginning the Season: First Practice

You may have had pretty nerve-wracking experiences with "first times" — the first time you rode a roller coaster, went on an airplane, or asked someone out on a date, for example. You don't need to include conducting your first lacrosse practice in that list, though.

Sure, if you've never coached a youth lacrosse team before, you may get sweaty palms just thinking about how you're going to handle all the kids. Being a little nervous is only natural, because you have a lot at stake when you step on the field to practice for the first time. The first impression you make sets the tone for the season and provides your kids a good indication of what's in store. But not to worry — we're here to guide you and to minimize any stress you may be feeling if this first practice is weighing on your mind.

The following sections explain how you should greet your team, introduce all the players and coaches, and run the remainder of your initial practice. Good luck!

Making a great first impression

First impressions are important, whether you're interviewing for a job or greeting your players for the first practice of the season. Establishing positive contact with the kids before they take a shot or catch a pass helps put them at ease and signals that they can expect a rewarding season.

Here are some tips to help you score big with your team at your first meeting:

- **Get there early.** Make sure you're the first person at the field. Being there ahead of time so that you can greet each player as he arrives sends a positive message that you're enthusiastic about getting started. If you pull up a few minutes before practice is supposed to start, and some players are already there, you give the impression that you're disorganized, too busy, and unprepared for all the responsibilities that coaching lacrosse entails.

- **Put the kids at ease.** A lot of youngsters are probably going to be a little nervous, so a friendly smile and warm greeting can go a long way toward squashing those jitters. Starting something new when you don't know a single person is uncomfortable for everyone. You don't want a child to stand off to the side, wondering whether she's at the right field. The more relaxing you can make the atmosphere, the more enthusiastic the kids will be about getting started.

- **Get the conversations flowing.** Begin establishing bonds with the kids right away. If time allows, talk briefly with the players as they arrive to find out a little bit more about them. Just keep the conversations general in nature and not too probing. Asking questions such as how long they've played lacrosse or what positions they've played in the past can help alleviate some of that first-practice stress. Taking a genuine interest in your players — which they'll recognize and appreciate — is the foundation for forging special relationships with them that can carry on throughout the season.

Coach and player introductions

You should start the first practice by formally introducing yourself and any assistant coaches you have. During your intro, share some tidbits about yourself, including the following:

> ✔ Whether you prefer being called "Coach," "Coach Jeff," or any other moniker (such as a funny nickname that will get a chuckle out of the kids)
>
> ✔ How long you've coached (or played) lacrosse and where
>
> ✔ Whether one of your own children is on the team

After introducing yourself and any assistants, ask each child to say her name. You want to keep the player introductions short and to the point. Some kids are going to be overly shy, and the last thing you want to do is traumatize them before practice has even begun.

You may have more than a dozen kids on your team, which makes learning all their names a little challenging. Giving each player a name tag to wear during the first practice or two speeds the process. Slap a name tag on yourself and on your assistant coaches so that the kids know you're all in this together. Team bonding can't start too early!

The skills to focus on first

Well before the first practice, you should know what drills you want to begin with and how those drills will lead into the more intensive practices to come. It's a good idea to keep a practice notebook where you log all the drills you use and make notes on which ones the kids really like and that achieve the results you are looking for, as well as those that flop and shouldn't be used anymore. For the scoop on some basic drills for beginners, flip to Chapter 7. If you're looking to upgrade your drills, Chapter 14 offers some advanced ones to incorporate into your practices.

If you're coaching a beginning-level team, chances are that many of your kids have never played lacrosse (or any other organized sport, for that matter). Because of the somewhat complex nature of the game — from the fundamentals of holding the stick for passing and catching to defending an attacking player — your best bet is to ease into the first practice by focusing on some basic skills, such as maintaining possession of the ball while moving.

Using the first couple of practices to cover fundamental skills establishes a solid foundation that you can build on throughout the season without overwhelming your players in the process.

If you're coaching players who have a little more experience, you can use the first week of practices simply to refresh them on the basics. Use the first couple of practices to evaluate your players individually and your team's strengths and weaknesses overall (see Chapter 5). You can cover the most basic elements quickly, but then you should move on to more-advanced techniques, such as executing shots and passes while on the move with a defender guarding them closely. In subsequent practices, you can include other advanced skills, techniques, and strategies to help your players upgrade their level of play.

When one of your players arrives late, don't immediately send her into the drill that is taking place. This rule is especially important for an older player who hasn't gone through the proper stretching and warm-ups that the rest of the team completed. Instead, have her work on an aspect of the game that can be done along the sideline to help get her loosened up before she steps on the field and goes full speed during the practice. Perhaps some light running while holding the ball if she's a beginner, or working on pivoting with the ball (check out Chapter 11 for more details on executing this move) if she's an advanced-level player. If you're coaching a team of older players who are more susceptible to muscle strains and pulls, make sure the late player goes through proper stretching before you allow her on the field. Just because a player is late doesn't mean that she can overlook this important aspect of the game. You don't want to put her at unnecessary risk of suffering an injury that could have been avoided.

Making practice a pleasure

Every day at school plays an important role in helping a child learn and develop, and the same applies to your lacrosse practices, which is why planning them is so important. Simply planning a practice isn't enough, however: You also have to follow through with successful execution.

Because you may have a dozen or so kids on your team, making sure that every player benefits from your practices can be quite a challenge. This section provides some tips that you can use to turn all your practices into fun-filled, dynamic sessions.

Revving up the warm-ups

When you're able to set a fun tone while the kids are stretching and getting loose for the practice, that helps them transition into your drills and creates a relaxed atmosphere that's conducive to learning — and having an enjoyable day of lacrosse. While they are loosening up, pick a number between 1 and 100 and then go around the group and have each player pick a number. The one who picks closest to yours gets to choose a practice drill that the team will run that day. Or, you could make that youngster the honorary team captain for the day, where she gets to lead off each drill, or has some other special privilege. By making the stretching period exciting you'll grab the players' interest the moment they take the field.

Starting and ending with fun drills

A little creative thinking on your part is all you need to open and close your practices in a positive fashion. If you're coaching a beginning-level team, for example, a fun way to start your practices is to give each player a ball, which he must carry in his stick while trying to run around the field and tag you. (See Chapter 7 for some more drills you can use with younger kids.)

If you're coaching older kids, you can pair them up and give each twosome a ball. Start the players in each pair about 15 yards apart, and have them jog down the field, passing the ball back and forth. This drill also helps loosen up the players and gets their hearts pumping so that they're ready to participate in practice.

One way you can close practice is to get the parents involved (see "Putting parents on the field," later in this chapter). You can also use scrimmages to end things on a high note (see "Picking the right times for scrimmages" section later in this chapter.)

Putting parents on the field

Your players' parents can be much more than just chauffeurs to practices and games. Your players (especially at the younger age levels) will get a kick out of having their parents on the field with them. Getting involved in practice will also be fun for the parents — much more so than sitting on the sidelines watching drills, we're sure.

You can involve as many interested parents as you want in your practices. Here are some ways you can bring them in:

- **Give them notice.** Let the parents know well in advance that you'd like to involve them in a practice. Give them options for dates and times. If you give busy parents time to plan, they'll likely be happy to join in.

- **Stir up excitement.** Set a fun tone for the practice involving the parents by talking about it to your players during the preceding practice. Be enthusiastic about the drills you have planned, and show your excitement about the adventure, so that the players will be equally pumped up to have Mom or Dad sweating on the field with them.

- **Set up a parent–child scrimmage.** The kids will really love seeing their mom playing goalie or their dad trying to stop them on the attack. You can play a quick game at the end of practice to conclude the day on a fun note, or you can devote a midseason practice to the scrimmage as a nice break from routine.

- **Pair kids and parents in drills.** Parents can help you liven up a routine drill. You can run a one-on-one drill, for example, in which the child has to go against her parent and try to break free to deliver a shot on net. Then have the parent try to beat her child with a move to get open. The kids will love the challenge of going against Dad or Mom.

Putting sedentary parents in the game

Not every parent is going to want — or be able — to participate in practices. Some parents have busy schedules that don't allow them to hang around for practices; others have physical problems that prevent them from running around. And some kids, for whatever reason, may not want their parents involved. That's OK, because having even a few parents involved gives your practice a different look and the kids another type of drill to participate in. Parents can participate in many ways, from keeping score during mini-contest drills to bringing a boom box to play music during warm-ups and cool-downs.

Coming to practice prepared

Your players need come to practice prepared, and so do you. You should have your practice plan ready the day before practice, along with the drills you want to run and how much time you plan to allot to each activity.

Your preparation should also include a properly stocked first-aid kit, which is a must for running a safe practice. (Check out Chapter 17 for more information on recognizing and treating player injuries.)

Bringing balls and other equipment

One basic rule for running a quality lacrosse practice is that you can never have too many balls. The more balls you have, the less practice time is wasted retrieving them or forcing players to wait to run a drill until a ball is available for them. You can make it a team rule that each child must bring a ball to practice. Just have each player put his initials on his ball so that he can take it home afterward.

If the program you are coaching in doesn't provide a lot of practice equipment, check with your local sporting-goods store about purchasing some new or even used balls.

Nothing sabotages a practice quicker than players arriving without the proper equipment. During your preseason parents' meeting (covered in Chapter 4), emphasize what kids are responsible for bringing to the field.

Creating Fun Practices for the Whole Season

Any time you are in a leadership position, whether it's overseeing a staff at work or a group of kids on the lacrosse field, being prepared is vital for achieving success. As a youth lacrosse coach, you must prepare your practice plans and then carry them out to have success with the kids on the field. You need to map out the skills you want to teach during the season (often depending on the age and ability level of your kids; see Chapter 2), and based on how many practices you can have with the kids this season, you need to determine what areas you can cover in each practice and how much time you can devote to each one.

As your season gets under way, you have an enormous amount of information to cover with your players — everything from passing and receiving techniques to the rules of the game. You'll be tempted to try to cram everything in. Your best bet, however, is to choose some of the most important aspects of lacrosse that you want to teach and then do your best to work in some of the other stuff as the season rolls along. You don't want to unload so much information on the kids that you actually end up detracting from their experience.

The following sections help you map out a great practice plan for your season. From the planning and drilling stages to the adjustments you need to make, we cover the big picture of planning for a youth lacrosse practice.

Setting the tone

Do you remember your involvement in sports or other activities when you were a child? You'll likely agree that the ones for which the leaders made learning fun and interesting were the most memorable for you. Making that same type of connection with your players comes down to the tone you set from the start of the season. You'll have the season headed in the right direction if you build it around positive feedback, encouraging words, an upbeat approach, and a good sense of humor.

One tip for running productive practices is exuding positive energy and enthusiasm, no matter how well or badly the session is going. We all have bad days, but you should never show up for practice in a bad mood, because your poor state of mind will interfere with what you are teaching the kids. When your players see that you're in a good mood and happy to be at the field, they'll practice and play in the right frame of mind, too.

When you prepare your practices, focus on setting a fun tone. If the kids don't look forward to attending practices, you're probably not doing a very good job, and more than likely, they're not learning many skills either. As you put together your practice plans, ask yourself whether the drills are fun and whether you'd like participating in them. If you answer "Yes," chances are that your players would, too — which is good news for everyone involved.

Determining practice length and frequency

Most youth lacrosse leagues, particularly at the younger age levels, have specific policies regarding how often and how long teams can practice. Before you can begin creating your practice plans, you need to know the program's stance on this. (Check out Chapter 2 for more advice on checking out your league's rules before the season.)

Following the league's schedule

Here's a breakdown of the typical practice allotments for different youth leagues:

- **Ages 5 to 7:** At the beginning levels, you typically get a one-hour practice with your team each week, along with one game per week.

- **Ages 8 to 12:** In the middle age groups, you're typically allowed one to two practices a week, with a game mixed in.

- **Ages 13 and older:** For the older kids, you often play a couple of games a week, as well as hit the practice field once (and sometimes twice) a week.

You can accomplish a lot during a one-hour practice if you come prepared. So stick to that time frame when running your practices. Only at very advanced levels should your practices run any longer than an hour.

Setting your own schedule

If you coach in an advanced league that leaves practice frequency to the coaches' discretion, use your best judgment in devising your team's practice schedule. Don't go overboard and monopolize the kids' time by cramming the calendar with practices. Overloading them with too many practices can throttle their interest in playing. (If you're interested in being on the field coaching most days of the week, overseeing a travel team may be for you. Check out Chapter 19 for more details on coaching travel teams.)

Sometimes, due to weather factors, games are postponed and made up at a later date. Any time your schedule features two or three games in a week, be sure to modify your practices accordingly so that you don't overwhelm your players.

Distribute your practice schedule during the preseason parents' meeting (see Chapter 4). The parents will appreciate the advance notice — which also helps reduce the amount of practice time your players miss, because parents will have time to alter their schedules to accommodate their child's season.

Picking the right times for scrimmages

Sometimes, just to mix your practices up a bit and keep the excitement levels high, you can conduct intrasquad *scrimmages* — informal games between two units on the same team. Scrimmages can be useful tools to give kids some gamelike experience. They often work well at the end of practices to give kids a chance to work on the skills that they practiced during the session.

Here are a couple of tips to keep in mind regarding scrimmages:

- ✔ **Alter the rules.** Use your creativity to target specific skills you want players to work on by changing the rules. If you've noticed a lack of teamwork in previous games, for example, run a scrimmage in which at least five different players have to touch the ball before anyone takes a shot. This rule forces the kids to work together, because they must rely on passing to be successful.

- ✔ **Conduct smaller-scale scrimmages.** Instead of going with a full-scale scrimmage, split the field, and run two scrimmages at the same time. Even if you have only enough kids to play three-on-three or four-on-four games, you'll be giving all of them more opportunities to pass and catch the ball, as well as to shoot and defend.

Don't fall into the trap of using scrimmages at every practice; use them only in moderation. You can't become lazy and rely on scrimmages to fill valuable minutes of practice time because you don't want to plan or run drills. Overusing scrimmages takes away from your individual teaching and instruction. Spend most of your practice time running the kids through drills that zero in on particular areas of their game; rely on scrimmages only as a tool to break up your practices for a few minutes from time to time.

Keeping practices consistent

You have a limited amount of practice time with your kids each week, so if you can establish a practice routine as soon as possible, your sessions will be more efficient and effective. When players know what to expect when they get to the field, they can mentally prepare themselves and be ready to go. On the other hand, if you bombard them with changes every time you get together with them, valuable practice time will be wasted, because the players will be forced to stand around and listen to your instructions regarding the changes.

Changing some of the drills you run from week to week is a good idea, because the best way to help youngsters learn new skills and improve others is to give them a challenge. You should cling to a core group of drills that focus on the fundamentals of the game, though. (For some drills that focus on the fundamentals, turn to Chapter 7.)

Here's a plan for preparing your practices:

1. **Determine your prepractice warm-up, which stays the same from week to week.**

   Sticking to the same warm-up and stretching routine at the start of each practice sets a comfortable agenda for the kids before they jump into a session. Because some of your drills will change from week to week as your focus shifts to different parts of the game, establishing and maintaining a routine at the outset of practice can set the stage for a productive outing.

2. **List the skills you want to focus on.**

3. **List the drills you want to use to teach each skill.**

4. **Insert appropriate times for water breaks.**

   You want to have regularly scheduled water breaks throughout your practices so that the kids understand they'll have plenty of chances to get a drink.

   Any time you're switching to a different drill, encourage the kids to grab some water. This way, they'll know that every 15 minutes or so, they'll have a moment to consume fluids. (For more on hydration, check out Chapter 17.)

5. **Save a few minutes at the end of each practice to talk about any changes in the schedule or to recap what the players performed well that day.**

Getting the Most out of Practice Time

One goal you should have on your mind going into each practice is making sure that all the players — and we stress *all* — benefit from their time with you that session. Granted, this task can be challenging; you're coaching a group of kids who have varying skills and who may be at vastly different levels of development. But rest assured that you're qualified to give your whole team a good experience in practice, and that you'll get a real sense of satisfaction from making it happen.

Following are a few helpful pointers that can make practices effective for the kids and trouble free for you:

✔ **Don't allow standing around.** All your drills must enable the players to feel like that they're an integral part of practice and that they're accomplishing something that will help the team when game day rolls around. Do whatever you can to make standing around at your practices nonexistent. The players are at the field to run, pass, shoot, and defend — not stand in line waiting to step in for a few seconds of action, followed by heading to the end of the line for more standing, watching, and waiting. After all, the kids came to *practice,* right?

✔ **Split up the drills.** If you have assistant coaches or parent volunteers, you can run at least a couple of different drills in different areas of the field at the same time. (For tips on choosing assistants, check out Chapter 4.) Running multiple drills lets children get in more repetitions. If you're running the team solo, try to focus on specific drills in which the kids work in smaller groups; this setup gives them more touches of the ball or more opportunities to defend, depending on what skill the drill is targeting.

✔ **Keep everything moving.** Avoid lengthy pauses between your drills, which sabotage the energy level and enthusiasm you want to maintain throughout the session. Strive for constant motion so that you can keep your practices going at a good pace and increase the skill development that takes place. Constant activity holds the kids' attention and gives them less chance to think about something that has nothing to do with lacrosse.

An added benefit of this approach is that the kids will become better conditioned. Conditioning really pays dividends later in games (especially at the more advanced levels) if your players are able to perform as effectively as they did in the opening minutes.

The following sections touch on some more areas you need to be aware of to maximize your practice time, and give you tools you can use to make every practice productive and fun.

Building skills

Coaching youth lacrosse requires you to work your way along a logical progression, building kids' skills one at a time. Showing a youngster how to shoot the ball makes little sense if you haven't already addressed the proper way to hold the stick when carrying the ball. Neither does it make sense to devote 50 minutes of a one-hour practice to offense and only 10 minutes to defense. The best practices allow kids to gain valuable experience performing a wide variety of skills.

View every practice you conduct as a building block in your team's development. Every time you practice, first reinforce what you've taught so far; then, if the players are ready to move forward, you can add to what they've already learned. This plan takes concentrated effort on your part; you have to refrain from jumping too far ahead if you want your youngsters to grasp the basics.

If you've been working on executing passes to stationary players in your previous practices, and the kids have a pretty good grasp of that skill, you can spend a couple of minutes at your next practice having them perform that skill as a refresher. Then, to continue their learning, you can take that skill to the next level — by introducing how to pass on the move, to a teammate who is moving, or while a defender is nearby, for example. By taking this approach, you can gradually begin incorporating other aspects of the game that your players can work on.

Evaluating your team and making the proper adjustments to fit your players' needs allows you to teach the fundamentals in the proper order and build on each skill in your practices. (Chapter 13 covers the art of evaluating your team and making midseason adjustments.)

Helping players who need a hand

No matter how great a coaching job you're doing (or are preparing to do, because you're taking the time to read this book), you're bound to run into some challenging situations in which players struggle to pick up parts of the game. Lacrosse requires a fairly extensive list of skills, so many players experience difficulties from time to time.

Whenever a child is having any type of problem learning a skill, you need to acknowledge his efforts in trying to get a handle on the technique. If you stick by him, encouraging and motivating him every step of the way, he'll pick up the skill eventually or at least get better at it.

Adjusting their training

When a player really struggles with a particular skill, sometimes you can trace the problem back to how you're teaching it. Be willing to accept the fact that you may need to adjust your approach. Just because the other players picked up on the skill doesn't mean that a better teaching method wouldn't make a difference with this child. Try the following techniques:

✔ **Modify your instructions.** Sometimes, just shifting the emphasis of your instructions to a different aspect helps put everything in clearer perspective for the child and produces the desired results.

Suppose that when you're going over shooting techniques, your instructions focus on the position of the player's hands. If those instructions aren't clicking with the child, and her shots are straying from the mark or aren't generating a lot of force, modify the points you're stressing. Instead, focus on her footwork, and talk to her about stepping toward the target. By changing your instructions, you can help her enjoy improvement.

✔ **Break the skill down into smaller parts, and work on them individually.** Teaching a child how to execute a pass on the run, for example, involves mastering several components. Instead of overwhelming the child with all of them at the same time, break the skill into smaller steps.

You can begin by focusing on how the player should position his stick while running with the ball. When he has a good handle (sorry; we couldn't help ourselves) on holding the stick while he's on the move, you can work on the next phase, which is delivering the ball to a teammate who is stationary. From there, you can build on making a pass to a teammate who is on the run. Next, you can incorporate a defender guarding the passer and then add a defender covering the intended pass recipient. Gradually keep building on his skills by taking them one at a time.

✔ **Bring in a new drill.** Perhaps the drill you're using isn't getting the job done, and introducing a new one can help the child catch on.

Boosting their morale

Remaining positive and upbeat is vital, whether the technique you are teaching is catching on or presenting difficulties for the team. You'll get much farther with the players, and they'll enjoy playing for you much more, if you say something like this: "That was excellent, how you kept your eyes focused on the attacker as she came down the field with the ball. Just remember to keep your weight on the balls of your feet so that you're able to move quickly in any direction she goes." This approach is much more effective than saying something like "You didn't keep up with her again."

Any time you're devoting a little extra time to a particular player, don't let practice come to a standstill for the remainder of the team. If you've got assistant coaches helping you, make sure that they keep drills going so that the other players aren't standing around. If you don't have any help, start a drill that the kids know well and that doesn't require any instructions; then spend a few moments with the child who is having difficulty.

Youngsters who don't pick up skills as quickly as their teammates do may get frustrated with themselves, perhaps with you, and even with lacrosse. You can help minimize their disappointment by making sure that you acknowledge even the slightest improvement in their play. If a youngster is really struggling to catch passes, but the ball is beginning to bounce out of the pocket of his stick rather than missing it altogether, he's making progress, which you should recognize so that he can build on that momentum.

Resist the temptation to tell a struggling player to watch how one of her teammates performs a skill. By doing so, you may send the message that one player is better than another.

Praising good play

Whether we like to admit it or not, we all love recognition for doing something well. Your young lacrosse players are certainly no different. Being praised for performing a skill well — especially in front of teammates — can be really uplifting and a great source of motivation to your players to continue learning and striving to do their best.

Following are a few ideas on giving positive feedback to your players:

✔ **The earlier you praise, the better.** Your warm-ups represent a good time to provide some positive feedback to kids. As you oversee the stretching exercises, for example, you can mention to a youngster that you're really impressed with how quickly he picked up a certain skill in your last practice and that you're eager to watch him put the skill to use today.

✔ **Use creative acknowledgments.** Your players will really enjoy creative praise, and they'll probably play even harder to receive it. Instead of giving an ordinary high five, for example, try a low five, or make the high five a little more exciting by having both of you jump in the air before slapping hands.

✔ **Ditch the negatives.** Lacrosse has no place for negative body language or tones unless you're dealing with a discipline problem. (For more on handling that situation, flip to Chapter 18.) Focus on making all your interactions positive. If you allow negative words to creep into your conversations or display negativity in your body language, you may paralyze a child's ability to react naturally to situations, because she'll be afraid of making additional mistakes that will generate more unfavorable reactions.

✔ **Specific praise works best.** When you're recognizing good plays, general comments like "Attaboy" and "Way to go" are OK, but you can pack a more powerful punch by zeroing in on exactly why you're applauding the player. Saying something like "Great job following through to your intended target on that pass" hits home and is more likely to stick in the child's head when he attempts another pass in the future.

✔ **Rely on the sandwich method.** We're not talking about tuna on wheat here, but an effective approach in which you surround your corrective comment with a pair of positive remarks.

When you're talking to your goalie, you can say, "Susan, your stance was perfect before the shot was taken, but then I saw you take your eye off the ball for a split-second when you peeked at that player cutting near you. Remember, you can't take your eyes off the ball at any time. And I loved how you kept your stick in proper position throughout the shot." This way, the child receives important feedback on a skill she isn't performing the right way, as well as a confidence boost on the skills she is handling correctly.

✔ **Halt practice.** Don't be afraid to interrupt practice for 10 to 20 seconds to praise a child or group for doing something really well. Think about the pride you'll give those youngsters who passed the ball accurately all the way down the field and generated a quality scoring chance if you stop practice and praise them right in front of everyone for their great execution.

✔ **Don't go overboard.** Of course you want to praise your players to make them feel good about what they've done (or tried to do to the best of their ability). But don't throw out praise at an assembly-line rate just for the sake of doing so. Praising without merit takes away some of your credibility and believability with the team. If a player isn't hustling at full speed to scoop up a loose ball, and you applaud him for his effort anyway, you're sending a bad message that giving 100-percent effort isn't important to you, and the child may develop some bad habits.

Make it one of your goals to praise every child on the team during every practice. You can praise anything — from the way she hustled to get back on defense after a player got past her to the way she demonstrated great teamwork by congratulating a teammate for a nice play. You can ensure that you distribute your praise equally by carrying a roster in your practice planner and making a mark next to a player's name every time you make a positive remark.

When discipline is in order, never push it to the side because you want to retain "pal" status with the player. No matter what happens on the field, you're still the coach and leader, and you don't want the team to lose respect for you. You can be demanding while maintaining a positive tone and disposition. Along with your encouragement, you can provide constructive criticism that helps your players improve in all areas of their game.

Wrapping Up on a Positive Note

Ending your practices on a positive note is just as important as how you kick them off. How you choose to start a practice sets the tone for the entire session; how you end it goes a long way toward setting the kids' frame of mind the next time you gather them for a practice or game. When you're able to send players home with smiles on their faces, filled with enthusiasm and desire to get better, you've done a great job of wrapping up your practice.

Luckily for you, we have some secrets to share for achieving this goal. To finish your practices on a strong note, consider these suggestions:

✔ **Save the best for last.** Use one of your most popular drills or scrimmages at the end of practice. If this method goes over really big, you may have trouble coaxing the kids off the field. That problem is a really nice one to have, because it shows how into the game your players are — and how much fun they're having.

✔ **Give a quick wrap-up talk.** Let the kids know that you appreciate the hard work and effort they put in and that you're pleased to see the strides they've made. Keep this talk general and focused on the entire team. This chat usually isn't the time to recognize individual efforts, because you run the risk of alienating the other kids.

Never use your postpractice chat to provide constructive criticism or rehash a drill that didn't go well. After practices in which nothing goes right — and you'll have days like that — search for some nugget to highlight that allows you to focus on the positives. You can pin your praise on all sorts of areas, such as the players' work ethic or the way they encouraged their teammates during a drill.

✔ **Review the upcoming schedule.** If the next time you'll see the players is at a game, make sure that everyone can attend so that you can plan your lineup and structure your substitution patterns for game day.

✔ Thank the team for their hard work, and conclude with a team cheer (if you have one). You can call it a day after the excitement dies down!

Chapter 7

Getting with the Drills

Getting your team excited about playing lacrosse on game day usually doesn't require a whole lot of effort, simply because kids are pretty keyed up for the action. Generating the same type of enthusiasm for your practices may be a little more tricky. The secret — which we divulge to you in this chapter — is running drills that are fun, interesting, and great at pushing skills to the next level.

In this chapter, we take care of all your needs in this area. We run down all sorts of offense, defense, and goaltending drills that you can slip into your practices all season long. You can easily tweak these drills, making them easier or more challenging, based on the ever-changing needs of your team from week to week.

Before you have your players running up and down the field performing these drills, of course, you need to put them through a proper warm-up to help prevent injuries, as well as to prepare their bodies to perform at their best. So you find valuable information on the basics of stretching in this chapter as well.

Warming Up Right

For many kids, stretching is about as appealing as eating a big bowl of Brussels sprouts. After all, youngsters arrive for practices and games eager to take shots on goal, make passes to teammates, and defend against opponents who are attacking their team's goal — not to spend time stretching hamstrings and loosening up neck muscles. Yet your practices should always begin with a segment devoted to warming up and stretching. Warming up is the springboard to developing healthy young bodies, and bodies that are loosened up properly are less likely to be injured during the course of the session.

Completing warm-ups and stretching exercises before engaging in intense physical activity on the lacrosse field boosts muscle temperatures and increases flexibility — catalysts for building skills and helping players advance in the sport. Players, especially older ones at the more-advanced levels, are susceptible to injury when their muscles are not loosened up properly before they step onto the field. Exercises that develop muscle flexibility also reduce injury risks by preventing those muscles from tiring easily.

Your warm-up sessions should always begin with light exercise, such as a moderate-paced jog. A basic lap around the field or a jog back and forth between the goals gets the job done and clears the way for some stretching.

One way to make the warm-up more beneficial for the kids is to have them pass the ball back and forth to a partner while they're jogging. This way, they can work on some important skills while getting their bodies ready for practice. At the youngest levels, simply having the kids carry a ball with their sticks while jogging helps them become more comfortable maintaining control of the ball while on the move.

Stretching basics

The two primary types of stretches are

- **Static:** These basic stretches involve placing the body in a specific position and holding that position for several seconds.
- **Ballistic:** These stretches rely on momentum, so the player has far less control of ballistic stretches than static stretches.

If you're coaching youngsters who are relatively new to lacrosse or any other organized sport, start them out with static stretches to get them used to preparing their bodies for activity. As they get older, you can incorporate the ballistic approach to prep them for competition.

Players should have designated spots for the stretching exercises at the start of each practice. If you're coaching a large team, having assigned positions for everyone on the field lets you spot a player's absence easily. This system also gives you more time to adjust your practice drills to fit the number of players present.

Keep the stretching exercises consistent. You don't want to waste valuable practice time introducing new stretches each week of the season. Design a basic warm-up and stretching routine that the kids can stick to all season long.

In addition to the warm-up, each practice should wind down with a 5-minute period of light exercise to help players' bodies return to their normal resting state. Run a specific play at half speed, or work on defending an attack; then conclude with a couple minutes of stretching the large muscles. The cool-down doesn't have to be nearly as focused as the warm-up session, because the purpose is to wind down from the activity rather than build up to it.

Warm-up fundamentals

Here are some additional warm-up fundamentals to keep in mind:

- ✔ **Begin every practice with a warm-up.** Always start your practices with a warm-up and stretching. Repetition is critical; when youngsters know that they'll be stretching at every practice, they learn that stretching is an important aspect of being a lacrosse player.

- ✔ **The younger the kids, the simpler the stretches.** For young kids, the stretching period can be basic and quick. You just want to introduce them to the concept of stretching and get them into the habit of doing so before any activity. Some basic arm windmills and toe touches are all you need at this level.

- ✔ **Hit 'em all.** You want the stretches to cover all the major muscle groups that the kids will use during the practice, which means stretches for the hamstrings, calves, neck, arms, and back.

- ✔ **Don't let the kids strain while stretching.** Bouncing and straining to reach a desired position can result in injury. Instead, stress moving slowly to the desired position, just slightly beyond discomfort; holding that position for a short period; and then relaxing. Players want to bend down slowly and touch their toes, count to 5, and then relax and return to an upright position. Remind kids that mild tension — not pain — is what they should strive for in any type of stretch.

  Youngsters should ease into the stretches while inhaling through the nose and exhaling through the mouth. Sharp, sudden movements can injure muscles and sideline a child.

- ✔ **Assume an active role.** During any stretching exercises, make sure that you have one-on-one contact with all the kids at some point. This contact is particularly important for youngsters who are new to lacrosse or to the whole concept of stretching before participating in an activity. When a child is stretching out his hamstrings, for example, place his hand on the back of his leg so that he can feel the exact area of his body that's being stretched and prepared for competition. This technique also helps ensure that the kids are following proper form.

- ✔ **Eliminate messing around.** The stretching period isn't a time for kids to be goofing around. It's a valuable part of your practice time, and kids need to treat it that way. Keep their attention focused on the stretches and concentrating on performing them correctly.

> ✔ **Don't forget to stretch out *your* muscles, too.** As the coach, you're running all over the field teaching skills, demonstrating techniques, and providing feedback, so joining the kids (and your assistants) for stretching serves a couple of useful purposes: It helps protect you from being sidelined with a strained or pulled muscle, which affects your ability to work with the kids; and it's a good opportunity to bond with your players by getting on the field with them.

Warm-up drills for everyone

Maintaining and improving children's flexibility is essential not only for preventing injuries, but also for giving them a solid foundation of strength, balance, and coordination. Incorporating a variety of stretches and strength-building exercises is a key factor in preparing youngsters for the physical demands of lacrosse. This section describes several stretches you can use during your warm-ups to help prepare youngsters' bodies for practices and games.

The more flexible players are, the greater their range of motion, which usually translates into improved play on the field. A youngster who has tight hamstrings, for example, is limited in how fast she can move down the field. If you help that child gradually stretch out her hamstrings and gain increased flexibility, she can enjoy a fuller range of motion, which leads to greater speed — a valuable asset for any position on the lacrosse field.

Standing squats

This stretch works the quadriceps. The child starts with his feet shoulder width apart and his hands on his hips (see Figure 7-1). He squats into a deep knee bend, keeping his body upright and steady, and centering his weight over his heels. In a slow, controlled motion, he pushes up into his starting position.

Figure 7-1: Players can strengthen their leg muscles by using standing squats.

Make sure that the child's weight isn't distributed over his toes, which places excessive stress on the knees. Also make sure that the child maintains good posture and doesn't relax his upper body, which places too much stress on the lower back.

Forward lunges

The child begins with her body in an upright position, her arms relaxed at her sides. She steps forward as far as possible with one leg. Bending her knees, she lowers her back leg toward the ground, stopping just before the knee touches (see Figure 7-2). The knee of the lead leg should be aligned directly over the heel. Using the hamstrings (back of the thigh) of the lead leg, she pulls the rear leg forward and returns to the starting position. She repeats with the opposite leg.

Watch the child's form. If the youngster doesn't step forward far enough, the knee of the lead leg can pass over her toes, placing stress on the lead knee. Pushing off the rear leg to return to the starting position eliminates the benefits of working the hamstrings. Also make sure that the child maintains good posture throughout this stretch; bad posture places unwanted stress on the lower back.

Figure 7-2:
Forward lunges help youngsters stretch out their hamstrings.

Calf raises

The child begins with his feet shoulder width apart and his hands on his waist. He rises onto his toes on both feet and slowly lowers himself toward the ground. He stops just before his heels touch the ground and then repeats the upward phase of the stretch.

Make sure that the child distributes his weight evenly across his toes; if he doesn't, he's working only part of the calf muscle. Don't let the child lock his knees, which reduces the effectiveness of the stretch.

Hamstring stretch

While sitting, the child assumes the hurdle position (see Figure 7-3) by extending her right leg fully and bending her left leg, placing the bottom of her foot along the inside of her right thigh. While keeping her back straight, she leans forward slowly, bringing her chest toward her right knee and reaching toward her toes with her right hand. Depending on how much flexibility the child has, she either places her hands on the ground alongside her left leg or holds her toes. She holds the stretch for a couple of seconds and then releases. Next, she repeats the stretch with the left leg.

Make sure that the child isn't lunging for her toes. She shouldn't feel any pain — just a slight stretch in her muscles.

Figure 7-3:
The hurdle position helps players stretch out their hamstrings.

Quadriceps stretch

The child grabs his right foot or ankle and lifts it behind his body (see Figure 7-4). He presses the top of his foot into his hand while pressing his hips slightly forward.

His lower leg and foot should be directly behind his upper leg, and there shouldn't be any twisting in or out. Make sure that the child doesn't rest his foot against his buttocks.

If any kids have trouble balancing on one leg for the quadriceps stretch, have each player put his free hand on the shoulder of a stretching partner to balance.

Groin stretch

The child sits on the ground and places the soles of her feet together, with her knees to the sides (see Figure 7-5). Leaning forward, the child presses forward slowly until she feels mild tension in the groin.

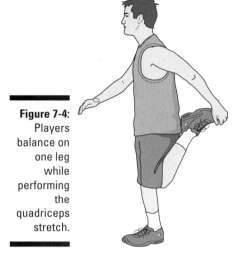

Figure 7-4:
Players balance on one leg while performing the quadriceps stretch.

Figure 7-5:
The groin stretch is a key element of any stretching session for older players.

Waist/lower back stretch

The child stands with his feet beyond shoulder width apart, arcs his left arm over his head, and points to the right while his right arm rests against his right knee (see Figure 7-6). Then he reverses to the other side, using his right arm pointing to the left. Perform several repetitions in each direction.

Upper back stretch

The youngster stands and stretches both arms behind her back, clasping them together while puffing her chest out (see Figure 7-7). She holds the stretch for a few seconds and then releases.

Figure 7-6:
A properly stretched lower back enables players to move freely.

Figure 7-7:
A stretched-out upper back allows players to move their arms easily.

Neck stretch

The child stands and slowly turns his head all the way to the left; next, he slowly turns his head all the way to the right. Then he tucks his chin to his chest to stretch out the back of his neck.

Always caution the kids to perform the neck stretch slowly. You don't want them straining or pulling something by being too forceful.

Knee bends

While the child is seated on the ground, she bends her left knee and places her left foot flat on the ground. She follows by placing her right foot and ankle on her left thigh, just above her knee. She places her hands on the ground behind her hips and presses her chest toward her knee and foot until she feels a stretch in her groin (see Figure 7-8).

The child's upper torso, neck, and shoulders should remain open and straight; don't let her round her upper back.

Hip flexor stretch

The child stands with his feet in a lunge position (see Figure 7-9), with both feet facing forward and his front knee slightly bent. He briefly pushes up onto his toes on his back foot. He also presses his hips forward while tightening his buttocks and then slowly lowers his body until he feels a stretch in the front of his hips. While he performs this stretch, his upper body remains upright and centered directly over his hips.

Arm stretch

The youngster stands with her feet shoulder width apart, interlaces her fingers, and stretches her arms straight up over her head. Her palms are facing up.

Figure 7-8:
Knee bends are another way to stretch out the groin area.

Figure 7-9:
Stretching the hip flexors enables players to run faster.

Warm-up drills for older players

For the older kids, you can use some more-aggressive stretches to help get them ready.

High knees

The child takes an exaggerated high step forward, lifting his knee as high as possible while simultaneously pushing up on the toes of the opposite foot (see Figure 7-10). The arm opposite the leg being lifted swings up to chin level. This move works the hips and shoulders, and also stretches the quadriceps, glutes, shoulders, and lower back.

Have the kids go 25 yards down the field performing these stretches; then have them turn around and repeat the move on the way back.

Figure 7-10: High knees stretch out both the upper and lower body.

Lunges

The youngster begins by placing her hands behind her head, with her fingers interlaced. She takes a long stride forward, placing her foot flat on the ground while coming up on the toes of her back foot (see Figure 7-11). The knee of her back foot is barely off the ground. The front knee should be at a 90-degree angle. She brings her back leg up and stands upright before repeating with the opposite leg.

Lunges stretch the glutes, hamstrings, hip flexors, and calves. Have the players do 10 to 15 repetitions for each leg.

Figure 7-11:
Performing
lunges
works the
hamstrings,
hip flexors,
calves, and
glutes.

Straight leg kicks

These moves stretch the hamstrings, calves, and lower back. The youngster begins by kicking his right leg up as high as it'll go; then he reaches out his left hand to touch his toes (see Figure 7-12). The player's extended arm should remain parallel to the ground. Then he repeats the stretch with the opposite leg and arm.

Have players perform ten repetitions for each leg.

Figure 7-12:
Straight leg
kicks
stretch the
hamstrings,
calves, and
lower back.

Running butt taps

This move gives the quadriceps and hip flexors a good stretch. The child begins running, flexing her knees so that each time she lifts her foot off the ground during the run, her heel comes all the way back and contacts her butt (see Figure 7-13). While performing this stretch, the youngster should be leaning slightly forward, with her arms swinging close to her body.

Have the kids complete 20 total kicks within 10 to 15 yards, or have them do this stretch while running in place. You can also have them carry a ball in their sticks to get them used to handling the ball while on the move.

Figure 7-13:
Youngsters stretch out the quadriceps with the running butt tap.

Running carioca

This movement stretches the abductors, glutes, ankles, and hips. The youngster begins on the balls of his feet and twists his hips while crossing one leg in front of the other. He brings his back leg through and crosses his lead leg behind the back leg (see Figure 7-14). His shoulders remain square through the entire drill.

You can have the players use this move to go across the width of the field and then return to their starting position.

Figure 7-14:
The running carioca stretches the glutes and hips, among other areas.

Going on the Offensive

Moving the ball down the field and generating quality scoring chances against opponents require each player to be comfortable with the offensive basics of the game: moving with the ball, passing and catching it while standing still and while moving, and taking accurate shots. The better your players execute these skills — especially when defenders are harassing them on game day — the more enjoyment they will gain from playing.

In the following sections, we take a look at a variety of drills you can use to help your players get a good grip on the offensive fundamentals of lacrosse.

Concentrating on cradling

Maneuvering on the field with the ball in the pocket of the stick — known as *cradling* — is one of the most basic elements of lacrosse. Regardless of what position a child is playing, she needs cradling skills to have any measure of success in playing and enjoying the game. The drills in this section zero in on this fundamental skill.

Cone Weave

The better players are at making sharp cuts while maintaining possession of the ball, the more success they'll enjoy getting by defenders and creating more scoring opportunities for themselves or teammates. This drill is perfect for improving footwork — a key skill for lacrosse players at all levels.

What you need: Pylons or other safe markers (such as plastic bottles or towels). A ball for each player.

How it works: Set up pylons randomly around the field to create a course that the players maneuver through while cradling a ball, cutting back and forth from their right to their left. Set some pylons close together to force players to make sharp cuts back to back; leave bigger gaps between other pylons so that players have to run several yards, building up speed, before making a move.

Coaching pointers: Make sure that the kids keep their heads up, rather than look down at their feet, so that they develop the habit of scanning the field at all times. In the older age groups, you can add a competitive element by timing the players to see who can negotiate the course fastest.

You don't want to waste a lot of valuable practice time forcing kids to stand in line waiting to do this drill. If you have enough markers and a couple of assistants to help you supervise, you can set up a few courses so that more players can participate at the same time. You can also speed things up by starting players off at 10-second intervals so that you have several players weaving through the course at the same time.

Motion Mania

If your players can move efficiently in any direction with the ball, without bobbling or losing control of it, defenders will have difficulty sticking with them. This drill helps players improve their cradling techniques.

What you need: One ball for each player.

How it works: Line the players up facing you, with at least 8 feet between players. If you have a big group of kids, you can have several rows; just make sure to have that 8-foot space on all sides. Each player begins by cradling a ball in his stick. To start the drill, signal a direction with your hand, and have the group run quickly in that direction. After just a couple of seconds, indicate another direction, thereby forcing the players to stop and change directions.

Coaching pointers: Be sure to mix up your directions so that players get plenty of practice moving not only left and right, but also to the front and back. Watch the players' heads to make sure that their heads are up, not down and taking peeks at the ball. You want to get players comfortable moving in all directions without glancing at the ball; otherwise, they may not see an open teammate or a good scoring opportunity because their vision isn't on the field, where it belongs.

Pumping up the passing and catching

The better your team is at passing and catching the ball, the more chances it has to score goals. The following drills zero in on this important aspect of offense.

Use tennis balls in some of your passing and catching drills to help players develop "soft hands," which are a real asset in performing these important skills during games.

Partner Passes

This drill is useful for helping players hone their stationary passing and catching skills.

What you need: One ball for each pair of players.

How it works: Break the team up into pairs, and give each twosome a ball. Have the pairs stand 15 yards apart, facing each other. On your command, the partners start passing the ball back and forth. To help the kids concentrate on making catches, have them keep track of how many catches their twosome has by calling out the number of each reception as they make it.

You can add a competitive twist by seeing which pair can make ten catches first or (to prevent the players from rushing to make passes) can make the most catches in a row.

Coaching pointers: You want players to be using the proper overhand technique (covered in Chapter 9). Make sure that they are following through toward their target, not chopping the follow-through short or coming across their bodies with their sticks while they're releasing the ball.

Stationary Passes

During games, you can't expect players to make pinpoint passes every time, especially when a defender is charging at them or Grandma is stationed on the sideline attempting to take a good action picture. So players have to be able to move to their left and right to snare passes that stray off target. This drill helps them get used to making these types of grabs.

What you need: One ball for each pair of players.

How it works: Break the team into pairs, and give each twosome a ball. Have the kids face their partners with about 10 to 15 yards between them. The player with the ball begins by intentionally passing the ball to his partner's right side. His partner catches the ball and delivers a pass back to his partner's right side. The next passes are made to the left side. The pairs continue rotating between sides. Have them see how many passes they can complete in a row.

Coaching pointers: During games, players will be forced to deliver passes to teammates who are covered tightly, so they have to be capable of working the ball in different directions. These passes are often a little more difficult for youngsters to execute, because they don't have a natural target, so make sure that they are stepping toward the intended area, which should be about 3 feet to their partner's left or right.

Knock-'Em-Out Pairs

This competitive drill helps players concentrate on making accurate passes and catches with something at stake — great practice for performing in close games, in which an errant pass or dropped ball can be the difference between a win and a loss.

What you need: One ball for each pair of players.

How it works: Break the team into pairs. Position the players so that they're facing their partners, about 5 yards apart. Be sure to leave at least 10 feet of space between each of the pairs. One player in each twosome has a ball and begins the drill by making a pass to her partner. If the ball touches the ground due to a poor pass or drop, that pair is knocked out of the drill. If the pass is caught, the player who delivered it moves back 2 yards. Keep moving the passer back 2 yards every time a successful exchange is made until only one pair remains.

Coaching pointers: Be sure to have another drill set up so that the kids who get knocked out of this one can jump into the other drill. Or simply have those players practice passing the ball to one another so that they're ready to go if you've set aside time in your practice to run this drill a few times.

During the drill, keep a close watch on the kids who are passing the ball to make sure that they follow through when releasing the ball. Sometimes, kids tend to stop their sticks as soon as the ball leaves their possession, which can lead to passes that fail to find their intended targets.

Rapid Receptions

Players who are skilled at catching the ball, as well as getting rid of it quickly when they spot open teammates, can make game day tough on opponents. This drill enables players to develop a quick release that can help turn up an offense's effectiveness several notches.

What you need: One ball for each pair of players.

How it works: Break the team up into pairs, and give each twosome a ball. Spread the pairs around the field, 15 yards apart. On your command, the kids begin passing the ball back and forth with their partners as quickly as possible. You can turn the drill into a fun team competition by seeing which pair can complete the most passes during a 2-minute period.

Coaching pointers: Make sure that your players aren't sacrificing proper technique in an effort to speed their passes, which sometimes happens in a drill that has a time element involved. If you choose to go the competitive route with this drill, use different time periods — such as 30 seconds or 45 seconds — to help hold the players' interest.

Shooting for perfection

For many young lacrosse players, nothing is more exciting than scoring goals, although some players at the beginning level derive more satisfaction from chasing grasshoppers during practices and games. Slip the following drills into your practices to help all your players hone their shooting skills — and have lots of fun doing so, too.

Target Shots

This drill helps players learn to pick out a specific area of the net and direct shots there.

What you need: One player, one goalie, and a bucket of balls.

How it works: The goalie takes his position in the net, and the offensive player stands about 15 yards in front of the goalie. You stand behind the net, out of the goalie's sight, and signal where you want the player to take the shot: upper left or right corner, lower left or right corner, or through the goalie's legs. Continue picking different locations before each shot.

Coaching pointers: Make sure that after you give the signal, the shooter doesn't reveal his intentions to the goalie by looking directly where he intends to shoot.

You can make this drill a fun competition for the entire team by giving each child 10 shots and awarding a point for every goal that is scored in the location you chose.

Shots on the Go

The most dangerous shooters — and the ones who get to celebrate goals with teammates most often — are those who are capable of delivering accurate shots while on the move. This drill helps them learn to get a good handle on this skill.

What you need: Four players, one goalie, and a bucket of balls.

How it works: The goalie takes her position in the net. Position two players to the left of the goalie and two players to the right; they should be about 10 yards away from the goalie and several yards off to the side. Have several balls in front of each twosome.

Figure 7-15 shows the action. On your command, the first player to the left of the goalie sprints across the field (1), cuts in toward the goalie (2), and takes a shot on net while moving forward (3). After taking the shot, she continues across the field to the other side (5). As soon as the shot is released, the player on the opposite side darts across the middle (4), cuts toward the net (6), releases a shot, and continues on across the field (7). The drill continues with players on each side of the field taking turns racing into the middle and delivering shots.

Figure 7-15:
The Shots on the Go drill helps kids develop shooting accuracy while moving.

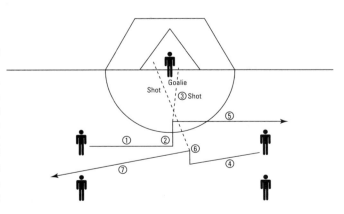

Coaching pointers: Make sure that the players are keeping their heads up and on the goal, rather than looking down at their feet, because under game conditions, they need to be aware of where their teammates and defenders are.

To increase the difficulty of the drill as the players sprint across the middle of the field, you can determine when they must cut toward the net by calling out "Cut!" This requirement forces the players to react quickly, much as they have to during games.

Catch and Shoot

Many times during games, players must rely on teammates to get them the ball when they are open. Players who are good at catching these passes and getting off shots pose problems for defenders. This drill helps them become more proficient in this aspect of the game.

What you need: Three players, one goalie, and a bucket of balls.

How it works: The goalie takes his position in the net. Two players stand behind the net, with one off to the goalie's left and the other off to the goalie's right. Each player has several balls in front of him. The other offensive player takes a spot about 10 yards in front of the goalie. On your command, the player on the goalie's right delivers a pass to the player out in front, who catches the ball and quickly takes a shot on net. As soon as the shot is released, the player on the goalie's left passes him a ball, which he catches and then shoots. Continue the drill, alternating between the two passers.

Coaching pointers: Keep a close watch to be sure that the player receiving the passes and taking the shots is watching the ball, not taking his eye off it in his enthusiasm to get off a shot. You want to keep this drill moving at a fast pace, but don't allow the passers to sacrifice accuracy by rushing so much that their passes are veering off target. Be sure to rotate the kids so that each player gets a chance to be both a passer and shooter.

One-on-One

The ability to beat a defender one-on-one and create an opening to shoot or pass is a real asset for any player to have in her offensive arsenal.

What you need: Two players and one goalie. A ball.

How it works: The goalie takes her position in the net. Position one player with a ball about 20 yards away from the goalie. A defender begins 5 yards away from the offensive player. On your command, the offensive player tries to maneuver past the defender and get off a shot on goal.

Coaching pointers: Make sure that the defender isn't committing any penalties. You want to keep your eye on the offensive player to ensure that she is protecting the ball properly. To increase the difficulty of the drill for the offensive player, allow only 5 seconds before a shot must be taken.

Facing off

Face-offs represent valuable opportunities to gain possession of the ball that (ideally) lead to scoring opportunities for your team. The following drills help your players get some quality practice in this important aspect of the game.

Dueling Partners

The ability to win face-offs and gain possession of the ball is key to building a successful offensive attack. This drill helps refine those skills.

What you need: Four players and one ball.

How it works: Split the four players into two-person teams. Have a player from each pair line up to take the face-off, with his partner about 10 feet behind him. On your command, the players face off for the ball and attempt to gain possession of it. Whichever team secures the ball tries to control it as long as possible, while the team that didn't secure it tries to take control. Run the drill for a minute or two, and limit the playing area so that the pair that gains control can't run all over the place.

Coaching pointers: Another fun twist that incorporates a passing element is that the twosome who gains control receives a point for each pass it completes. Run the drill for a minute, and see over the course of the drill which pair is able to accumulate the most points.

Mystery Moves

Players can employ several face-off techniques (check out Chapter 9 for the basics). This drill is good for helping younger players learn how to execute face-offs.

What you need: Two players and one ball.

How it works: The two players take their positions for the face-off. You whisper in the ear of one player what type of face-off technique you want her to use. On your command, the players vie for the ball.

Coaching pointers: Keep a close eye on the players' technique to ensure that they are executing the face-off properly. Also, be sure to give all the kids a chance to try to win the face-off by using the techniques you whisper to them.

Staying Alive

This competitive drill for older players is a fun way to close out practice.

What you need: The entire team. A ball.

How it works: Randomly pair the players up, and conduct a quick mini-tournament to determine which player is best at winning face-offs. Call each pair up, and conduct a face-off. The player who secures possession of the ball stays alive; the other player is knocked out of the competition. Continue pairing up the kids who win their face-off battles until only one youngster remains.

Coaching pointers: When conducting this drill, you want to run through it quickly, because you don't want the kids who are knocked out to be standing around long. If you have a large group of kids on your team, have another drill for those who get knocked out to participate in.

Scooping up the ball

Any time a ball is loose on the field during a game, you want your players hustling to gain control of it as quickly as you would pounce on a $50 bill lying on the sidewalk. The following drills focus on this part of the game.

Ball Chase

Whenever a ball is up for grabs on the field, you want your players giving it their all in battling the opponent for it. To help instill that mentality in your team, turn to this drill.

What you need: A bucket of balls.

How it works: Break the team up into pairs. The drill begins with a player standing on each side of you. You toss a ball in any direction. As soon as the ball is thrown, the two players race after it to see who can come up with possession of it.

Coaching pointers: Make sure that the players, in their exuberance to scoop up the ball, aren't committing penalties. To turn the drill into a fun team competition, split the kids into two teams, and keep score to see which team snags the most balls. This competition helps get the kids really enthusiastic about doing well, as well as cheering on their teammates, which usually spices up a practice and leads to increased skill development.

Retrieve and React

One of the many neat aspects of lacrosse is that players must switch from offense to defense — and vice versa — in the blink of an eye. This drill helps players make that transition.

What you need: Three players, one ball, and a goal.

How it works: The goalie takes his place in the net. You begin standing about 30 yards away from the goal, with a player standing on either side of you. Throw the ball several yards out in front of the players. As soon as you release the ball, the two players chase after it and vie to gain possession. The player who scoops up the ball assumes the role of the attacker; the other plays defense. The attacker tries to move in on the goalie and get off a shot; the defender works to prevent a shot.

Coaching pointers: Make sure that players use only safe techniques that are within the rules as they contest for the loose balls. To keep the drill moving, give the player who gains possession of the ball only 10 seconds to get off a shot. This restriction ensures that players don't hold onto the ball for long periods, trying to create an opening to get off a shot.

Drilling on Defense

Defending opposing players requires a variety of skills that are much different from those needed when your team has possession of the ball. Being an effective defender requires the ability to adapt and react to what the opponent is doing. The following drills are designed to help your players (regardless of the positions they play) enhance their defensive skills, deny opponents goal-scoring opportunities, and get the ball back for their team.

One-on-one action

Disrupting an opposing player who is on the attack requires a broad range of skills. The following sections provide some one-on-one drills to help your players improve those all-important defensive techniques.

Dodge and Roll

This drill tests players' abilities to react to sudden moves and to defend against attacks.

What you need: Two players, one goalie, and one ball.

How it works: The goalie takes her position in the net. Designate one player to play offense, and give her a ball. She stands about 10 yards away from the goalie, with her back to the goalie. The defender begins 3 yards away from the offensive player, facing her. On your command, the offensive player spins to her left or right and tries to get off a shot before the defender can prevent it from happening.

Coaching pointers: Make sure that the defensive player isn't committing any penalties. Also, encourage the offensive player to use fakes to get the defender off balance.

If you're coaching in a boys' league that allows checking, you'll want the defender to use that technique to help counter the offensive player's moves.

Read and React Tag

This drill is a fun one to use with younger players to help them learn to follow the player they're guarding.

What you need: Two players and one ball.

How it works: Break the team up into pairs, and designate one player in each pair as offensive and the other as defensive. Give the offensive player a ball to carry. The offensive player stands at the midfield line, with the defensive player 10 yards away from him. On your command, the offensive player takes off; the defender must chase him down and touch him with his stick.

Coaching pointers: You can run this drill in 1-minute intervals all over the field that so many players can participate at the same time. You want the offensive players to use their speed, as well as fakes and cuts, to avoid getting tagged by the defender. Remind your defenders to keep their heads up and their eyes focused on the offensive players' chests, which will cut down on the defenders going for fakes and taking themselves out of position.

Corner Checks

If you're coaching in a boys' league that allows checking, this drill helps defenders learn to use the technique to their advantage.

What you need: Three players, one goalie, and one ball.

How it works: Break the kids up into groups of three, and designate an offensive player and two defensive players. The goalie takes his position in the net. The offensive player begins standing about 25 yards away from the goal. The two defenders face him, standing about 5 yards away. On your command, the offensive player tries to maneuver toward the net and get off a shot; the two defenders check him to keep him away from the net. Give the offensive player a set amount of time — such as 30 seconds or 1 minute — to get off a shot.

Coaching pointers: At the older levels of play, this drill can turn pretty aggressive, so make sure that the defenders use proper checking techniques at all times.

Goalie moves

Quick reflexes, excellent hand-eye coordination, and superb footwork are some of the most important ingredients young goaltenders should focus on developing. The following drills will help your goalies excel in the net.

Shooting Shuttle

The ability to stop shots from all angles is a necessity for success for any goalie. This drill gives your goalies a chance to defend a barrage of shots in a short period, which also enhances their hand-eye coordination.

What you need: Three players, one goalie, and 15 balls.

How it works: The goalie takes her position in front of the net. Position three players about 10 yards away from the goalie, with about 10 feet separating those three players and with five balls in front of each player. On your command, the three players scoop up a ball. The player on the left shoots first, so the goalie moves into position to defend the shot from that angle. After the shot is taken, the goalie quickly slides into the middle to face the shot from the player in the center, and as soon as that shot is taken, she moves over and gets into position to stop the shot from the player on the right. Continue with all the shots in rapid succession until no balls remain.

Coaching pointers: With so many shots coming at them, some young goalies tend to get sloppy with their footwork and the positioning of their hands. Make sure that the goalie keeps her body facing the shooter and that her glove hand is in the proper position to knock away shots.

Mystery Shots

During games, goalies never know when or where shots will come from, so this drill is ideal for helping them learn to react quickly to shots.

What you need: Two players, one goalie, and a bucket of balls.

How it works: The goalie takes his position in the net. Two players position themselves about 15 yards away from the goalie, with approximately 10 feet between them. Each of the two players possesses a ball. You stand off to the side, out of the goalie's sight. You signal to the two players which one you want to shoot the ball on net. On your command, both players move their sticks into shooting position, but only the designated player actually continues through with the shot; the other player simply fakes a shot. The goalie must react to the actual shooter and attempt to stop his shot.

Coaching pointers: Make sure that the goalie's head is up and that his eyes are focused on both players. You don't want him to focus on only one shooter and guess who will be taking the shot; you want him to read both players and react as soon as the shot is released.

Besides being a good exercise for your goalies, this drill helps your other players enhance their fakes, which they can use during games to get defenders out of position.

High and Low

The most effective goalies are those who are comfortable stopping both high and low shots. This drill helps goalies become more proficient at stopping both types of shots.

What you need: One player, one goalie, and a bucket of balls.

How it works: The goalie takes her position in the net; the offensive player begins approximately 15 yards away. The player scoops up a ball, and you say either "High" or "Low." The player must then take a shot at that height. You can have the player take several shots in a short period.

Coaching pointers: Because the goalie knows the type of shot that is coming, she'll be able to develop some confidence making stops. If she's pretty good at stopping the majority of the shots, you can increase the difficulty by moving the player in several feet closer. You can also turn the drill into a competition by awarding a point to the shooter for every goal scored and a point to the goalie for every shot that doesn't find the net.

Putting It All Together: Sample Practice Plans

Now that you have some drills to incorporate, you're ready to put a practice together. A sample one-hour practice for a team of beginning players could look something like this:

- ✔ **5 minutes:** Warm-up. Get your players into the habit of warming up at the start of each practice with some basic jumping jacks, arm windmills, and leg stretches.

- ✔ **10 minutes:** The Cone Weave gets the kids' legs churning and their hearts pumping, and helps set the tone for an energetic, productive practice.

- ✔ **10 minutes:** Passing and catching the ball is a key skill for playing any position, so go with the Partner Passes drill.

- ✔ **5 minutes:** After you have the kids work on their passes, run the Knock-'Em-Out Pairs drill as a fun way to wrap up work on these particular skills. Just be sure to have the kids who get knocked out of this drill continue working on their passing and catching off to the side with their teammates who are also no longer alive in the drill.

✔ **15 minutes:** All kids love shooting drills, so run the Shots on the Go drill on one half of the field and the Target Shots drill at the other end of the field. Be sure to rotate the kids so that each player gets a chance to participate in both drills.

✔ **10 minutes:** Defensive-oriented drills should always be part of your practices, so at one end of the field, use the Dodge and Roll drill, and at the other end, go with the Read and React Tag drill. After 5 minutes, rotate the kids so that they all have a chance to participate in both drills.

✔ **5 minutes:** Have the players cool down with some light stretches. While they're performing these stretches, take time to applaud them on their effort throughout the practice and to acknowledge their improvement in different areas of the game.

Here is a look at another practice plan you can follow using the drills introduced in this chapter:

✔ **5 minutes:** Warm-up. Every practice should start with this to help prepare the young bodies for physical activity.

✔ **10 minutes:** Run the Stationary Passes drill. This is a nice follow up to the stretching, and allows the kids the chance to work their way into the practice.

✔ **5 minutes:** Go with the Rapid Receptions drill. Run a series of one-minute mini tournaments and see which pair can complete the most passes in a row.

✔ **15 minutes:** At one end of the field run the Catch and Shoot drill to help players develop their skills of catching the ball and releasing shots quickly. At the opposite end of the field run the Ball Chase drill. Be sure to rotate the kids so they have a chance to participate in each drill.

✔ **10 minutes:** The Cone Weave drill. Break the kids up into groups of three, and see which group is the fastest by combining each of their times. This will incorporate a team element and have the kids cheering for their group partners.

✔ **10 minutes:** At one end of the field run the Shooting Shuttle, and at the other end go with the Mystery Shots drill. Rotate the players so they have a chance to do both drills.

✔ **5 minutes:** Conclude your practice with a cool down.

You can be flexible with your practice schedule and tweak it based on how the session is unfolding. If you find that a particular drill is far too easy for the kids, for example, you don't need to continue it, despite how much time you may have allotted for it in your practice plan. Instead, jump to your next drill, or fall back on a backup drill that you have ready to go in case another doesn't go as expected.

Chapter 8

Making Game Day Memorable — For the Right Reasons

Game days are exciting times for players, because they get the chance to use the skills and techniques they've been practicing so hard all week (and to slip on the cool uniform, too!). Those days are equally enjoyable for you if you're prepared to handle the flood of responsibilities that come your way.

Coaching a youth lacrosse team on game day requires you to wear many hats, and this chapter runs down all your tasks. We share the details on meeting with the opposing coach and referees; delivering pregame pep talks and remaining a constant source of motivation throughout the game; substituting players; instructing kids in a positive fashion during the action; making halftime adjustments; and ensuring that you send the kids home happy, regardless of what the scoreboard says. As you can see, a lot goes on during game day, and this chapter makes sure that you'll be on top of it all.

Taking Care of Pregame Business

Before you can send your players out on the field to compete in the game, you have to tend to some important pregame responsibilities, which range from inspecting the field to meeting with the opposing coach and the officials. Read on for more details to make sure you have these areas covered.

Checking the field

Ensuring the safety of your players, as well as those from the opposing team, should always be a top priority of any youth lacrosse coach. So before the game, inspect the playing area for broken glass, rocks, raised sprinkler heads, loose pieces of sod, and any other hazards that pose an injury risk to players. You can ask your assistant coaches or some parents to help you check the field so that the inspection doesn't monopolize all your time.

Don't rely on the opposing coach or the grounds crew to do the field inspection. Every step you can take to help ensure the kids' safety is crucial.

In many lacrosse programs, games are played in rapid succession, but don't skirt the pregame field check just because another game was just played there. Even if someone has already checked the playing area, having another set of eyes look it over never hurts. Also, all the traffic on the field may have torn up chunks of grass that could trip young players if the grass isn't replaced properly before the next game gets under way.

Meeting with opposing coaches and referees

Before the ball is in play and your players are tearing up and down the field, head over to meet the opposing coach and shake hands with him, as well as any assistants. This meeting is a wonderful demonstration of good sportsmanship; it also sets a good example for the players on both teams, as well as for the parents and other spectators. While you're over there, take the time to find out whether any players on the opposing team have any special needs that you and your players should be aware of or any accommodations that need to be made.

Meeting with the referees who will officiate your game provides another example of some good pregame sportsmanship. When introducing yourself to the officials, let them know that you want to be informed if any of your players (or parents) says or does anything unsportsmanlike during the course of the game. You want to work with the officials — not against them. Even though they're wearing striped shirts and you're donning a coach's cap, you're all involved in youth lacrosse because you care about kids and want to make the experience as rewarding as possible for them.

During your meeting with the officials, alert them if any child on your team has special needs. Officials can make the proper adjustments when they know this information beforehand. If one of your players has a hearing problem and won't be able to hear a whistle, for example, the official knows to use a hand signal for this child to get her attention.

Getting Their Game On: The Pregame Team Meeting

A team meeting helps get everyone in the right frame of mind before the game gets under way. In the following sections, we take a look at all the areas you need to cover during this meeting to help set the tone for a great day of lacrosse for all your players, as well as yourself.

Checking equipment

Amid all the excitement surrounding game day, kids sometimes forget an important piece of equipment, such as a mouthpiece. During your talk with the team, do a quick equipment check to make sure that all the players have what they need. Beyond the obvious equipment basics — such as sticks and head gear — check to verify that the players have their mouth guards and water bottles on hand, too.

It's a good idea to enforce a team rule that every child must bring a water bottle to all practices and games, with his name clearly marked on the bottle. Besides being important so kids remain hydrated during the game, you don't want them spreading germs by drinking out of the same bottles.

At the more advanced levels of play, make sure that the kids have cleats that meet league regulations. As we discuss in Chapter 2, children should never be allowed on the field to participate in a practice or compete in a game without all the proper safety equipment.

Inspiring the players with your pregame talk

As a lacrosse coach, you want your players to be excited about playing and ready to give everything they have when the game begins. Sometimes, though, kids require a boost to get motivated to chase down those loose balls or sprint back on defense after an opponent bursts past them. That's where the pregame motivational talk comes in.

Getting the best effort out of your players every time they take the field will be a challenge at times, but you're fully capable of meeting the challenge. Just keep in mind that your motivational talk needs to pull the players together as a team. Following are some tips to ensure that your pregame words hit home and produce the responses you are aiming for.

Minimize distractions

Kids have short attention spans, so any time you're speaking with them, you don't want to be competing with anything that can monopolize their attention and detract from what you're trying to get across. Whenever you're having a pregame chat, gather the kids in the spot that has the fewest distractions. Your players won't be the least bit interested in what you're saying if they can see their parents or other family members milling around nearby.

Also, keep your distance from the other team. Kids naturally want to check out the opposition, which is another distraction you don't want to contend with.

Keep it short

Always keep in mind that the kids didn't show up on game day to listen to you talk or to be subjected to long-winded speeches. They're there to play a game. Keep your talk to less than 5 minutes. Anything longer than that, and you risk defusing their energy and enthusiasm for the game.

Swipe the good material

Reflect on your playing days in lacrosse (or any other sport) and the pregame talks that really made an impression on you. Steal from the good ones, and stay away from those that left a bad impression, and you'll have the makings of a pregame message that fulfills your intentions.

Make the message fit the audience

Target your message to your audience; otherwise, you're wasting your players' time. The younger the players on the team, the more basic your words must be. At the more-advanced levels of play, you can get a little more in-depth on what you want to address with the players.

Dump the clichés

Clichés like "No pain, no gain" will probably produce more than a few blank stares from your players. Just go with your instincts, and speak from the heart with genuine passion. You don't need to resort to worn-out phrases, which are more likely to cause confusion.

Make it all about your team

Center your talk on your team, your players, and your confidence in them. Positive reinforcement of their skills can provide them the extra boost of confidence they need to perform up to their capabilities. It also has more impact than covering the strengths and weaknesses of an opposing team that they may know very little about.

Blanket the conversation in positives

Make sure that everything that comes out of your mouth is positive and uplifting. Talk about areas of the game in which the team has excelled lately, and tell your players you can't wait to see them put those skills into action. Don't allow any doubts and insecurities to creep into the players' minds.

Deliver it just before the game

Make sure that you deliver your chat moments before the game instead of before your warm-ups. You don't want to waste your words by pumping up the players for their warm-up; you want the kids heading into the game riding a wave of positive energy.

Relax — and remind the kids to have fun

Speak to the team in a calm, relaxed manner. If you're nervous or uptight, your players will be, too, which infringes on their performance. If you're smiling and laughing, the players will approach the game in a much more relaxed way, which usually leads to better play on the field.

Be clear that you want the kids to have a good time playing, whether they're up by six goals or trailing by that many. When kids genuinely believe that having fun is important, they play more loosely — and usually more effectively — because they're not afraid of making mistakes or losing games.

Briefly recap the warm-up

Verbally run through the pregame warm-up quickly to refresh the kids' memories on the order of the drills so you don't have to waste valuable time explaining them once you're on the field. (For more on the type of warm-ups your players should be performing to get properly loosened up for competition, check out Chapter 7.)

Emphasize sportsmanship

You want the team you put on the field to model good sportsmanship at all times, regardless of the score of the game or what is going on in it. That includes respecting the officials, regardless of what calls they make. Remind players of the importance of being good sports and being a team that others in the league will strive to emulate each time out.

Wrap up with your team cheer

Conclude with a team cheer, such as "One . . . two . . . three . . . team!" or "Together!" The cheer's a symbolic gesture reminding the players that they need to work together.

Warming up

Although injuries are part of a contact sport like lacrosse, and they're out of your control when the game begins, pregame warm-ups help minimize the risk. The older the players on your team are, the more susceptible they are to pulling or straining muscles. A well-designed, pregame warm-up stretches the kids' muscles, loosens their bodies, and gradually elevates their heart rates. It also helps them perform to the best of their ability during the game.

The goal of any pregame warm-up is to prepare kids for competition, reduce the chance of injury, and prep them to perform their best. Warm-ups conducted in a positive environment can give players confidence and have them looking forward to performing similar skills during the game.

During your practice sessions leading up to game day, spend a few minutes going over your pregame warm-up. You don't want to waste valuable time before the game organizing players, introducing drills, and giving lengthy instructions on how to perform certain stretches.

Keep the following tips in mind when putting together your pregame warm-up:

Before beginning the stretches, be sure to have the players do some light running in place or some jumping jacks to get their bodies warmed up.

- **Hit all the major muscle groups.** The stretches need to cover all the major muscle groups, including the hamstrings, calves, neck, arms, and back. See Chapter 7 for some specific stretches you can use.

- **Pump up the kids' confidence.** While your players are stretching, work your way around the group and provide a little extra encouragement that they can take with them onto the field that day. A pat on the back, a wink, or a general comment about how you're looking forward to watching them play gives them an extra little shot of confidence that can make a big difference in their play and how much they enjoy the game. Even general comments directed at the entire team can produce positive results when the game action heats up.

- **Keep the drills light.** After the kids are stretched out, you want them to work into the drills gradually. When attackers are running with the ball, for example, you want them moving at half their normal speed for several repetitions and working their way up to top speed. If kids go full speed throughout the entire warm-up, they'll be gasping for breath by the time the game begins.

✔ **Cover all the skills.** Besides getting your players loosened up, you want to get them comfortable performing all the skills that will be required of them during the game. You don't want to send your attackers out on the field without having caught a pass on the run — a skill they'll be counted on to perform throughout the game. And your defensive players will be unprepared if they begin a game without having done any type of running and cutting in different directions — a skill that they'll use often during games to stick with attacking opponents who charge down the field with the ball.

You simply want to loosen the kids up for competition — not have them run around as they would during an actual game.

✔ **Allow time to drink fluids.** Don't conduct your warm-ups right up until the start of the game so that kids don't even have a chance to catch their breath. Give players a minute or two to get a drink of water and compose themselves before they head onto the field.

Coaching a Great Game

We're confident that your pregame talk will motivate your players to perform at their top level and that your quality warm-up will get them loosened up the right way, prepared for competition. But when the game begins, all sorts of new challenges fall squarely on your shoulders, some of which you may not have given much thought to. Motivating players, orchestrating substitutions to ensure equal playing time, communicating plays, and making changes in strategy are just some of the areas you need to take care of during the heat of the action.

This section shows you what awaits you and how you can fulfill all your responsibilities to help your players benefit from their participation.

Motivating your players

A great pregame speech that excites the kids and has them charging out onto the field ready to play is a great way to begin the game, but you need to keep that energetic level of play going all game long, even on those days when nothing seems to go your team's way. Being a constant source of motivation for the players helps keep them involved in every aspect of the game at both the offensive and defensive ends of the field.

Keep the following tips in mind to help motivate your players throughout the game.

Give them freedom to make mistakes

That's right — mistakes! Because mistakes are part of lacrosse and can't be prevented, allow your players to make some during the course of the action without showing any frustration on your part.

Give them some space

Giving instructions every second of the game puts the brakes on players' development; they need some space to think and react on their own to what is unfolding in the game. Giving youngsters freedom to play and to make some decisions of their own fuels their growth, enhances their learning, and deepens their love of the game.

Rest the vocal cords

Grabbing for the throat lozenges after games isn't a good sign. Part of being a good coach is keeping your emotions in check and refraining from spending the entire game shouting instructions to every player on the field.

Constantly hearing your voice can wear players down. Sure, sometimes you need to get a player's attention, and increasing the volume is warranted. Just be sure to convey the instruction in a calm manner, because the louder your voice, the less effective the message may be for a young player. Also make sure that you deliver your message in a positive fashion.

Limit your sideline running

Don't use game day as a chance to fit in exercise by running up and down the sidelines. At specific points in the game, you may want to encourage your team to push the ball down the field quickly by running along the sideline, exuding positive words of encouragement and clapping your hands. That's perfectly OK. This type of behavior becomes a problem only when you're doing it the entire game, which can be a major distraction to players who are doing their best to focus on the game.

If you find yourself covering as much ground during the game as your players do, give yourself a breather. That move will be healthy for both you and your team.

Be positive with your feedback

Keep in mind that how players respond to your feedback during games can much different from the way they react during a midweek practice, simply because of all the extra people around. It can be upsetting for a youngster to get singled out in front of family members, strangers, and the opposing team; choose your words carefully so that the youngster's psyche isn't damaged.

If an attacker isn't following through on his passes, for example, offer some instruction in a positive manner. Say something like this: "Cameron, remember to follow through toward your target just like you did so well in practice this week." By taking this approach, you provide the player feedback that enhances his play during the game — and also give him a boost of confidence by pointing out how well he performed the skill earlier in the week.

Applaud hustle

Players can't control how many goals they score or limit an opponent to a specific number of scores. The one factor that they *do* have full control of is how hard they play and hustle on both offense and defense. You never want your players to be outhustled by the opposition; effort isn't controlled by talent or athleticism, so a team really has no reason to get outperformed in that area.

Your least talented players can have the greatest impact on the game by hustling and giving it their all. So applaud your players' work ethic enthusiastically, and reward their hustle with applause and praise. When you instill this attitude in your entire team, they'll reward you with their best effort at all times. You can always correct improper techniques or missed assignments, but only the players themselves control how much effort they put into every play and how deeply they really care about doing their best. Let kids know that even though they'll make mistakes, you want them to make those mistakes going at full speed and with 100-percent effort.

Communicating plays

Any time your team has possession of the ball, it has an opportunity to score a goal, so you always want the players focused on getting the best possible shot. Sometimes, you'll want to run a play in an attempt to create a scoring chance. At advanced levels of play, you may notice a defensive tendency of the opposition that you can exploit with a particular play in your arsenal. (For a rundown on some of the types of plays you can run, such as using checks to create openings and attacking from behind the net, check out Chapter 15.)

Whatever method you use to communicate plays, be sure to use it during your practice sessions, too. Just as kids need practice passing and defending, they need practice deciphering your hand signals from the sideline and executing the play.

At the beginning levels of play, children are there simply to learn the basics of lacrosse and have fun chasing up and down the field. Steer clear of bombarding them with an avalanche of plays that they won't be able to remember when game day rolls around. At more-advanced levels, you can introduce a series of plays for the kids to learn and use against opponents. Experienced players will enjoy the challenge of learning plays, practicing them during the week, and putting them in action on game day — and perhaps seeing their efforts pay off in goals.

Making player substitutions

Most lacrosse programs allow coaches to make unlimited substitutions during games, particularly at beginning levels of play, to help ensure that the kids receive an equal amount of playing time and don't feel that they're stranded on the bench for unbearable amounts of time. Being familiar with your league's rules (which we discuss in Chapter 2) is crucial that so you know whether any special rules regarding substitutions are in place.

When making substitutions, try to bring kids out after they do something well rather than when they make a mistake or simply get beaten by the opposing player on a move. If you bring a player to the bench shortly after she made an errant pass, she'll relate making mistakes to losing playing time, which can make her less assertive on the field.

When you bring a player to the sideline, give him a pat on the back or a high five recognizing all the effort he's putting forth. Kids love those kinds of receptions, and those gestures keep their enthusiasm running high so that they'll be eager to re-enter the game and continue giving a strong effort.

Employing advanced strategy for older players

The older and more advanced the players on your team are, the more chances you have to incorporate more sophisticated offensive and defensive techniques. At higher levels of play, you can introduce plays to set up when your team crosses midfield or when it's attacking from behind the net, for example. Picks are also a great way to free up players for open shots. You'll find details on executing these types of plays in Chapter 15 and the scoop on how to defend them in Chapter 16.

During your practices, you want to work with your team on running several types of plays so that regardless of the situation, you've got something to call for them to run during a game. But spend a little extra time nailing down one or two plays that your team is confident about performing. These plays are the ones you'll rely on when your team is trailing by a goal late in the game. When a team has a special play to turn to when the game is on the line, it has a greater chance of depositing the ball in the net.

When working on plays with your team during your practices, don't fall into the habit of designing them all for your most talented player to wind up shooting the ball. You want to spread those shots around. By doing so, not only do you include more players on your team in the action and make them feel that much more valued and appreciated for their efforts, but a team that possesses a balanced scoring attack that can shoot from anywhere on the field — from any player's stick — is much more difficult for defenses to stop. If an opponent always knows that shots are going to come from one particular player, it will adjust accordingly, and your offense won't have many options at its disposal if you haven't practiced a variety of plays that feature several different shooters.

Pumping Them Up: The Halftime Speech

During the first half of a game, you'll see everything from players scoring goals (ideally, for your team) to passes being dropped and penalties being called (ideally, on the other team). If you're coaching beginning-level lacrosse, you may even witness goalies checking out birds in the sky rather than the ball rolling past them into the net. A lot happens during the course of play, so when halftime arrives, you have a lot of information to sift through — and usually not much time to chat with the team before it returns to the field for the second half.

Following are some tips to keep in mind when gathering your troops during halftime to help ensure that the time is productive, enlightening, and beneficial, and that it leads to a strong team effort for the remainder of the game:

- ✓ **Rehearse what you want to say.** Because halftime breaks usually are short, you typically won't have a lot of time with your players. On your way to the locker room or the bench area where teams gather for the break, think about what you want to get across. That way, you'll know exactly what you want to say when you stand up in front of the kids and won't waste time searching for the right words.

- ✓ **Make sure the players consume fluids first.** Give players time to drink some fluids before you begin your halftime talk. Having a chance to quench their thirst and catch their breath makes them more receptive to your comments.

✔ **Keep the message short and simple.** What you say during your halftime chat should be clear, concise, and uplifting. Your players were just out on the field, and they know what happened, so don't waste valuable time recapping everything that transpired. If you limit the amount of information you throw at your team, your words are more likely to sink in. The last thing you want to do is send your team back on the field overwhelmed and confused about what you want them to do.

✔ **Match the team's mood.** The most effective halftime talks are those that match the mood of the team. If your team is trailing by several goals, for example, many of the kids may have their heads down in disappointment. You've got to revive their enthusiasm, using positive, uplifting words to get them to believe in themselves again. Even though the players may not have scored as many goals as they would have liked, point out the positives in their play and remind them that through hard work, they'll be able to capitalize on scoring opportunities a little better in the second half.

Conversely, if your team played a great first half and has a comfortable margin to work with, you don't need to give a rah-rah speech. Instead, acknowledge how well everyone performed, and remind the players to maintain their concentration and focus on duplicating that effort when they get back on the field for the second half.

✔ **Keep your emotions level.** Even if you're frustrated by how the team is playing — and all lacrosse coaches will endure those days from time to time — never let the team know, because that can kill morale and wipe out any chance for the kids to bounce back and play a better second half. Losing a grip on your emotions detracts from your ability to coach and interact effectively with your players. Whether your team is way ahead or way behind, maintain a positive attitude and demeanor.

✔ **Make necessary adjustments.** At the more-advanced levels of lacrosse, one of your biggest halftime challenges is making adjustments based on what went right — and not so right — during the opening half of play. Focus on finding solutions and fixing problems rather than making speeches.

✔ **Solicit input from players.** You can't possibly monitor every single thing that takes place on the field. If you're coaching an advanced-level team, your players can help. Asking them whether they have any suggestions to employ in the second half reinforces your respect for them and their knowledge of the game, and you may gain some valuable feedback that benefits the team.

✔ **Factor in the field conditions.** Sometimes, you have to tweak your strategy to fit the weather or the condition of the field. If the playing area has become wet and slippery, and your team typically plays a very aggressive style of defense, you may have to resort to a more-passive approach, because the conditions don't allow them to maintain their footing as easily.

> ✔ **Adjust to the striped shirts.** Different referees officiate games different ways, and your players have to adjust accordingly. Make note of how the game is being called, and make any necessary adjustments in your team's approach. If the referee is calling a lot of penalties, for example, your team will be better off toning down its aggressiveness just a bit so that it doesn't put itself in difficult short-handed situations.

Being a Good Sport

One of the many interesting aspects of playing a lacrosse game is that every contest produces a winner and a loser (except in beginning-level programs, which don't keep score). Showing your team how to win and lose with class and dignity transcends your instructions on the proper way to deliver a check or make an accurate shot on goal from long distance. Children must understand that they can leave the field feeling good about themselves — regardless of the score — if they gave 100-percent effort and performed the best they could.

Have team chats in which you discuss the importance of playing fairly, abiding by the rules, and behaving gracefully in both victory and defeat. Review the right ways to congratulate a winning team and how to behave when they're celebrating a victory themselves. Ask your players how they want to be treated when they've lost and how they should treat their opponents when they're the winning team. Opening the door to these types of discussions helps your players clearly understand what acceptable behavior is and clears the way for them to exhibit manners that make you proud.

Winning gracefully

Lacrosse teams are remembered not only for how well they played in the game, but also for how they behaved in it. Youth lacrosse has no place for showboating or excessive celebration. Considering all the readily available examples of poor sportsmanship by professional athletes, showing children the art of winning with grace may be one of your most challenging tasks as a lacrosse coach.

Lacrosse is a physical game, and any time contact is involved, emotions tend to run high. You need to show your team how to celebrate good plays without coming across as taunting the opponent. Your players need to know that celebrating a goal is OK. After all, kids are naturally excited about performing well in a game, and you don't want to curb their enthusiasm for doing well. The key is making sure that the excitement and energy are shared among your team, not directed at the opposition. When one of your players scores a goal, for example, she can high five her teammates, and they can congratulate one another. The celebration crosses into the territory of poor sportsmanship if the player who scored the goal looks over at the opposing goalie while celebrating or makes any type of comment or gesture to any player on the opposing team.

Sometimes, you'll find a pretty significant gap between the skills of the players on the competing teams, so being a good sport when these mismatches are in your favor is important. If your team is dominating an opponent that simply doesn't have the talent or skills to compete, do everything you can not to pile on the goals and embarrass the other team. That behavior reflects terribly on you and your team, and it serves no purpose in the development of your players. Remember, next week your team could go up against a vastly superior opponent, and you wouldn't want your kids to be demoralized.

If you find yourself in a lopsided game, consider some of the following approaches to keep your team's interest level high, work on a broad range of skills, and avoid humiliating the opponent in the process:

- ✔ **Sit the starters.** If you're coaching an advanced-level lacrosse team, put your starters on the bench, and give the kids on the second and third string (the nonstarters) plenty of action.

- ✔ **Rotate players.** Give kids the chance to play positions that they haven't had a lot of experience with to this point in the season. This change allows them to work on different aspects of their game and provides new challenges.

- ✔ **Practice a new defense.** If your team is stopping the opposition's attack with ease and forcing lots of errant passes, switch up your defense. If you've been playing man-to-man, mix up your approach by going with a zone defense that you haven't been able to devote much time to in practice. (For more details on coaching defense, flip to Chapter 16.)

- ✔ **Work on weaker skills.** Encourage your players to focus on areas of their game that could use additional work. If a player isn't proficient at making passes to a player on the move, for example, have him look for teammates who are on the move and then try to deliver the ball to them.

Losing gracefully

Learning to win with grace is a fairly easy lesson; losing with class can be a little more challenging for young players. You and your players would love to win every time you take the field — what coach or team wouldn't? — but that's simply not going to happen. The best coaches and the best teams suffer losses.

There's nothing wrong with losing a game, but there's plenty wrong with behaving as though losing is the worst thing in the world. Crying, throwing equipment, blaming the officials, swearing, and refusing to shake hands with the opposing team are examples of behavior that you simply can't tolerate. (Jump to Chapter 18 to find out more about dealing with some of these types of behaviors.)

Regardless of what transpires on the field, have your players line up and shake hands with the opposing team at the conclusion of the game. This display of good sportsmanship can be difficult for players who just gave their best efforts and came up short. Yet showing respect for opponents is important for your players' overall development — not only as lacrosse players, but as people, too. Encourage your players to acknowledge a well-played game by the opposition. Remind them to keep everything in perspective; next time, they could be on the winning end.

Regardless of how arrogant the opposing team may be, your players should always rise above that type of behavior. As difficult as this is at times — and that goes for you, too — always offer a congratulatory handshake or high five to the other kids. Being sincere in the face of adversity or a loss is a great attribute. The same thing goes for shaking the officials' hands after the game.

Sending Them Home Happy: The Postgame Talk

What you say to your team following a game and how you say it have a big impact on the kids, because that message resonates in their heads until the next time they take the field. Regardless of how the game turns out, one of your most important tasks is sending the players on their way feeling good about themselves. Pats on the back, lots of encouraging words, and genuine smiles are always well received by kids in any postgame chat. When they feel appreciated for their efforts, playing for you gives kids a real sense of satisfaction.

Keeping the focus on fun

Ensuring that every child has fun every time he steps on the field is one of your top priorities. Be sure to keep a close eye on whether the entire team had an enjoyable experience.

A great way to gauge the fun factor is to ask players randomly whether they had fun. Ideally, you'll get a chorus of enthusiastic responses. If so, poll the players to find out what they enjoyed most about the game. If some kids don't answer quite as enthusiastically as others, immediately find out why they didn't have the same amount of fun.

After you gather this information, be sure to make any necessary adjustments to ensure that all your players will have smiles on their faces at your next game.

A child may not have enjoyed the experience on the field for a variety of reasons. Maybe she was really hoping to score a goal while her dad was in the stands, and she misfired on a good opportunity. Or perhaps he got knocked to the ground hard by an opposing player. Always take the time to solicit feedback, gauge feelings, and probe for answers when you sense that a child did not derive much satisfaction from game day. Sometimes, part of being a good lacrosse coach is being a detective, so keep those communication lines open. Find out whatever information you can to make sure that your players' experience continues to be fun — or returns to being fun — before your next game.

Accentuating the positive

Never rely on the scoreboard to dictate your mood when you interact with the team following a game. How much your team won or lost by doesn't define its effort, how it's improving, or how much fun it had playing. Following losses, fight the urge to dwell on the negative and everything the kids did wrong. Just push those thoughts to the side. Your players were out there on the field running around and are well aware of what happened. They certainly don't need a recap of their errant passes or their lapses on defense that led to goals by the opposition.

Whether the team played its best game of the season or got clobbered, part of your job is pointing out good things that happened that the team can build on. Perhaps your defense did an outstanding job of keeping the opponent away from the middle of the field, or maybe your attackers made quick, accurate passes that kept the opponent off balance. By keeping your comments positive, your body language buoyant, and your tone of voice upbeat, you can send kids home feeling good about themselves. They'll also be eager to return to practice in the coming days to continue working on their game.

Recognizing good sportsmanship

Your team's ability to execute the fundamentals of the game is a direct reflection on you as a coach, as is how they behave toward the opponents and their coach during and after games. So be sure to touch on sportsmanship in your postgame chat.

Recognizing the kids who made the spectacular defensive plays or executed the passes that led to the goals is the easy part, because they stand out in your mind after the game. A little more difficult, but equally important, is recognizing the displays of good sportsmanship that occurred during the game. Showing your appreciation for good behavior reinforces the importance of displaying good sportsmanship at all times.

Always be on the lookout for examples of good sportsmanship, and make mental notes when they occur during the course of play. One of your players may have said "Nice save" to an opposing goalie after she stopped a good scoring chance from in close, or she may have congratulated an opponent who turned in a really strong performance. You can even mention displays of good sportsmanship by the opposing team, which further reinforces how important it is to you. Making your players aware of sportsmanship sends the all-important message that good conduct is as important as good passing, shooting, and defending.

Part III:
Basic Training: Teaching Lacrosse Skills

The 5th Wave   By Rich Tennant

"Just how much do you think you can embarrass me? If you think I'm going to the lacrosse game with you wearing those ridiculous socks, you're sadly mistaken!"

In this part . . .

This part is where the real fun of coaching lacrosse kicks into high gear. Here, you find out how to teach the basics of this great game — which include cradling, passing, catching, shooting, defending, and goaltending, among other assorted offensive and defensive skills.

Chapter 9

Scoring with Offensive Fundamentals

Good lacrosse coaches possess many good qualities — patience, caring, and enthusiasm, to name a few — but if you're not also a competent teacher of skills, you'll be about as successful as Wile E. Coyote was trying to nab the Road Runner.

In this chapter, we start from square one, covering the basic offensive skills that every young lacrosse player needs to enjoy some level of success on the field. We go over the chief skills pertaining to cradling, passing, catching, shooting, scooping up loose balls, and winning face-offs.

Focusing Your Approach for First-Timers

When children are learning how to spell, teachers don't start them with multisyllable words; instead, they start children with basic, one-syllable words like *cat* and *dog*. You should stick with the same approach in coaching the offensive skills of lacrosse. You want to start with the basics of the game — not what's taught at the high-school or college level — and slowly build on those skills and techniques.

More than likely, you'll be with your team for just a few hours each week, so be realistic in your expectations. Coaches typically have younger children for only one practice and one game each week, which doesn't leave time to cram a lot of information into their young heads, so the more basic you can keep your instructions to them, the better.

Lacrosse has a unique language all its own, and using unfamiliar terms and phrases may confuse kids. Stick to terms that you've taken the time to explain clearly and that you can confidently say all the kids on the team understand. (For more on the basic terms and rules of lacrosse, check out Chapter 3.)

Mastering the Basics

No question about it — kids enjoy having the ball and being on the attack much more than they do trying to stop an opponent from scoring. To take advantage of possessions, though, they must have a good grasp of the offensive fundamentals. When players don't understand the basics of cradling, passing, and catching, for example, those chinks in your team's offensive armor will lead to turnovers and missed opportunities. This section covers all the offensive basics that your players need to enjoy success when they get their sticks on the ball.

Cradling

A player who can't move around the field without losing control of the ball isn't going to be very effective or have much fun playing lacrosse. Read on to get the lowdown on the proper techniques for executing a variety of cradles, as well as the best opportunities for using them and ways to troubleshoot problems that kids are having with them.

Helping kids execute different cradles

How important is cradling? Very. It allows players to move around on the field at top speed while carrying the ball or to control the ball in heavy traffic while defenders try to swipe it. Players won't be effective in passing or shooting until they master the basics of cradling, which the following sections review. Different situations during the game dictate the types of cradle techniques that players should use.

Horizontal cradle

A *horizontal cradle* (sometimes referred to as a *small cradle*) is a basic motion of the arms and wrists that players use while controlling the ball; it's the easiest cradling technique to learn. A player uses a horizontal cradle primarily when he wants to move the ball to the top of the pocket on his stick to deliver a pass or take a shot. Here's how it works:

1. **The player holds the stick in front of his body (see Figure 9-1).**

   His bottom hand holds the end of his stick, and his top hand is near the throat of the stick.

2. **He rolls the wrist of his top hand upward toward his chest.**

3. **He rotates his arm and wrist back toward the field (see Figure 9-2).**

   This motion creates the centrifugal force that holds the ball in the pocket.

Figure 9-1:
The horizontal cradle is the most basic cradling technique.

Figure 9-2:
The player rolls his wrist toward his body and then releases toward the field.

Because this position isn't the best one to shoot or pass from, players can also use the horizontal cradle at shoulder height. A left-hander would execute it the following way:

1. **The player places her right hand at the end of the stick (see Figure 9-3) and holds the stick horizontal to the field.**

   Her left hand grips the stick just below the midpoint.

2. **She rotates the wrist of her top hand side to side.**

   This motion allows her to get a feel for where the ball is in the pocket of her stick — without looking at it — before setting up to shoot or pass.

Figure 9-3:
The player
keeps
her stick
horizontal
to the field.

Two-handed vertical cradle

When players are on the move, either running down the field with the ball or attacking in the opponent's end of the field, the two-handed vertical cradle is the primary option. Here's how it works:

1. **The player holds the stick near the throat with his top hand (see Figure 9-4), with the pocket above his shoulder and at ear level.**

   His bottom hand grips the butt end of the stick.

2. He rotates his top wrist first toward his body and then away from it.

This motion keeps the ball in the pocket of the stick.

Figure 9-4:
The player keeps his stick vertical to the field.

One-handed vertical cradle

When players are attacking the net, this technique provides maximum protection of the ball and makes the defender's job much more difficult. Here's how it works:

1. A left-handed player holds the stick with his left hand near the throat (see Figure 9-5) if he's attacking to his right.

The thumb points up, while the other fingers grasp the stick.

2. He holds the ball at about shoulder level and uses his free arm to protect his stick. (See Figure 9-6.)

Figure 9-5:
The one-handed cradle is effective for attacking the net.

Figure 9-6:
Players can use their free arm to protect their sticks from defenders.

Correcting cradling problems

The No. 1 problem kids have with cradling is keeping their eyes glued on the ball when it's in the stick. As a result, they can't see the defender charging toward them or a wide-open teammate downfield who is in great scoring position. During your drills, hammer home to players the importance of keeping their heads up and their eyes scanning the field. Encourage them to resist the urge to glance back at their sticks; eventually, they will know by feel where the ball is on the stick.

Passing

Some kids enjoy passing the ball about as much as being told to clean up their bedrooms, simply because when the ball isn't on their sticks, they don't have a chance to shoot it. Yet the better your team is at passing the ball, the more chances everyone will get to score goals. Make that point clear to your team and then get to work showing them the techniques of passing.

Grip

Both hands are important in passing, so holding the stick properly is key. A right-hander relies on her right hand to control the direction of the pass, because that hand is her top hand on the stick; the left hand generates the bulk of the force for the pass. The bottom hand grips the butt end of the stick.

Stance

Players keep their feet shoulder width apart to maintain good balance. In boys' leagues that allow checking, this stance also makes it more difficult for opponents to knock the player off balance.

Stick position

When a player is ready to deliver a pass, she cradles the ball so that it gets positioned in the center of her stick's pocket (see Figure 9-7). While she is positioning the ball, she brings her stick back behind her head.

Figure 9-7:
Players move the ball to the middle of the pocket before passing.

Delivering the ball to a teammate standing still

When the player has the ball in the proper position and the stick behind his head, he's ready to execute a pass. Here's how he gets the ball to his target:

1. **The player extends his top hand and follows through toward the target, using his bottom hand to pull the shaft of his stick down and toward his body.**

2. **He turns his body slightly and steps toward the target with the foot opposite his top hand (see Figure 9-8). A right-hander, for example, would step with his left foot.**

Figure 9-8:
Players step
toward their
intended
target when
passing.

Delivering the ball to a teammate on the run

Often during games, players are forced to deliver passes to teammates who are on the move, which presents a few more challenges than passing to a stationary player. The secret of making an accurate pass to a moving player is picking out a target at stick height in front of the player, based on how fast she is moving. This technique is difficult to teach, because the passer must factor in how far she is from the player, as well as judge how fast she is moving. All skills require lots of practice for players to become comfortable performing them in the heat of the action on game day — particularly this one. Be sure that your practices incorporate lots of drills in which players must pass the ball to moving teammates. (Check out Chapter 14 for a sampling of some drills that you can use.)

When a player misfires on a pass, you prefer him to miss by delivering it too far out in front of his teammate, rather than behind him. When the ball is passed too far out in front, the intended recipient still has a chance to beat the defender to it and secure possession, but when the ball is passed behind him, the opponent can scoop it up and race in the other direction with it.

Executing passes on the move

Players rarely have the luxury of passing while standing still during games, because defenders will force them to be on the move, looking for openings. Here's how to make accurate passes while on the move:

1. **The player pulls her stick back to the top-hand side of her body.**

   A right-hander with her right hand on top of the stick, for example, positions the stick on her right side (see Figure 9-9).

Figure 9-9:
A player pulls the stick back toward her body while making passes on the move.

2. **She twists her body slightly to the right.**

   This move helps protect the ball from defenders.

3. **She steps forward with her left foot toward the target, twisting at the hips and rotating her shoulders to face the target (see Figure 9-10).**

4. **She delivers the pass and follows through with her top arm pointing at the target.**

Figure 9-10:
The shoulders must face the target when a player is passing on the move.

Sidearm passes

When players are being pressured by a defender, the sidearm pass is an effective way to get the ball to a teammate. Here's how it's done:

1. **The player grips the butt end of his stick with his left hand, if he is a right-hander, while his top hand grabs the stick at about its midpoint (see Figure 9-11).**

Figure 9-11:
The sidearm pass works well against heavy pressure from opponents.

2. **When his right hand is on top of the stick, he steps toward the target with his left foot.**

3. **He flicks the wrist of his top hand toward the target while uncoiling his body in that direction.**

Flip passes

This pass is similar to the sidearm pass but is delivered below the waist at a lower angle. This pass is a good one to use when players are covered tightly and need to get the ball to a teammate in close quarters. Here's how it's executed:

1. **The player drops her stick below waist level (see Figure 9-12).**

Figure 9-12:
Players drop the stick below waist level to execute the flip pass.

2. **She angles her stick toward the ground, with the pocket of the stick facing the sky.**

3. **When her right hand is on top, she steps forward with her left foot (see Figure 9-13).**

4. **She snaps her right wrist up toward the target while releasing the ball.**

Figure 9-13:
The player steps toward the target while delivering the flip pass.

Correcting passing problems

Delivering passes to teammates can be a challenging skill to learn, simply because of the many types of passes and the many aspects involved in executing them. The following tips can help your players overcome some of typically passing problems:

- ✔ **Passes don't have much force behind them.** The secret of getting a lot of force behind passes is using the legs. Many kids stand still while delivering passes, which drains all the power out of the passes. Remind players to step toward their target, using the foot opposite their main shooting arm. (A right-handed passer steps toward his target with his left foot, for example.) The problem can also be the result of a youngster's failure to snap the wrist of his top hand as he releases the ball from his stick.

- ✔ **Passes are hooking.** This problem usually can be traced to the fact that the child is releasing the ball from her stick while it is still behind her body. This release produces a low, curving pass that either misses the mark or is more difficult for a teammate to handle. To correct this problem, have the player focus on hanging on to the ball and not releasing it until it is next to, or slightly in front of, her body.

- ✔ **Passes are missing their intended targets.** When passes are off target, the problem usually is the player's follow-through. When the youngster's stick doesn't end up pointing at the target after he releases the ball, the pass usually doesn't hit its mark.

- ✔ **Passes are delivered behind a moving player.** Youngsters tend to aim passes at their teammates' sticks, so by the time the ball arrives, it is well behind a player who is running. Remind them to get the ball out in front; it's better to miss there than behind the other player, because she'll have a better chance to retrieve it.

Catching

Catching passes in lacrosse requires a variety of components: good hand–eye coordination, proper footwork, and quick reaction to passes that veer a little — or a lot — off target. (For a refresher on the proper grip, stance, and stick position for catching passes, check out Chapter 5.) No matter how skilled your players are at passing the ball, the offense will sputter if they aren't equally proficient at catching it. Share the following information with your players so they can — we have to say it — catch on to this aspect of the game.

Instill in your players the habit of stepping toward the ball to receive passes. When players stand still and wait for the ball to reach them, the opponent has extra time to step in and intercept the pass, or at least get a stick on the ball and knock it down.

Making weak-side catches

A weak-side catch (also known as a nonstick-side catch) is a useful technique when a defender is nearby; the player can use his body to shield the opponent and make the catch. Here's the method players should use:

1. **The player turns toward the direction of the pass, bringing the stick across his body (see Figure 9-14).**

   The wrist of his top hand faces his body; his bottom hand is on the bottom of the stick; and his feet are shoulder width apart.

2. **As he receives the ball, he twists his upper body toward his stick and pulls his arms in toward his body to absorb the pass (see Figure 9-15).**

Figure 9-14:
Players
must be
able to
catch
passes in all
directions.

Figure 9-15:
The player's
arms help
absorb the
force of the
pass.

Making catches on the run

When players are breaking down the field, and someone makes a long pass, the only way to get a stick on it may be an over-the-shoulder catch. The over-the-shoulder catch is one of the most difficult to pull off, but here's how it's done:

1. **The player runs while turning her head toward the ball.**

   Her bottom hand holds on to the base of the stick, and her top hand is on the midpoint of the stick.

2. **She reaches her stick out away from her body (see Figure 9-16).**

3. **She keeps her eyes on the ball and watches it go into the pocket of her stick.**

Figure 9-16:
A player keeps the stick away from her body to make an over-the-shoulder grab.

Correcting catching problems

Becoming comfortable making catches takes a lot of hard work. Here are some of the most common difficulties kids encounter while learning this skill:

✔ **The ball bounces out of the pocket of the stick.** This problem results when the player holds his stick too rigidly when the ball arrives. To correct it, have the child pull the stick back toward his body just slightly on impact. This move helps cushion the force of the pass and allows the ball to settle into the pocket of the stick rather than carom out.

✔ **The player is unable to get her stick on passes.** The culprit here usually is a lack of preparation on the youngster's part. Often, the reason is that the child is carrying her stick too low, so when a pass does come her way, she wastes time raising her stick to react to it. During practices, when you see players' sticks dipping below waist level, remind them to get the sticks up so that they are always in the best position to react to passes.

✔ **The player has trouble catching long passes.** Most likely, the player is twisting his entire body around to locate the ball, which drains a lot of his speed. Remind him to keep his body facing forward and to simply turn his head to spot the ball over his shoulder.

Shooting

Children who are new to lacrosse must know how to shoot the ball correctly so that when they find themselves in good scoring position, they have the confidence to make an accurate shot. (For a recap of the basic fundamentals involved in shooting, turn to Chapter 5.) Following is information on other types of shots that players will find useful to have in their arsenal — and that will keep defenders on their toes, because they won't know what to expect when your team is on the attack.

Taking a sidearm shot

The overhand shot (check out Chapter 5 for the basics of executing it) gives players the best chance of directing the ball where they want it to go. The sidearm shot is another option that players can use to generate more velocity on their shots, though it sacrifices some accuracy. It's also more difficult than the overhand shot to execute on the run. Here's how the sidearm shot works:

1. **The player drops her stick to around mid-chest level.**

2. **With her right hand (if she's a left-handed shooter) on the butt end of the stick, she slides her left hand down the stick (see Figure 9-17).**

Figure 9-17:
The sidearm
shot can
generate a
lot of force.

3. She steps toward the goal with the foot opposite her top hand.

4. She pushes her stick forward with her top hand while pulling her bottom hand toward her body.

5. The player completes the follow-through by swinging her stick across her body, keeping the stick parallel to the field (see Figure 9-18).

Figure 9-18:
The player's
stick follows
through
across her
body.

Taking a long bounce shot

These shots — when executed properly — pose double trouble for goalies, who must deal with the angle the shot is released from, and decide whether the shot will bounce up high or skid along the ground. Help your players master this shot (which also works well in close), and opposing goalies will have a tough time stopping it:

1. **A right-handed shooter grips his stick with his right hand on top and his left hand on the butt end; his left shoulder points toward the goal (see Figure 9-19).**

2. **The player keeps the ball above and behind his head.**

3. **He steps forward with his left foot toward the goal.**

   He pushes the stick forward and down with his right hand, while his left hand pulls the bottom of the stick in toward his stomach.

4. **Keeping his left elbow pointed away from his body, he flicks his top wrist forward to release the ball at a downward angle (see Figure 9-20).**

Figure 9-19: The bounce shot is difficult for goalies to handle.

Figure 9-20: The bounce shot can also be taken from in close.

Taking accurate shots on the run

Players stick to the same fundamentals to execute shots on the run and while standing still, holding the stick above the head and adjacent to the ear, and keeping the hands about 12 to 18 inches apart on the stick. Maintaining proper balance is especially important to maximize power and accuracy.

When your players slip past a defender and have an opening to take a quick shot, they can use the pop shot, which works well in traffic; the shot requires no backswing, so a defender a couple of steps behind doesn't have an easy opportunity to disrupt it. Here's how to take a pop shot:

1. **The player raises her stick so that the pocket is just above her top-hand shoulder. Another option is to move the pocket of the stick in front of her face.**

2. **She pushes the stick forward with her top hand and then quickly pulls the stick down toward her body with her bottom hand.**

3. **To complete the shot, she snaps her top wrist forward, toward the goal.**

Pop shots don't generate a lot of speed, because they have no backswing or follow-through, so players should use them only when a defender is chasing them closely from behind.

Correcting shooting problems

Kids love scoring goals, so any time they are having problems with their shots, frustration can set in rather quickly. Review the following common shooting problems so that you are prepared to help get your players' shots back on track:

- ✔ **Shots lack power.** Sure, shots are released with the arms, but some of the power comes from the legs, too. Remind your players to step toward the goal with the foot opposite their top hand to help generate more force — and cause more difficulty for the goaltender.

- ✔ **Goalies are stopping all their shots.** Young players shooting the ball often stare at the area of the net they are aiming at, which goalies will pick up on. During your shooting drills, train your players to scan the entire net, not lock their eyes on one spot. This technique forces the goalie to defend the entire net without being able to cheat in one direction or the other.

Facing Off

Excelling in the face-off circle can be parlayed into more time possessing the ball and additional opportunities for the team to score goals. This section describes how face-offs are handled.

Grip

One of the most common face-off grips is placing the right hand on the throat of the stick, with the palm facing the sky. The left hand is about 12 to 18 inches away, palm facing down (see Figure 9-21).

Figure 9-21:
The proper grip for taking a face-off.

Stance

When taking a face-off, players want to crouch low so that they can spring out of their stances on the official's whistle and generate enough force to gain control of the ball. Here's a glance at the proper stance:

1. **The player positions his right elbow inside his right knee and leans slightly in that direction (see Figure 9-22).**

   His knees are bent, and most of his weight is on the balls of his feet.

2. **He keeps his head down and his eyes on the ball.**

Figure 9-22:
Players get into a low crouch before taking a face-off.

Stick position

Using the right grip and taking the proper stance aren't going to be as effective if a player doesn't have her stick in the correct position. Keep the stick flush against the field. The player's gloves also touch the field.

In girls' lacrosse the referee tosses the ball up in the air, and the players raise their sticks above their heads to go after the ball, similar to a jump ball in basketball.

Following are some additional tips to help your players enjoy more success handling face-offs:

- ✔ **Capitalize on assets.** Some players possess outstanding quickness; others' strength is their . . . well, strength! Whatever a player's strongest qualities, he should rely on them most often to enjoy the most success.

- ✔ **Mix up the moves.** The less predictable players are in the face-off techniques they use, the less likely opposing players are to get a read on them. Keeping the opposing player off balance helps shift the odds of controlling the ball in your team's favor.

> ✔ **Maintain focus.** The player taking the face-off must focus all her concentration on the official's whistle and on grabbing control of the ball. If she's peeking at the positioning of her teammates or opposing players, or looking at you on the sidelines, she is less effective.

Using the trap

The key to executing this technique is performing two moves simultaneously: drawing the ball backward while rotating the wrist of the top hand over so that the stick is flat on the field. If a player executes this move quickly enough, he'll trap the ball in the pocket of his stick, and he can drag the ball away from the opposing player and scoop it up (see Figure 9-23). The stronger players are, the more successful they tend to be with this technique.

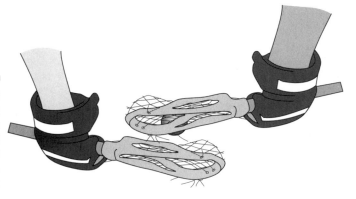

Figure 9-23:
Executing the trap requires quick reactions.

Using the draw

To use the draw technique, the player positions the throat of his stick as close to the ball as possible before the face-off. On the official's whistle, he quickly pulls his stick straight back toward his body. When a player executes this move correctly, the ball is pulled (or drawn) by the netting on the stick to his side of the circle.

Using the block

Players use this technique when the opponent is attempting to trap the ball. To execute the block, a player pushes the tip of his stick against the opponent's (see Figure 9-24). This move prevents the opponent from turning his stick over and trapping the ball. Then the player pulls his stick toward his body, sweeping the ball with it.

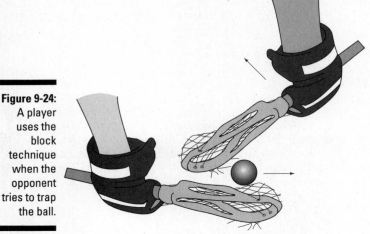

Figure 9-24:
A player
uses the
block
technique
when the
opponent
tries to trap
the ball.

Correcting face-off problems

Teaching kids face-off techniques can present some challenges, partly because these skills are affected by the ways that opposing players react in game situations. Here are a couple of problem areas that may pop up among your players while you provide instruction on this skill:

✔ **Not reacting quickly on the official's whistle:** Kids have short attention spans, and a big part of being effective in the face-off circle is maintaining focus. Work with your players to keep their minds on the task at hand. Even if their minds wander for just a second, that second may be all the advantage an opponent needs to win the face-off.

✔ **Problems executing the trap:** Have the player slide his top hand closer to the throat of his stick. This maneuver allows him to use his glove to block his opponent's stick and trap the ball with his own stick.

Scooping Up Loose Balls

The team that wins the majority of the loose-ball battles generally wins the game, simply because more possessions translate into more chances to score goals. (In Chapter 5, we cover the basics of scooping up a loose ball.) Read on to find out how to show your players the best approach for outdueling opponents over loose balls:

1. **The player turns her back to the defender to shield that player from the ball (see Figure 9-25).**

   She holds her stick at waist level and keeps her feet shoulder width apart to maintain her balance so that the defender can't move her out of position and swipe the ball.

2. **If she's unable to scoop the ball due to defensive pressure, she pushes the ball farther away from the defender with the end of her stick before making a play on it (see Figure 9-26).**

Figure 9-25: A player faces away from the opponent to shield the opponent from the ball.

Figure 9-26: Using the stick to push the ball helps keep it away from an opposing player.

Here are some other points to keep in mind regarding scooping:

- ✔ **Control the stick.** Young players are often tempted to take one hand off the stick to reach for loose balls. Scooping up a ball one-handed is difficult, though, and even if a player does pull off this maneuver, an opponent can knock the ball loose more easily.

- ✔ **Attack the ball.** As you've always heard, the shortest route between two points is a straight line. Instruct your players always to run straight toward a loose ball, because the more steps they have to take, the less likely the ball is to end up on their stick.

- ✔ **Communicate with teammates.** When a player recognizes that he's in the best position to scoop up a loose ball, he should alert his teammates by shouting "Ball!" If he reads the situation correctly and makes the call quickly enough, his teammates can get a jump on their opponents and move down the field quickly to catch the defense off guard.

Helping a Child Who Just Can't Catch On

Regardless of how talented or motivated players are, they all encounter struggles picking up skills. How you handle kids when the learning path becomes a little bumpy is the true barometer of your coaching ability.

Keep the following points in mind when working with kids who encounter difficulty catching on to certain skills:

- ✔ **Reevaluate your approach.** Take a closer look at how you're interacting with the kids who are having difficulty. Are you spending too much time talking and not giving them lots of opportunities to practice the skill? Are you filling their heads with too many thoughts about what to do instead of keeping the instructions as simple and straightforward as possible? If the kids are giving maximum effort, the problem probably is more of a teaching problem than anything else.

- ✔ **Keep it simple.** Keep your instructions short and to the point. Don't stray off into long-winded instructions. Children learn more, and improve faster, by performing skills than by listening to you talk about how to perform them.

- ✔ **Rev up the repetitions.** The more reps the kids get, the better. Standing in line watching teammates perform a skill doesn't compare with doing it themselves over and over.

- ✔ **Move players around.** Maybe the youngster who's struggling had her heart set on being a defender, rather than an attacker. Mix things up for the youngster; playing a new position may rejuvenate her enthusiasm and get her more interested in learning all the skills you're teaching.

✔ **Never embarrass the child.** Don't allow your tone of voice or body language to reveal frustration or disappointment, and never make a spectacle of a child who's struggling. Most children are well aware of how their skills stack up to their teammates'; they don't need you making their deficiencies stand out even more by signaling them out for extra work on the sidelines. Try demonstrating the skill again yourself. Besides being a good refresher for the other players, this just might be enough to help the youngster who's struggling.

✔ **Check to see whether they really like playing.** Some children simply don't enjoy contact sports. Nothing's wrong with that. A child could be struggling simply because he's tired of being knocked to the ground — especially in a boys' league that allows checking. If his parents seek your advice about whether he should continue with lacrosse, be honest. You may want to suggest other sports that can provide their youngster better opportunities for fun, rewarding athletic experiences.

Recognizing physical problems

Sometimes, extra factors hamper a child's ability to learn some of the skills of lacrosse. One of the most important reasons to hold a preseason parents' meeting is to find out about any children on your team who have special needs that you need to be aware of. (Check out Chapter 4 for more details on conducting the meeting.) Be on the lookout for the following conditions; if you spot them, you may be able to make a difference for the youngster.

✔ **Attention Deficit Hyperactivity Disorder (ADHD):** A child's lack of focus and ability to comprehend instructions may be the result of ADHD. Some common characteristics of ADHD are distractibility, poorly sustained attention to tasks, impaired impulse control, and excessive activity and physical restlessness. If you think someone on your team is displaying signs of ADHD, talk to her parents about your concerns.

✔ **Vision problems:** A child who continually drops passes or has difficulty delivering the ball to teammates may have a vision problem that can be corrected easily with glasses or contact lenses. If you suspect a vision problem, tell the child's parents.

✔ **Hearing problems:** A child who has difficulty following instructions may have a hearing problem. If a player relies on reading lips, make sure that anytime you're explaining or demonstrating a technique that you speak loud and clear, and look directly at the child.

Chapter 10

Setting Defensive Fundamentals

*T*his chapter focuses on the fundamentals of good defense. Here, you find the best ways to help your players grasp the important role of defense in lacrosse, as well as lots of detailed information on defending opposing players. We also cover assorted types of checks: the poke, slap, and (if you're coaching in a boys' league that allows it) the much more physical body check. And we provide a gold mine of information to help your young goalies learn their challenging position.

Because some kids may encounter difficulties with some of these defensive skills, we also provide handy troubleshooting tips for diagnosing what went wrong and what to do to get the players back on track. (For some general guidelines on the best ways to help players who aren't catching on to skills as quickly as most of their teammates are, head to Chapter 9.)

Stressing the Importance of Defense

Because your players will spend roughly half of each game trying to prevent the opposing team from scoring goals, the better they understand fundamental defensive techniques, the more success they'll have. Playing good team defense — the kind that rattles opposing teams, forcing them to make bad passes and low-quality shots — paves the way for your players to get more enjoyment out of the game.

Teaching the basics of good defensive play doesn't have to translate into a miserable experience for the kids — and a frustrating one for you — as long as you approach it the right way. Following are a few tactics you can use to emphasize the importance of playing defense:

✔ **The payoff of playing good defense is more time on offense.** This statement usually is enough to grab kids' attention and show them the benefits of executing at the defensive end of the field. The better they become at defending opposing teams and derailing attacks, the more opportunities they'll get to go on the attack themselves and take shots on goal.

✔ **Playing defense has to be fun.** Your job is to persuade the kids that you are interested in helping them perform well both offensively *and* defensively. You must be as thrilled when a player makes a nice defensive play and creates a turnover as you are when he deposits a shot in the opponent's net for a goal.

✔ **Run plenty of defensive drills.** Pack your practices with a variety of drills that emphasize defensive components. (Chapters 7 and 14 provide some great drills that you can incorporate into your practices.) Whenever you are running a drill that focuses on offensive skills, don't neglect coaching the defensive element and encouraging effort in that area, too.

If you're coaching an older, more-advanced team, adding a competitive element to the drills — such as who can make the most defensive stops in a 2-on-1 drill — helps fuel interest and rev up enthusiasm levels. It also reminds your players how important good defensive play is to you and how it affects the team's overall performance.

Mastering the Basics of Defense

To thrive on defense, players should know how their footwork affects their ability to stick with an opposing player all over the field, make an opponent's shot more challenging, and steal passes, among many other aspects of the game. Read on for tips on pumping up your players' defensive tenacity.

Grip

Players who use their sticks the right way enhance their effectiveness defensively. The stick-on-stick and cross-handed techniques are the two basic ways players can handle their sticks while playing defense.

In the stick-on-stick technique, the defender carries her stick in her right hand when the opposing player's stick is in her left hand (see Figure 10-1). With the cross-handed method, the defender's stick is in her left hand when the opponent has her stick in her left hand, too. (See Figure 10-2.)

Stance

A defender's top objective should be to keep himself positioned between his team's goal and his opponent's stick. Here's how he sets up:

1. **He keeps his feet at least shoulder width apart, with the foot opposite the opponent's stick side positioned slightly back (see Figure 10-3).**

2. **He distributes his weight evenly and bends his knees slightly.**

3. **He tries to maintain about a stick length's distance from the player he's covering.**

4. **He keeps his head up and his eyes on the defender.**

   He can swivel his head from side to side on occasion so that he knows what is happening behind him, as well as rely on communication from his teammates to alert him to any plays the opponent may be setting up.

Figure 10-1:
The stick-on-stick technique is a popular choice for kids playing defense.

Figure 10-2:
Some defenders prefer using the cross-handed method on defense.

Figure 10-3:
A good
defensive
stance is a
prerequisite
for
successful
coverage.

Footwork

The better your players' footwork is when they're defending an opponent's attack, the less likely they are to surrender good scoring opportunities. Check out "Sticking with a player on the move," later in this chapter, to gain insight on the popular shuffling technique that players can use to cover opponents on the move.

The real essence of team defense is lending support when it's needed. When a teammate gets beaten, and the opponent she was covering is a threat to attack the goal or take a shot, her teammates nearby must recognize the situation and slide over to provide defensive help.

Guarding a player standing still

Good defensive play doesn't happen by coincidence or pure luck; excelling in this area of lacrosse takes a dedicated effort on each player's part. Your defense will be only as strong as your weakest player. Help your players keep the following pointers in mind when dealing with an opposing player whose feet aren't on the move:

✔ **Favor his stronger side.** Defenders can make it more difficult for the attacker by slightly favoring the opponent's stronger hand. If the attacker's top hand is his right hand, for example, he will pose more of a threat running to his right, so the defensive player can dilute some of the attacker's effectiveness by moving slightly in that direction and forcing the opponent to attack from the left. If the player does decide to attack from the right, the defender will be in great position to impede his progress.

- ✔ **Be aware of what's going on behind you.** Just because the player the defender is guarding isn't attacking at that moment, she shouldn't be lulled into a sense of complacency, because the opponent may just be waiting to set up a screen or pick play. (See Chapter 16 for more details on defending these types of offensive maneuvers.) Communication among teammates is crucial in counteracting these types of plays.

- ✔ **Pay attention to tendencies.** If the opponent the defender is guarding always fakes to his right and cuts left from a stationary position, the defender can make a subtle adjustment in his positioning to account for this trait.

Sticking with a player on the move

When an attacker is moving around the field at a slow to moderate speed — usually while she is surveying the field and determining when or where to attack from — defenders should use shuffle steps to track her movements. *Shuffle steps* are simply short lateral steps. The defenders must be careful not to cross their feet so that they can remain near the attacker.

When the attacker's pace picks up, defenders ditch the shuffling technique and opt for running.

Any time a defender gets beaten by an opponent, he must try to recover as quickly as possible. The faster he gets back into the play, the less time the opponent has to capitalize on the advantage.

Dealing with a player taking a shot

Goalies in lacrosse have a challenging job, so they appreciate anything their teammates can do to help them keep balls out of their net. Besides keeping attackers as far away from the net as possible, defenders can lend a helping hand by blocking shots. Even if a defender is unable to deny a shot, if she can get her stick into the path of the shot and alter it, the ball has less chance of reaching the net, and if it does, it arrives with at least much less force.

Following are the basic elements of disrupting shots:

- ✔ **Good defensive positioning:** By keeping the attacker in front in full view, the defender can react more easily to shots. Any time the attacker has a step on the defender, he has the advantage, and disrupting his shot is more difficult.

✔ **Anticipation:** This skill can't be taught, but players pick it up over time simply by being involved in a lot of games. Gradually, players begin to recognize situations and get a feel for when opponents are setting up to take a shot.

✔ **Quick recovery:** Instill in your players that even when they have been beaten, they are never out of the play if they hustle. Players who recover quickly enough can still deny an attacker's shot if they are only a couple steps behind him, especially if the opponent takes a big backswing on his shot. A defender can get his stick in the path of the shot and knock the ball to the ground.

Stealing the ball

The most obvious benefit of stealing the ball is that it takes away an opportunity for the opposition to set up a shot on goal; it also can translate into a fast-break opportunity by catching the opposing team off balance and out of position.

Here are a few techniques your team can use to create turnovers, which can pay off in scoring opportunities:

✔ **Watch the passer's eyes.** Youngsters handling the ball often lock their eyes on the teammate to whom they want to pass. Telegraphing a pass this way allows defenders who are paying attention to get a jump on the pass and pick it off, or at least to bat it down with their sticks. At the more-advanced levels of lacrosse, offensive players rely more on fakes, looking one way while passing in another direction.

✔ **Adjust strategies.** At the advanced levels of lacrosse, employing different strategies takes on greater importance and often has a greater impact on games. If you recognize that a particular opponent isn't quite as efficient at passing or handling the ball, you can adjust your defense accordingly and take a more-aggressive role. Conversely, if the opponent features excellent passers and ball handlers, your team will be better off taking a less-aggressive approach, because attempting to make a lot of steals against a talented team is risky.

✔ **Pick up on patterns.** Sometimes, an opposing team gets into the habit of running the same types of plays or attacking from the same part of the field each time it gains possession of the ball. You can alert your players to these patterns so that they can adjust accordingly. If the opponents generally set up their attack from behind your team's net, for example, and the passes come predominantly from the right, recognizing this pattern lets your players get a jump on the passes and perhaps pick some of them off, or at least make them more difficult to execute.

Whenever you pick up on an opposing team's tendency, you want to refrain from letting your team know about it before the team is able to capitalize on it. If you know that a particular attacker generally throws long passes to a player on her right, for example, you don't want your defenders jumping into that passing lane so early that the opponent sees the adjustment and has a chance to deliver the ball elsewhere. You want your defenders to be patient and allow her to release the ball; then they can get a good jump and sprint to pick off the pass.

Correcting problems with defensive form

Defensive fundamentals are often more challenging for players than the basics of offense (covered in Chapter 9), simply because some of the techniques are based on reacting and adjusting to what an opponent is doing. This section looks at a few areas of defensive play that tend to present problems for young-sters and what you can do to help them overcome those problems:

- ✔ **The player is unable to maintain defensive coverage on an opponent.** This situation happens all the time in youth lacrosse, for many reasons. Pay close attention to your defender's footwork, which is the root of many defensive deficiencies. Also make sure that she isn't crossing her feet while shuffling from side to side; the moment a defensive player gets her feet tangled, she gets off balance and out of position, giving the opponent the green light to attack.

- ✔ **The player loses his stick when executing stick checks.** If a player has only one hand on his stick, he's not going to be able to generate much force on his checks, and he runs a greater risk of losing control of the stick, dropping it, or having it knocked away by an opponent.

- ✔ **An attacker gets by the defender easily.** This problem usually is easy to correct: Analyze the spacing the defender keeps between herself and the attacker. Ideally, you want your defender to stay about a stick length's away. If she's any closer, the attacker can use cuts and spin moves (covered in Chapter 11) to slip past her. By maintaining a distance of about the length of a stick, the defender gives herself a little more time to react to the opponent's moves and deny her penetration.

Teaching Checking Techniques

Players on offense can turn to a variety of moves and techniques, and so can the defenders who are trying to stop them. These techniques vary for girls' and boys' teams, however. One of the most notable differences between boys' and girls' lacrosse is that the boys' game is much rougher and allows a lot of contact;

the girls' game doesn't allow players on opposing teams to make contact. (For other differences between boys' and girls' lacrosse, check out Chapter 3.)

In girls' lacrosse, the two types of checks that are allowed are stick checks and body checks. In the girls' game, the term *body checking* refers to how the defender positions her body in relation to the attacker. Being an effective body checker requires recognizing the path the attacker wants to take and then forcing her to alter her route.

A good body check forces the attacker to move in the direction of the bottom hand on her stick.

When a defender steps into the path of an oncoming attacker, she must allow the attacker enough time to adjust her course. If she fails to give the attacker enough time to react, the official can call a blocking foul on the defender. If the defender allows the attacker time to change directions, but the attacker still runs into her, the official can call a charging foul on the attacker. (For more on fouls, flip to Chapter 3.)

Stick checking

A *stick check* is simply a controlled hit against the opponent's stick in an effort to dislodge the ball from his stick. The key to making good contact is using the head of the stick to make contact with the pocket of the opponent's stick and — if the check is effective — dislodge the ball.

Grip

During your practices, encourage players to experiment with their grips while handling their defensive responsibilities. When a player moves her top hand up closer to the pocket, she gets a lot more control of the stick but sacrifices leverage and reach. Run through a bunch of different drills with your players, encouraging them to place their hands in different positions on their sticks; gradually, they will get a feel for what works best for them.

Stick position

Defenders want to maintain good defensive position and keep both hands on their sticks so that they can execute stick checks as quickly and efficiently as possible.

Footwork

There's just no substitute for good footwork and being in proper defensive position. Focus on giving your players a strong foundation in these skills; then build on those skills by showing the players the checks that are covered later in this chapter.

Make sure your players know that their sticks are not weapons and should never be used with malicious intent. Keep a close eye to ensure that the kids keep their sticks under control at all times. Any time you spot players wielding their sticks carelessly during a practice or game, pull them aside immediately to make them aware of what they did wrong.

Executing a poke check

The poke check is one of the most popular stick checks, and it should be in every defender's bag of moves. A bonus of the poke check is that players can use it with virtually no risk. Usually, they can maintain good position between their goal and the opposing player because they aren't lunging or trying to make a big play; they're simply jabbing their sticks at the opponent's stick, trying to force a turnover.

Here's how the poke check is executed:

1. **The player maintains proper defensive position by being about a stick length from the opponent who's handling the ball.**

2. **The defender makes a jabbing motion with his stick, by pulling his stick back slightly and then moving it at the opponent, attempting to dislodge the ball from the opponent's stick.**

   He targets the ball handler's bottom hand (see Figure 10-4). The hand on the bottom of the stick generates the force.

3. **The stick slides through his top hand, which guides the direction of the poke check.**

Figure 10-4: The poke check requires a jabbing motion.

Whenever a ball carrier swings his stick around in front of his body, a defender has a perfect opportunity to use the poke check. Because the attacker isn't using his body to help shield his stick, the defender has a free shot to dislodge the ball.

Executing a slap check

The slap check is another technique available to defenders. When defenders are shadowing opponents by using the shuffle step, they can use the slap check to try to knock the ball free. To make the slap check work for your players, share the following techniques with them:

1. **The defender holds her stick at approximately waist level, parallel to the field (see Figure 10-5).**

2. **She snaps her stick across the opponent's stick, keeping it parallel to the field (see Figure 10-6), and follows it up with a couple more quick taps in rapid succession.**

3. **She pulls her stick back toward her body after making contact.**

Make sure that your players use a series of taps — executed quickly — rather than a single motion when attempting to knock the ball free from the opponent's stick.

Correcting stick-checking problems

Understanding how to use the stick to their advantage when they don't have possession of the ball can be a little tricky for youngsters to pick up, especially when they're new to lacrosse. Following are a few problems that can trip youngsters up and tips on how you can help them become more comfortable wielding their sticks to their advantage:

- ✔ **The attacker gets past the defender whenever he uses the poke check.** This problem usually occurs when the defender takes a step toward the opponent while delivering the poke check. Moving forward puts the defender slightly off balance and creates openings for the opponent to burst past him. Remind your defenders to keep their feet shoulder width apart while using the poke check; that stance cuts down on opportunities for attackers to get past them.

- ✔ **The slap check isn't effective.** Many times, in their eagerness to knock the ball free, youngsters take a big backswing with their sticks. Not only is a wind-up unnecessary, but it also alerts the ball carrier to what is coming, giving her extra time to react. Work with your players so that they don't pull the stick back more than 2 feet before bringing it toward an opponent.

- ✔ **A player has trouble controlling the stick.** Have the child slide his top hand a little farther up his stick, toward the pocket. Right away, he should notice a difference in his control of the stick.

✔ **A player has difficulty reaching the attacker she intends to stick-check.** Inspect the player's footwork first, making sure that her feet are shoulder width apart and that she's facing the opposing player. If she's using proper footwork, have her slide her top hand down the stick closer to her other hand. This technique helps her extend her reach with her stick.

At advanced levels of play, encourage defenders to use a variety of checking techniques so that the attackers will be kept off balance, unable to predict which moves are coming.

Figure 10-5:
Defenders keep their sticks parallel to the field for the slap check.

Figure 10-6:
The defender slaps her stick across the opponent's.

Body checking

Body checks are allowed only in boys' lacrosse, and only at the more-advanced levels of the game. Be sure to check with the director of your league to find out whether body checking is allowed. (For more details on what you should check on concerning your league's rules, flip to Chapter 2.)

Grip

The player's bottom hand grips the butt end of the stick. The end of his stick should not be exposed. His top hand is approximately halfway up his stick.

Stance

The player maintains a strong base, with his feet about shoulder width apart. His shoulders are square to the player he intends to check. Being square to the target simply means that the player is facing the opponent and isn't at an angle, with one shoulder leaning out in front of the other.

Footwork

The defender stands on the balls of his feet — a stance that allows him to exert more force.

Executing a body check

In delivering a body check, a defender fares best if he keeps himself under control. Here's how to execute this type of check:

1. **The defender moves his stick to the side of his body, keeping his head up and looking straight ahead (see Figure 10-7).**

2. **He lowers his shoulder, targeting the middle of the opponent's chest.**

3. **With his arms in close to his body and both hands on his stick, he plants his feet approximately shoulder width apart.**

4. **He drives his body into the attacker (see Figure 10-8).**

Making contact in cross-checking

To help ensure that a check does what it's intended to do, remind your players to focus on the opponent's mid-section when they execute a check. If they focus on the opponent's head, they can be thrown off balance by the attacker's fakes and are less likely to make solid contact.

WARNING!

Delivering body checks to opponents above their shoulders, below their knees, or from behind is illegal. Also, those types of checks put kids at unnecessary risk of injury. Always teach only proper and safe techniques. Any time you see an illegal check delivered during your practices, be sure to go over with the player what he did wrong so that he doesn't carry that play over to game day and put himself — or his opponent — in harm's way.

Figure 10-7:
The defender keeps his head up while delivering the body check.

Figure 10-8:
The defender drives his shoulder into the attacker's chest.

Correcting cross-checking problems

Following are some of the problems boys typically deal with when learning how to deliver body checks:

- ✔ **The defender misses making solid contact.** Typically, this problem occurs when the youngster is out of control, lunging at the player he's attempting to check. A good rule to share with your players is that if they wouldn't be able to take a step and land on the opponent's shoes, they're probably too far away to attempt a body check. At older levels of play, as kids gain more skills and quickness, they become comfortable delivering body checks from a little farther away.

- ✔ **The defender loses his balance easily.** All good defensive play originates with the feet. If a player's body checks are leaving him off balance, make sure that his feet are about shoulder width apart and that his knees are slightly flexed on contact.

Anyone with possession of the ball has a bull's eye on his chest in leagues that allow checking. The same goes for any player within 5 yards of a loose ball, who also can be body-checked legally. (For a rundown on the rules of lacrosse and the penalties for various infractions, check out Chapter 3.)

Training in Goaltending Techniques

The goaltender position in lacrosse requires a wide range of skills that are much different from anything else you're teaching the rest of your players. Goalies must be able to stop shots from all angles — and at all speeds — using their arms, legs, stick, and glove. They also must contend with shots that bounce in front of them or that are deflected by opposing players and even their own teammates. Because the position is so difficult, youngsters who play it must gain a sound grasp of the fundamentals.

Grip

The hands are as important to a goalie as a chainsaw is to a lumberjack. Good work with the hands — especially in holding the stick — leads to good goaltending. The goalie's top hand should be at the throat of the stick, or at least very near it. Her bottom hand should be approximately 12 inches down from her top hand. Both palms face her (see Figure 10-9).

Stance

A goalie who is in the proper stance before the opponent ever gets into good scoring position is prepared to deal with any type of shot that comes her way. The goalie's feet should be shoulder width apart, and her knees should be slightly flexed. (For a refresher on the goalie's stance, turn to Chapter 5.)

Hands

Although the goalie's stick stops the majority of the shots, her hands make everything come together. Whenever a shot is taken, the goalie's hands move toward the ball; this momentum carries her body directly to the ball. She uses her bottom hand to rotate her stick down so that the head of it faces the ball to stop the shot.

Figure 10-9: In the proper goalie grip, the palms face inward.

Making stops

When the opponent has the ball out in front of the net, the goalie's top responsibility is to keep his body directly between the player's stick and the middle of his net. If he's off center even just a step to either his left or right, he opens up more space in the net for the shooter. At the advanced levels of lacrosse, good attackers can exploit the smallest weaknesses, so establishing good fundamental goalie play at the beginning levels is important. (Jump to Chapter 12 to take a look at how goalies can play different angles.)

When the opposing team operates its attack from behind the net, and an attacker maneuvers near the post, the goalie must keep his stick vertical so that the pocket of the stick is above the net. This position helps prevent easy passes to players out in front of the net. The goalie's bottom hand should grip the end of his stick, and his top hand should be positioned in the middle of it.

Although his grip doesn't vary, he can position himself in several ways to defend:

- **Middle position:** The goalie turns to face the attacker (see Figure 10-10). When the attacker is on his left, the goalie places his right foot in front of the goal line and angles his left foot toward the opponent.

- **Near post position:** The goalie moves to the post nearer the attacker (see Figure 10-11). This position prevents the attacker from being able to beat his defender and take a shot toward the near post.

- **Far post position:** The goalie moves to the far post and takes a step away from it (see Figure 10-12). His feet are angled toward the attacker.

Figure 10-10:
The goalie can stay in the middle of the net when the attack is behind him.

Figure 10-11:
The goalie can protect the near post when the attack is behind the net.

Figure 10-12:
The goalie can position himself at the far post.

Correcting goaltending problems

Because of the difficulty of learning the goaltending position, kids commonly experience a variety of problems, such as these:

- **Lack of mobility:** The quicker and more mobile a goalie is, the more shots she'll be able to keep out of her net. Sometimes, goalies take a stance that is too wide, which detracts from their mobility. Make sure that those feet are kept shoulder width apart, and you should see improved play from your young net minders.

- **Fear of the ball:** It's certainly not uncommon for a young goalie to be afraid of the ball; after all, getting hit by a shot stings sometimes. To help a youngster overcome his fears, use a tennis ball during your practice drills to get him comfortable making stops again. That change usually is enough to help him regain his comfort level, as well as his confidence that he can make saves. Then you can go back to the ball your program uses to build on his progress.

- **Inability to get the stick on shots:** Check the positioning of the goalie's arms. If she keeps her elbows too close to her body, she limits her movement.

- **Difficulty stopping both low and high shots:** This problem probably is related to an improper stance. The goalie's hands may be too far apart on his stick, and his feet may be spread too wide (see Figure 10-13). Or perhaps his feet are too close together, and his hands are too close together on the stick (see Figure 10-14). In either case, he won't be able to react as quickly or be as effective in stopping shots.

Figure 10-13:
Goalies
shouldn't
spread their
hands and
feet too far
apart.

Figure 10-14:
Neither
should
goalies keep
their hands
and feet too
close
together.

Chapter 11

Playing Lacrosse Offense

Winning face-offs, marching down the field, and scoring goals are some of the ways in which offensive roles can be so much fun. Helping your players become a productive unit — one that evolves into a potent offense that applies pressure to opponents all game long — requires a thorough understanding of some of the more advanced elements of the game.

In this chapter, we go on the attack (forgive us; we had to say it) and dig in to the face-off techniques players can use to gain possession of the coveted ball. We run down techniques such as the inside roll dodge and outside pivot, which players can take advantage of to get by defenders, and provide some information on shooting. Here, you find details on executing long sidearm and long underhand shots, and faking out goaltenders.

Revving Up the Offense

Regardless of what ages or levels of lacrosse players you're coaching, adhering to some key offensive principles clears the way for your team to gradually build on skills and emerge as a more cohesive unit. As kids gain confidence and see themselves progressing in the game, they'll develop a deeper appreciation of lacrosse. Ideally, they'll be a little tougher for the opposition to defend along the way, too.

Attacking one-on-one

Lacrosse is a team sport, but players still have room to use their individual skills. Following are some tips to help your players attack defenders successfully (while sticking to your team concept):

- **Take advantage of tired bodies.** Out-of-breath defenders aren't going to have the energy to keep up with an offensive player who has some bounce in his step. When your players see that they have a tired defender in front of them, encourage them to raise their aggressiveness a notch, because chances are good that they'll be able to get by that defender.

- **Maximize the mismatches.** During a game, mismatches occur, such as a small player defending a bigger, stronger opponent. But if your players don't recognize an advantage when it unfolds, it goes to waste, and the defense is let off the hook. Help your players become aware of situations that develop on the field. The better your players are at seeing and capitalizing on mismatches, the more punch your offense will have.

- **Be unpredictable.** Being predictable is boring, and in lacrosse, predictability on offense makes players stagnant and less effective.

- **Force defenders to react.** Effective offensive players force defenders to react to their moves. A player who uses fakes to get a defender's feet moving has a greater chance of luring that defender out of position.

- **Play with confidence.** No matter a defender's size, speed, or strength, instill confidence in your players so that they continue playing hard and attacking. Just because a defender possesses some strong qualities doesn't mean that your players can't be successful with different moves.

- **Move in all directions.** Players who are comfortable moving to both their left and right are doubly difficult for defenders to get a read on. During practices, make sure that your players don't get into the habit of always attacking on the side that's most comfortable for them.

- **Keep moving.** Players who stand still are easy for defenders to track. Being on the move challenges opposing players to keep up. Also, defenders who are forced to run all game long eventually show signs of tiring, leading to additional opportunities for your players to attack.

Changing directions

The better your players become at changing directions, the more difficult they are to defend. Teach your players how to use fakes — both inside and outside moves — and they'll be freer to make passes and take shots (and maybe score more goals). Here are some tips for making the inside and outside cuts work.

Inside cut

This technique, also known as a split dodge or face dodge, is popular because it puts the ball carrier in the middle of the field — the prime position from which to attack the defense by shooting or passing. The key to making it work is getting the defensive player off balance. If the defender is leaning to the outside or backpedaling, he has less chance to stay with (or, in boys' lacrosse, to check) the offensive player. Check out these steps for making an inside cut:

1. **The ball carrier holds his stick close to his body.**

2. **He steps with his right foot, planting it outside the defender's left foot.**

   A right-hander turns his left shoulder toward the defender to fake that he is moving to the outside (see Figure 11-1).

3. **He pushes off hard with his plant foot and takes a large step toward the middle of the field with his opposite foot.**

4. **He dips his right shoulder and turns his body sideways (see Figure 11-2). This move helps shield the ball from the defender.**

5. **He takes another step with his right foot as he continues angling toward the middle of the field.**

Figure 11-1:
Beating a defender inside requires a good outside-fake move.

Figure 11-2:
The player dips his inside shoulder when cutting into the middle of the field.

Outside cut

Defenders are naturally most concerned with keeping players out of the middle of the field, so the outside cut is a good option to have in the offensive repertoire for attacking that area of the field. The move works this way:

1. **Keeping her stick near her body, the ball carrier plants her left foot outside the defender's right foot.**

   This move gives the defender the indication that she plans to attack the middle of the field.

2. **She pushes off hard with her left foot and takes a step with her right foot to the outside of the defender (see Figure 11-3).**

3. **As she cuts outside (see Figure 11-4), she turns her left shoulder to shield the defender.**

4. **Holding the shaft near the head of the stick, she moves her stick across her body with her right arm (see Figure 11-5) and uses her left arm to fend off the defensive player.**

5. **As she steps past the defender, she puts both hands on her stick.**

Figure 11-3:
The outside cut should be in every attacker's repertoire.

Figure 11-4:
The left shoulder shields the defender.

Figure 11-5:
The inside arm fends off the opponent when the player is cutting outside.

Mixing up the pace

The most dangerous attackers are those who have a variety of moves and can execute them at different speeds. Even if an attacker is a fast runner, if he moves at that same speed every time he has possession of the ball, defenders pick up on that habit and have a better chance of sticking with him.

The element of surprise is an effective offensive tool for keeping defenders off balance, and is an effective technique to employ at the older and more advanced age groups. When you mix up the speeds at which your players maneuver on the field — from full-out sprints to jogging, along with intermittent bursts — defenders will never fully know what to expect, which increases the chance that your players' attack will be successful.

Perfecting the roll dodge

Many times during the course of a game, ball carriers find themselves with their backs to the defender. Being able to pivot in either direction is important for getting by a defender and for creating opportunities for the whole team. The inside and outside pivots should be in every attacker's bag. Here's how these moves are performed.

Inside roll dodge

Good footwork is essential for executing this move:

1. **If the ball carrier is a left-handed shooter, he plants his left foot in the middle of the defender's feet (see Figure 11-6).**

Figure 11-6: Good footwork is key for executing the inside roll dodge.

2. He spins his back into the defender and rotates his right foot around so that his back is to the defender. His feet are slightly beyond shoulder width apart.

3. Holding his stick vertically and close to his head, he leans back into the defender while looking over his right shoulder (see Figure 11-7).

4. With his left foot, he takes a strong step toward the inside of the field, keeping his stick to the outside and using his body to shield the defender (see Figure 11-8).

5. He slides his top hand down on his stick so that he is in good shooting position.

Figure 11-7:
The attacker leans into the defender while peeking over his shoulder.

Figure 11-8:
Players hold their sticks to the outside when performing the inside roll dodge.

Outside pivot

Defenders are mostly concerned about protecting the middle of the field, so your players can use this pivot move to gain an advantage on the outside:

1. **The ball carrier plants her right foot between the defender's feet (see Figure 11-9).**

2. **She turns her body sideways, holding her stick vertically toward her left shoulder to help shield the defender.**

3. **She spins her left shoulder toward the outside of the field.**

4. **She moves her left foot outside the defender's left foot (Figure 11-10).**

5. **She slides her right hand about midway up the stick while taking her left hand off the stick. This move helps protect the ball from the defender.**

Figure 11-9:
The outside pivot works against defenders protecting the middle of the field.

Figure 11-10:
The attacker steps to the outside of the defender.

6. **She moves her left elbow onto the defender's back. This move gives her leverage to get past the defender.**

7. **As she moves past the defender, she brings her stick to the front of her body to protect it so the ball isn't knocked loose.**

Beating a defender

In boys' lacrosse, defensive players rely heavily on checking to slow an attacking player, bump him off his intended path, or create a turnover. Kids who can absorb a hit and continue on their way pose a lot of problems for defenders. Teach your players these techniques for dealing with contact, and opponents' checks won't be nearly as successful in disrupting your attack:

1. **As the defender comes closer, the ball carrier turns his body sideways. This move helps shield his stick from the defender and gives the defender a smaller target to check.**

2. **The ball carrier chokes up on his stick.**

   Choking up (check out Chapter 3 for terms of the game) means sliding his top hand closer to the head of the stick, which gives him more control.

3. **He moves his stick into a vertical position. This maneuver makes it easier to maintain control of the ball when the defender makes contact.**

4. **He leans in to the check.**

   Leaning in, rather than waiting for the defender to initiate contact, helps him maintain balance. As contact occurs, the ball carrier's weight should be evenly distributed on both feet, which should be shoulder width apart.

5. **He absorbs the check, maintains his balance, and moves past the defender.**

   As he moves by, he keeps his stick in the vertical position so that he can maintain possession of the ball until he's ready to pass or shoot.

Even though checking isn't allowed in girls' lacrosse (visit Chapter 3 for a run down of the rules of the game and the differences between boys' and girls' lacrosse) players can still rely on similar moves to create openings when their team is on the attack. If you're coaching a girls' team, you can teach any of the moves described here to avoid checks in the boys' game for your players to turn to to get past opposing defenders.

The more offensive moves your girls use, the harder they'll be to stop, and the more chances they'll have to create goal-scoring opportunities.

Shoring Up Shooting Skills

The more good jokes a stand-up comedian has at his disposal, the funnier he's going to be. The same principles apply to offensive players: The more shots they have in their arsenal, the more success they have in scoring. To help your players upgrade their shooting skills, work on the following shots.

Mastering straight shots

Determining the right time to take shots — in the heat of the action, with defenders breathing down your players' neck — has a big impact on a team's offensive productivity. Ingrain the following tips in your players' minds to help them deposit more shots in the opponent's net:

- ✔ **Be ready.** Players must be ready to shoot at all times, because they never know when openings will appear (and close down a second later). Taking advantage of openings the moment they appear translates into better scoring opportunities and usually more goals, too.

- ✔ **Don't get greedy.** A lot of times when a player maneuvers past a defender, she's in prime position to shoot or pass the ball to a teammate, but instead, she tries to beat another defender to get even closer to the net. Usually, this move results in a couple of defenders converging on her, and she ends up wasting the advantage she created seconds earlier. Remind your players that they don't have to be right on top of the goalie to be in scoring position.

- ✔ **Know the goalie.** Most shots on goal aren't deflected, so players can't count on their teammates to steer their shots into the goal for them. Instead, they must rely on making accurate shots on net themselves. Knowing the goalie's tendencies — a habit of leaning toward his left on straight-in shots, for example — can enhance your players' effectiveness with their shots.

- ✔ **Use a quick release.** The faster players shoot the ball when it's in their possession, the less chance the goalie has of setting up to make the save.

Zeroing in on long shots

Teams that can score goals from long distances are difficult and frustrating to play against. Scoring goals without having to string together several accurate passes to get close to the net can smother an opponent's morale. A couple of long-range shots that you can introduce to your players are the sidearm and underhand shots. (Check out Chapter 9 for the rundown on executing the overhand long shot and the long bounce shot.)

Long sidearm shot

This shot gives the goalie trouble judging where the ball is headed, because the shooter uses a whip action upon release. Here's how the shot works:

1. **The ball carrier places his feet shoulder width apart, with his left shoulder (if he's a right-handed shooter) facing the goalie and his hands together at the end of his stick.**

2. **His right hand is about halfway up the shaft, with his left hand at the bottom. He brings his stick back at waist level so that the head of the stick is past his right shoulder.**

3. **He takes the stick backward around his waist while stepping forward toward the goalie with his left foot (see Figure 11-11).**

4. **He follows through by bringing the stick around his waist and shifting his weight to his left foot, helping generate power.**

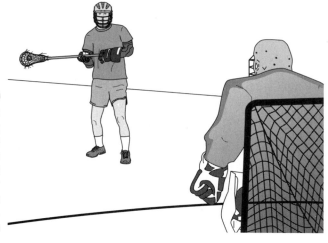

Figure 11-11:
The long sidearm shot can be deceptive and hard for goalies to stop.

Long underhand shot

The ability to execute this type of shot gives players the opportunity to shoot the ball low to the ground or up high. Here's how to make this shot:

1. **The ball carrier places her feet shoulder width apart, with her left shoulder (if she's a right-handed shooter) facing the goalie.**

2. **She slides her right hand up by her left hand at the end of her stick.**

3. **She brings the stick back about waist high while watching the net.**

4. **She rotates her hips toward the goalie while stepping forward with her left foot. As her weight shifts forward, she brings her stick around just above the ground. (See Figure 11-12.)**

5. **As the stick crosses in front of her feet, she rotates her wrists toward the goal to release the shot and follows through above her waist.**

Figure 11-12:
The long sidearm shot resembles a slap shot in hockey.

Finding the net with in-close shots

Scoring from long range requires a strong shot. But the closer your players are to the net, the greater role accuracy plays in whether they score. When a shooter moves in close on a goalie, he can attempt a shot or go with a stick fake to get the goalie to lunge out of position and create a gap to shoot at. Here are tips for when your players are in the shadow of the opponent's goal:

✔ **Quicker moves are better moves.** When a player is in scoring range, he doesn't have time to get too fancy with the fakes or the footwork. Usually, he's about to get checked by a defender, so the faster he releases the ball, the better chance he has of collecting a goal.

✔ **Keep the stick close to the body.** When they're playing in close, your players should hold their sticks close to their bodies so that they don't surrender possession of the ball to defenders, who are usually nearby.

✔ **Forgo fakes.** At the advanced levels of lacrosse, many goalies expect the attacker's first move to be a fake, so encourage your players to just shoot the ball sometimes instead of trying to get the goalie out of position.

✔ **Focus on the side opposite the head of the goalie's stick.** This is also called the off-side. Shooting at the goalie's off-side hip high is good because it forces her to move to block the ball with her body or rotate the head of her stick to the other side of her body to make a stick save.

Faking shots

Proficiency with fake shots — in which players attempt to convince the goalie that they are shooting the ball in a specific direction when they really intend to shoot it elsewhere — can increase your team's goal-scoring proficiency. Here's a glance at a standard fake:

1. **The ball carrier raises his stick above shoulder level and focuses on a spot over the goalie's right shoulder (see Figure 11-13). If the goalie is left-handed simply reverse the directions.**

2. **As the goalie leans in the direction of the fake, the ball carrier lowers his stick to waist level and steps to his right (see Figure 11-14).**

3. **He releases the shot.**

   Shooting the ball in one motion is important. Otherwise, the goalie has a chance to recover and get back into position.

Figure 11-13:
A shot fake helps get the goalie out of position.

Figure 11-14:
The ball carrier must make a quick shot after faking the goalie out of position.

Focusing on Face-Offs

A team's ability to win face-offs can change a game's outcome. Controlling face-offs leads to coveted ball possession and, through effective passing and one-on-one moves, often some good scoring opportunities too. Cashing in on opportunities, of course, requires strong shooting skills. Every face-off your team wins is one less possession for the opposition. If the other team doesn't have the ball, it can't score, and you just can't beat that for good defense!

When one of your players goes through a game in which she didn't fare well winning face-offs, chat with her about it at your next practice. Encourage her to analyze what the other player did that worked so well against her to help her identify some techniques that she can use herself.

Going with the up and over

Quick reflexes are real assets for winning face-offs, and players rely heavily on speed to execute the up-and-over technique. Here's how it works:

1. **On the referee's whistle, the player moves his stick over the ball — the faster, the better (see Figure 11-15). His goal is to get his stick between the opponent's stick and the ball.**

2. **When he achieves that goal, he rakes the ball back to a teammate, using the pocket on his stick.**

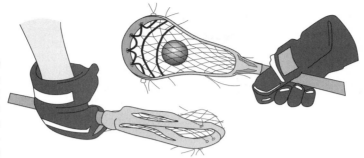

Figure 11-15:
The up and over relies on quick reflexes.

Executing the flip

This technique relies on several elements — such as trapping the ball, fending off the opponent's stick, and drawing the ball back. Here's how it works:

1. **On the referee's whistle, the player flips the back of her stick down on the ball by rotating her top wrist backward (see Figure 11-16).**

2. **She positions the top of the stick flat to the field and rotates her wrist so that as she traps the ball, she rakes it backward.**

Figure 11-16:
Players trap the ball and draw it back with the flip technique.

Running set plays

One of the most fascinating aspects of coaching lacrosse is that when youngsters have a fairly good grasp of the basics of the game, you can begin introducing strategies and plays for them to use on game day. Following are a few set plays that you can run off face-offs:

- ✔ **Send the ball to the goalie.** One of the most basic plays you can run is having the center midfielder send the ball directly back to the goalie.

- ✔ **Pushing the ball past the opposing center midfielder.** Your face-off man focuses on knocking the ball past his opponent. A teammate rushes forward to scoop up the ball and move the attack downfield.

- ✔ **Drawing the ball backward toward a teammate.** The center midfielder rakes the ball back toward a teammate. It's important that the players not involved in the face-off are ready to pick up a loose ball and don't allow nearby players from the opposing team to gain possession.

Chapter 12

Playing Lacrosse Defense

*W*atching your team push the ball down the field and score goals is rewarding for you and great fun for the kids, but you'll quickly realize that derailing an opposing team's attack and denying it the chance to do the same to you is equally satisfying. Showing your players how to transition from offense to defense, as well as how to handle their responsibilities when the opposition has the ball, has a big impact on their game-day performance and how much enjoyment they get out of participating in lacrosse.

In this chapter, we dig in to some key defensive elements that your players need to be well versed in, because they spend roughly half of every game on defense. We cover the different defensive styles your team can use and discuss many techniques that help comprise a sound defensive unit, ranging from defending cuts to (in some boys' leagues) picking up checks.

Also, because the goaltending position is so prominent in lacrosse, and because it's difficult to play well because of all the skills and nuances involved, we devote a large section ("Making Saves") to facing all sorts of shots.

Determining the Defense

When you choose the type of defense you want to play, you can go with either player-to-player or zone defense. The most commonly used defensive style is *player-to-player,* which is exactly what it sounds like: Each player is responsible for defending a specific player on the opposing team.

At the more-advanced levels of play, when kids have more experience with the game, you can introduce the *zone* defense. This style of defense is more complex and tougher to teach than player-to-player, because players are responsible for defending an area of the field rather than an individual. The following sections look at both defense styles.

Player-to-player

Player-to-player defense is the better type to use when you're coaching beginning lacrosse players. In this defensive approach, your defender covers the opposing player wherever he goes on the field.

A general rule to keep in mind: The closer an opposing player is to your goal, the closer your defender should be to her. When an opponent is 40 yards from the goal and doesn't have possession of the ball, your player doesn't need to be right on top of her.

You can make all sorts of modifications in player-to-player defense to fit the strengths of your team. You can choose an aggressive approach that applies more pressure to the opponent but also involves more risk, for example. This high-pressure type of play works well with quick-footed players who understand the game well enough to be able to slide over and help teammates who need defensive support. If your team's defensive skills are still in the developmental stages, you may prefer a less-aggressive style that doesn't expose your team's weaknesses as much, even though it allows the opposition to dictate much of the action by controlling the ball a little more easily.

Here are some additional coaching tips to keep in mind:

- **Communicate constantly.** Good communication skills are important in relationships, in the workplace, and when your team is defending an attack. Whenever a player manages to knock the ball away from an opponent and onto the ground, for example, he needs to yell "Ball!" to alert nearby teammates who might be able to make a play.

  Communication also plays a vital role when a defender gets beaten. In such a situation, yelling "Help!" lets the teammate nearest her know that she needs to provide defensive coverage so that the opponent can't roam free and take an uncontested shot.

- **Keep the head moving.** The best defensive players know what's going on all over the field, because they always know where the player they are guarding is, as well as the location of the ball.

- **Always be ready to help.** Lacrosse is a team game, so players must always be ready and able to help a teammate who has been beaten. Defenders can't be concerned just with the players they are guarding; they must also keep an eye on the other opponents and be ready to assist teammates whenever necessary.

✔ **Keep the sticks in the air.** Players can defend a lot more territory by keeping their sticks in the passing lanes, thereby limiting the space the offense has to operate in. When defenders hold their sticks close to their bodies, opponents can exploit that situation, because they have more space in which to work the ball around to create a good scoring opportunity.

✔ **Play on the appropriate side of the opponent.** When the opponent your player is defending doesn't have the ball, your defender should always play slightly to the side of him that coincides with the side of the field the ball is on. This maneuver allows the defender to gain a step if the opponent cuts toward the ball to receive a pass. If the opponent cuts away from the ball, any pass in his direction must go over the defender's head, which puts him in an advantageous position to intercept the ball or deflect it.

✔ **Cover quickly.** Whenever a pass is on the way to a player your defender is covering, she should step out to cover her opponent while the ball is in midair. This way, she's in position to defend as soon as the opponent gets possession. If she waits until the reception has been made to move forward, the opponent has more time to get settled and plan her move.

✔ **Be a constant distraction.** Whenever an opposing player has the ball, the defender responsible for covering him should be a constant source of aggravation.

In a boys' league that allows checking, the defender should use the stick check (see Chapter 10 for more details on executing stick checks), as well as keep his stick around shoulder height to cut down on passing lanes and make it more difficult for the opposing player to scan the entire field.

✔ **Don't be afraid of the ball.** Sometimes, for fear of being hit by the ball, youngsters turn their backs when an opposing player winds up to take a shot. This move is one of the worst mistakes a defender can make. By turning her back, she'll be taking herself out of position if the opponent is faking a shot, which will create an opportunity for that player to move past the defender and take a real shot even closer to the goal.

If some of your players have a fear of being hit, first use tennis balls in your drills to help get them comfortable facing shots; then work your way up to a regulation lacrosse ball. You may even want to consider using a tennis ball in some of your early-season practices to help the kids become comfortable before making the transition to the harder lacrosse ball.

✔ **Watch out for penalties.** Sure, penalties occur during games, but the key is keeping them to a minimum. Don't ignore penalties when they occur during your practice drills. Kids must understand what they did wrong so that those habits don't carry over to game day and put your team at a disadvantage.

Zone

You can use many styles of zone defense, based on what type of offense the opponent is running. The basic concept for any zone is that each player is responsible for a specific area of the field; whenever an opposing player enters that zone, the defender provides coverage. Whenever your team commits a penalty and must play a person short, a zone defense works well to compensate, because you are unable to put a defender on every opposing player.

A basic zone defense that you can use when your team is down a player is the 2-1-2 zone (see Figure 12-1). Two midfielders play at the top of the zone, farthest away from the goal, while three defenders surround the crease area. The players' primary focus is preventing inside shots, so whenever the ball is on the opposite side of their coverage area, they sag down to help deny inside penetration.

When one of your players makes a great defensive play, recognize the effort with a verbal comment during the game or a high five when he comes to the sidelines for a breather. Kids will understand the importance of defense — and give you a strong effort in that area of the game — when they sense that you place as much importance on it as you do on their play at the offensive end of the field.

Figure 12-1:
A 2-1-2 zone defense works well when your team is short-handed.

Goalie

Defense   Defense   Defense

Midfielder   Midfielder

Polishing Individual Techniques

Playing good team defense — the kind that smothers goal-scoring opportunities, keeps opponents off balance, and makes trying to work the ball down the field a frustrating experience — requires each player to understand and be able to use a variety of techniques. In the following sections, we look at some defensive skills that your players can use.

Picking up checks

If you're coaching in a boys' league that permits checking, your players will enjoy the defensive side of the game more, and have more success, if they understand how and when to check players (see Chapter 10 for techniques).

When you instruct your players on the role of checking in defense, emphasize these benefits:

- ✔ **It gives the opponent something else to think about.** A check doesn't have to knock a player to the ground or produce a turnover to be effective. The more checks your players deliver during the course of a game, the more the other team will think about those checks. When opponents know that they are going to get hit as soon as they catch a pass or try to move into shooting range, they'll start making adjustments by turning their bodies or making other moves to avoid some of the contact. Forcing opponents to perform these extra maneuvers takes away some of their effectiveness, because they're not able to attack quite as quickly as normal.

- ✔ **It cuts off the middle of the field.** Whenever an opponent drives toward the middle of the field, the defender must keep his body on the opponent and deliver a stick check to prevent him from taking a shot or passing to a teammate.

Closing out

A *close out* occurs when a defender is in such a position that she must charge toward the opponent who has the ball. This situation usually occurs in a cross-field pass when the defender has to get out on the player who's receiving the ball; otherwise, that player will be open to take a shot on net. In this situation, she must get her body in front of the player's stick while maintaining balance. If she is out of control as she runs toward the opponent, her momentum will take her out of position, as well as out of the play. If he fails to arrive on time, he should focus on the player's stick, and as it's being set up to take a shot, he should use his stick to knock the opponent's stick up or down to disrupt the shot.

Recovering when beaten

One strength of a really good defense is the players' commitment to hustling every second they are on the field and refusing to allow any easy scoring opportunities for the opposition. To achieve this type of play all season long, you must instill in your players the competitive desire to work themselves back into the play whenever they have been beaten and have lost contact with the player they are defending.

Just because an opponent gets by one of your defenders doesn't mean that she should give up and become a spectator, simply watching the action unfold. She must devote all her energy to chasing that player down, because she doesn't know what could happen. If she hustles back fast enough, she may be able to make a play on the opponent or at least distract him enough with a stick check where he can't get off a clear shot or pass. Remember, in girls lacrosse some leagues, at the more advanced levels of play, allow stick checking. Oftentimes, a modified form is allowed where the defender can check the stick if it is below shoulder level and as long as the defensive motion is downward and away from the opponent's body. Or maybe a teammate slid over to cover the opponent, and she can cover the player her teammate left unguarded to help minimize the chance that a quality scoring chance will develop.

Defending cuts

Whenever possible, you want your defensive players to force opponents to run toward the sideline, rather than toward your goal. When a player cuts to the middle of the field, he poses more of a threat to the defense than he does if he is on the outside.

To steer opponents to the outside of the field, a defender does the following:

1. **He positions himself in front of the offensive player with his inside foot about 6 inches in front of his outside foot.**

2. **When the opponent cuts to the outside, the defender pushes off with his front foot and takes a step backward with his back foot in the direction of the attacker (see Figure 12-2).**

3. **He keeps his stick at about waist level parallel to the ground.**

   This stance allows him to check the opponent, too, to keep him off balance and keep him from going where he wants to.

Figure 12-2:
Good
footwork is
required for
defending
cuts to the
outside.

Opponents who cut inside pose threats to the defense, because they are attacking a valuable piece of real estate that must be protected. When a player cuts to the inside, the defender counters with the following moves:

1. **She steps backward with her inside foot and shuffles both feet laterally in the direction in which the opponent is moving (see Figure 12-3), taking short, quick steps.**

2. **She keeps her feet spread about shoulder width apart to maintain a solid base.**

    This stance is important if he uses a check so that he keeps his balance.

3. **She holds her stick at about waist level parallel to the ground so that she can disrupt shots and deny passing lanes.**

Figure 12-3:
A defender
takes short,
quick steps
to defend an
opponent
who's
cutting
inside.

Positioning in the midfield

As soon as your team surrenders possession of the ball, whether due to a turnover or a shot on goal, every player must commit to playing strong defense. Many defensive breakdowns occur in the midfield area, which can lead to good scoring opportunities for the opposition. One of the most important elements of strong defensive play in the midfield area is having each player mark the player he is defending goal side — that is, keeping himself between the opponent and the goal.

When an opposing player has possession of the ball in the midfield area, the defender should focus on forcing her to her weak side. That means forcing a right-handed player to move to her left, and vice versa (see Figure 12-4). While shadowing the opponent, the defender holds her stick up in front of her. Her nondominant hand is at the bottom of the stick, and her dominant hand grips near the middle of the stick. She stretches her arms out to harass the opponent and to contest passes and shots.

Figure 12-4:
Good defense in the midfield area requires forcing opponents to their weak sides.

Making Saves

Playing the goaltender position in lacrosse is more challenging than working a Rubik's Cube blindfolded — at least, it can seem that way some days. The position requires a broad range of skills, many of which take years of practice before the goalie becomes proficient.

In this section, we help you begin to build your goalies' skills, covering everything from playing the angles and defending corner shots to stopping long and in-close shots.

Relying on reflexes

At the beginning levels of lacrosse, many young goaltenders are more interested in swatting the butterfly floating around the net than in stopping the ball heading their way, so expecting them to have the reflexes to react to shots isn't reasonable. But at the more-advanced levels of play, goalies must rely on their reflexes to turn away shots and deny goals to the opposition.

One of the best ways to build quick reflexes in your goalies is to use drills that force them to react to a flurry of shots in a short period. This technique helps build their hand–eye coordination and also helps them learn to anticipate where shots are headed as soon as they are released from a player's stick. (Check out Chapter 7 for some basic drills to use with your goaltenders.)

Good reflexes and being in the right position based on the angle of the opponent's shot are an effective combo for keeping balls out of the net. Read on to get the scoop.

Playing the angles

If you remember your days in geometry class, you learned a lot about angles (if you were paying attention and not flirting with a cute classmate, that is). Being an effective goalie requires understanding the angles of shots and where to be positioned in the net to defend them the best.

Here are a few additional coaching points to make regarding playing the angles:

✔ **Understanding angles saves a lot of work.** When a goalie is in the proper position based on the angle of the shot, he saves himself a lot of work, because he doesn't have to lunge or stretch to make quite as many saves. Because of his good positioning, many shots simply bounce off him.

✔ **Remain centered.** Playing the right angles requires starting from the center of the net before moving out on shooters. Remind goaltenders to watch their positioning as the play develops to ensure that they are between the goal posts and that they haven't strayed a step in either direction. This technique helps them take the proper angle as they step out to challenge a shooter.

✔ **Keep the post within reach.** You don't want the goalie straying so far out of the crease that she would have great difficulty recovering from a pass to a player around the front of the net area. A general guideline is that the goalie should be able to touch the *short-side post* — the one closer to her — with her glove-hand arm extended.

✔ **Experiment during practices.** During your drills, encourage goalies to test how far out of the net they are comfortable moving to challenge shooters. This experiment will give them a good gauge of what will work best for them on game day. Goalies who possess a lot of quickness may find that they can take two steps out from the net and still be able to cover it efficiently; others may find that one step out puts them in the best position to stop shots.

Your goaltenders must keep in mind that the deeper they play in the net, the more openings they provide for the shooter. When they move out of the net to challenge shooters, they cut down on the angle and provide a much smaller target for the opponent to shoot at.

Defending the corner shots

The goalie position requires constant movement — both side to side and up and back — when the opposition is on the attack. If a right-handed goalie (who holds the stick in his right hand) sees the ball go into the right corner, he slides his body in that direction and puts his outside foot against the goal post, with his leg pressed tightly against the post (see Figure 12-5). His arm holding the stick rests against the outside of the post, while the stick is between his legs. His head is upright and facing the player in the corner, though he should be constantly scanning what is taking place in front of him so that he's ready to slide over in case a pass is made to a player in that area.

Figure 12-5:
A goalie's body must be snug to the goal post when the ball is in the corner.

Stopping breakaway shots

When a goaltender faces a *breakaway shot* — one made by an offensive player who has a clear path to the goal with no defender nearby — her first reaction may be to say a quick prayer, because these shots are the toughest ones to stop. The advantage is tipped heavily in the shooter's favor. But your goalie has a couple of options:

- **Move out.** She can take a few steps out of the net, which takes a longer shot away from the opponent and forces her to move in closer before releasing the ball. Moving out also cuts down on the angles the shooter has available.

- **Focus on fakes.** Many shooters, as they close in on the net, go with a fake before taking a shot. Your goalie can play a hunch and not bite on the opponent's first move. This option works if the opponent did indeed fake the shot; it fails miserably when the opponent has no intention of faking and releases the ball into the net.

Maintaining positioning when the ball is behind the net

Many lacrosse teams' offensive plays originate from behind the net, so your goalie must be prepared to defend when the ball moves back there. Depending on the size of your goalie and the size of the net used in your program, this is the ideal position for him to be in:

1. **His right foot is pressed against the inside of the right post while his left hand (his glove hand) stretches toward the left post (see Figure 12-6). For left-handed goalies, do the opposite.**

2. **He keeps his back tight against the crossbar.**

3. **He keeps the stick positioned between his legs and lets it graze the ground.**

4. **He continually looks over his shoulder to monitor what the player with the ball is doing.**

5. **He keeps his body facing the play in front of him so that he is ready to make a save if the ball is passed out to the front area.**

Figure 12-6:
Maintaining good positioning is vital when the ball is behind the net.

Holding the proper position during face-offs

Lacrosse features several rules that your goaltenders must know to play their position most effectively during a face-off. (For a rundown on the basic rules of the game, check out Chapter 3.) During a face-off, the goalie should stand with one foot in and one foot out of her crease, or with both feet out of the crease. Because players can't pass the ball into their own crease, the goalie must be outside it in case a teammate needs to pass the ball back to her. She also must keep one foot in the crease in case she wants to draw a loose ball back.

Your goalies should keep in mind that if they go after a loose ball and leave their crease, they cannot return to the crease with it.

Stopping long shots

Players don't have to be right on top of a goalie to present a scoring threat; an opponent can be 20 yards from the goal and still score. Long shots can present problems for goalies because those shots typically are difficult to track, what with a maze of players moving between the shooter and the net. Also, when the opposing player has a strong shot, the ball can travel from his stick to the goal in what seems to the goalie to be the blink of an eye.

When you're coaching your goalies to stop long shots, emphasize the following points:

- ✔ **Step out.** The goalie should take one step forward toward the shooter. This move cuts down on the available space the opponent has to shoot at.

- ✔ **Move in an arc.** As the ball goes around the field, the goalie follows it by moving in an arc. If the ball is on the goalie's left, for example, and it has been passed to the right side of the field, the goalie takes one step off the left goal post, slides with a shuffle step to the middle of the net, and then takes a step back to the right goal post. While performing these steps, she maintains her ready stance and keeps her body facing the ball at all times.

Denying in-close shots

In-close shots are as problematic for goalies as kryptonite is for Superman. Whenever an opponent works the ball in close for a shot, the odds are in his favor, but that doesn't mean all hope is lost. If you show your goalies the proper techniques for contending with these shots — and showing them how to use their arms, legs, and stick to keep the ball out of the net — they can send opponents back down the field shaking their heads about how they weren't able to register a goal.

The most important point to keep in mind is that the goalie should stay a little closer to the net than he does when dealing with a long shot. If he steps out too far, the shooter may have a chance to put the ball over his shoulder for a goal.

Dealing with bounce shots

Sometimes, players' shots bounce short of the net — often because of an intentional act by the shooter — and these shots can pose new challenges for goalies. The secret to turning bouncing shots away is attacking the ball the way a hungry dog does a meaty bone. Work with your goalie to step forward and get her body in front of the ball as soon as she recognizes that the ball is going to bounce short of the net. You want her to have her stick out in front of her as the first line of defense. Then, if she misses the ball with her stick, she can rely on her legs and chest to block it. (Check out Chapter 14 for some drills on stopping bounce shots.)

Make sure that the goalie isn't lunging for the ball with his stick, which is a clear indication that his body isn't in the proper position to make the save.

Part IV:
Net Gains: Advanced Lacrosse Coaching

The 5th Wave   By Rich Tennant

"Hey! I said 'pick-and-roll,' not 'kick-and-roll!'
Everybody off the assistant coach!"

In this part . . .

One of the real trademarks of a quality lacrosse coach is the ability to propel players to higher levels of play. In this part, you find everything you need to do exactly that, such as information on adjusting to the ever-changing dynamics of your team and upgrading your drills to match the players' progress. The part also provides approaches you can use to make your offense more potent and to turn your defense into an even tougher unit to score against.

Chapter 13

Refining Your Coaching Strategies

*T*he group of lacrosse players you greeted at your first practice is dramatically different from the one you're working with at the halfway point of the season. After participating in a bunch of practices with you, and playing in games under you, your team will be more efficient at executing the fundamentals of the game. Sure, this progress is pleasing to see, but a word of caution: Don't hit that cruise-control button and think you can coast through the second half of the season. You want your team to be as strong in the second half of games as it is in the first half, and the same goes for your coaching.

In this chapter, we look at how you can adjust your coaching strategies to meet the ever-changing demands of the season. We give you tips on handling the tricky change in team dynamics that occurs. We also outline your key midseason responsibilities, including revising coaching strategies, adjusting practice plans, setting goals, and reviewing the progress of your players. If that's not enough, we also discuss how chats with parents can keep you in the loop on how your players really feel about lacrosse, the season, and you. Use the information presented in this chapter to finish the season on a positive note.

Adjusting to Changing Team Dynamics

Whether you're coaching in a six-week beginner league or a three-month advanced league, by the time your team reaches the halfway point of the season you have a pretty good idea of what areas your team excels in, as well as those aspects of the game that pose problems.

Even excellence can be a problem. Perhaps your players have greatly improved their stick-handling and passing skills, to the point where they drive defenses crazy with their ability to move down the field and score on a consistent basis.

In that case, you've got to adjust everything from your practice planning to your points of emphasis so you can raise the kids' defensive skills to match those offensive plays they've become so darn good at.

Regardless of what part of the game they involve, improvements and areas of weakness affect the makeup of your team. You must shuffle players into different positions, tweak your practice drills to account for the team's ever-changing skills and needs, and — if you're coaching an advanced-level team — probably even fiddle with some of your game-day strategies to account for newfound strengths and compensate for any weaknesses that come to light.

In the following sections, we help you gauge your team's overall development, and we assist you in revising your coaching plans to focus on areas you want to strengthen during the remainder of the season.

Never rely on the scoreboard in evaluating your team's performance or progress, because scores can be misleading. Even if your team lost by half a dozen goals, your players may have turned in one of their best performances of the season, with almost flawless execution of the fundamentals. Or perhaps your team won by a lopsided margin, but against a much weaker opponent and with a lot of sloppy turnovers due to poor passing technique. One of the underlying secrets of good coaching is ignoring the final score — win or lose — and putting the magnifying glass squarely over the kids' performances. Ask yourself questions centered on execution and the areas of the game you worked on in practice earlier in the week.

Recognizing improvements

As players pick up skills, show improvement, and gain knowledge of lacrosse, they'll become more proficient during your practice drills, as well as on game day when Mom and Dad are in the stands cheering them on. As a coach, you can't ask for much more than seeing the kids improve, progress, and enjoy varying levels of success on the lacrosse field. Player improvement will make you proud — and well it should, because making everything come together takes a lot of time, effort, commitment, and patience on your part.

Although you deserve a pat on the back for a job well done up to this point, the situation does present some new — and, we hope, exciting — challenges. The following list gives you a peek at some of the common challenges you face when coaching a team with improving players:

✔ **Shifting players around on the field:** After a few games and many practices, you may realize that kids you penciled in at certain positions are better suited to handle entirely different ones. During practices, pay close attention to the smallest details. If you notice that one of your midfielders transitions well to defense, for example, perhaps taking on a defensive role would suit him better and enhance the team too. By observing players as closely as a detective does a crime scene, you may discover that a young-ster would be able (and eager) to play a new position that would make the team more effective. At the very least, you can identify valuable backups if any players have to leave a game or get injured.

Any time you shift a player to a new position, be sure to alert the parents. Communicating regularly with parents (see Chapter 4) is important, because any news concerning their child is big in their eyes. It also reduces the chance of disputes. Tell the parents why you think their child is better suited for this new position and how the skills you've watched her develop in recent weeks make her a real asset to the team. Sometimes, this news will be well received; at other times, not so well. (For more on dealing with parent issues, flip to Chapter 18.)

✔ **Trimming the tension:** If you coach an advanced-level squad and deter-mine playing time by skill level, you may discover that youngsters who lose their starting jobs have great difficulty adjusting to their backup status or new positions if you simply move them with little or no explanation. After all, feelings get hurt when a player's skills are indirectly criticized in front of teammates, and many kids perceive a move this way. Make sure you take the time to explain to the player that he's a valued and important member of the team. Encourage him to keep working hard in practice and to support his teammates.

✔ **Diffusing disappointment:** A youngster who loses her spot to a teammate is naturally disappointed, much as you would be if you lost a promotion to a co-worker. Pay some extra attention to the child who lost her position to ensure that she remains passionate about the game and supportive of her teammates. Let her know that if she continues working hard, chances are strong that she can pick up the skills that will lead to more minutes on game day. Also, by working hard in practice and challenging her teammates during drills, she can help them improve and have a role in making the team a more efficient unit.

✔ **Making changes in your game-day approach:** As the season moves along, your team may become significantly different from the one that began the first practice — and you have to adjust accordingly. Maybe early in the season, the kids didn't have a good handle on the mechanics of checking (if you're coaching an advanced-level boys' team) or cradling (if you're coaching a beginning-level girls' team). Now, halfway through the season, all your advice and all the players' practice have come together, and the team has those areas of the game down pretty well. In that case, you should capitalize on these improved skills and tweak your game-day strategies to take advantage of them.

Keeping close tabs on each player's progress makes it easy for you to be there to deliver a high five whenever the kid learns a new skill or makes an improvement. Maybe the action is subtle, such as the youngster's positioning his feet properly to take a face-off, or maybe he is becoming consistent at scooping up balls on the run. Regardless, be sure to show plenty of enthusiasm, which is the fuel for spurring more learning. The goal of improving should be to build self-confidence and have more fun, which will help the players appreciate the game more and want to stay involved for years to come.

Revising your drills

There are many great aspects associated with coaching lacrosse, and one of the most enjoyable is revising practices and game plans to accommodate the ever-improving skills of their players and the ever-changing needs of their teams. Any time the kids are improving individual skills and the team is progressing as a unit, you want to embrace this special opportunity to help propel them even further in their development. You don't want to suffocate learning by turning to the same set of drills at *every* practice. Your kids will get the most out of their participation and improve fastest if you keep challenging them with new drills. (For some practice drills you can run to raise the level of play a notch or two, turn to Chapter 14.)

To keep your practices fresh and imaginative, and your players motivated, look for clever ways to tweak some of the most popular drills you've used in previous practices. If you do a shooting drill in which the players simply work on getting the ball past the goalie, try this slight alteration: Challenge the kids to score goals in a particular area of the net. This slight alteration in a basic drill introduces a new component that challenges the kids and grabs their interest because it's new and fun. Award bonus points for each goal scored in the area of the net that players are aiming at, and turn the drill into a fun competition to see which player fares best.

Conducting the Midseason Review

Halfway through the season, you'll notice all sorts of changes and improvements among your players. Ideally, you'll also see that your team has really bonded under your leadership. Don't stand pat on your successes, however: Take the time to review how the team is progressing.

Conducting a midseason review benefits both you and the players. It helps keep a headache-free season headed in the right direction, and it can rescue a season that's drifting a little off course.

We all enjoy getting progress reports — in school, at work, and in other endeavors — especially when we receive glowing feedback about how well we've been doing. Your players are no different. Pointing out their progress and improvement drives home the point that you have their best interests in mind and that you're committed to helping them get the most out of their experience this season.

The following sections explain how you can set goals for your players and the team; help you turn those goals into plans; and show you how you can evaluate progress from this point on.

Setting coaching goals

When done the right way, setting goals is one of the most effective coaching tools available. Goals push your players to reach their full potential by presenting challenges that they can have fun striving for and meeting. At the season's halfway point, put the knowledge you've gained from watching your players to good use by setting goals for them for the rest of the season.

Giving yourself pointers

To make midseason goal-setting successful, keep the following points in mind:

- **Encourage practice.** Encourage more advanced players to practice skills with their parents or friends at home. Just a few minutes in the backyard or park a couple of times a week can pay big dividends. Never force practice — you don't want to make it feel like dreaded homework — but nudge kids in the right direction with gentle reminders about polishing certain skills at home.

- **Find a balance.** Choose goals that are in between being too easy and too difficult so that you keep the child's interest, minimize frustration, and maximize his chances of success.

- **Be realistic.** Set only goals that fit within the framework of the team. (See "Fitting your goals to your team" later in this chapter.) Giving an attacker a goal of scoring three goals, for example, is unrealistic. The child has no control over individual performance numbers, such as how many goals she can score. Plus, that type of goal kills team chemistry because there is a chance she will look to shoot more to reach that goal, which means she could overlook open teammates who are in a better position to shoot.

- ✔ **Use short-term goals.** The younger the child, the shorter the attention span, so you're better off setting a series of short-term goals so that the child sees lots of progress right away. Long-term goals have a way of evaporating in a child's mind.

- ✔ **Go with several levels.** Set goals at varying levels so that if a player doesn't reach the top goal but makes strides toward it, she still gains a sense of accomplishment. Having just one goal to shoot for turns goal setting into an all-or-nothing proposition.

- ✔ **Get player feedback.** At the advanced levels of play you can make goal setting more effective — and more enjoyable for the kids — if you have a short discussion with the whole team on which areas of the game they want to improve. Giving players a voice in the goal-setting process helps drive their development.

- ✔ **Factor in injuries.** Any time a youngster has been injured during the season and misses some playing time, be sure to take that missed time into account when setting goals. Young players often take some time to get back up to their preinjury levels. After you sense that a player is back at his normal level after an injury, you can revisit his goals and adjust them to coincide with his improved health.

Fitting your goals to your team

Setting team goals that revolve around winning may seem like a good idea, but those goals can lead to all sorts of problems. If one of your team goals is to win the last three games of the season, for example, and you drop the first of those three games, the goal is suddenly unreachable. In terms of the goal, it doesn't matter whether your team played really well and simply lost to a better team or got edged out by a fluky goal in the closing seconds.

Team victory goals represent the proverbial double-edged sword. When the team wins, the players' confidence soars; when games don't end in victories, the players are blanketed in disappointment and doubt. Instead, steer team goals away from the win–loss record. Focus on weekly improvement and on playing hard at both ends of the field. Aim for team goals such as committing fewer turnovers than in the last game or committing fewer penalties than the week before. Positive team goals such as these make a real difference in helping kids raise the level of their game.

If you're coaching a beginning-level team, keep the midseason emphasis on having fun; downplay winning and losing. When you keep the goals realistic, you'll realize your share of wins — and more important, you create an environment that allows your players to reap the rewards of playing, learning, and achieving together.

Helping your players improve their skills

Any time you're mapping out the midseason review for your players, you start by establishing realistic goals that they can reach by working hard and following your lead. You want to set your players up for plenty of successes — not failures — and create an environment in which they can flourish. After establishing realistic goals, you act on them by creating plans to help your players achieve those goals.

Planning for player success

Putting together a skill-building plan requires working up to the goals one step at a time. If you build players' confidence with each step in the progression, your players reap the benefits. To help your youngsters gauge their progress, make sure that you compare their current performances with those from earlier in the season. Many times, kids tie their progress to how the team is performing, which isn't a good indicator, because wins and losses don't play a role in how a player has grown and developed in different areas of the game. Just because the team has won five games in a row doesn't necessarily mean that a child has become an accurate shooter. Conversely, simply because the team has been on the losing end of several games recently doesn't mean that the youngster couldn't be improving and playing some of her best lacrosse of the season.

Suppose that your midfielder has become good at catching passes while standing still or while moving just a couple of steps in either direction. Naturally, one of your next goals for him is to catch passes while running faster; this goal upgrades his skills and helps him become a more complete player. The more skills a player has, the more difficult he is to defend.

Putting the plan into play

Any plan is executed on the field over time. The following sample plan is a snapshot of the entire process, which may unfold over the course of a few weeks:

1. **Position yourself several yards away from the player, and throw the ball several yards in either direction.**

   This drill forces the youngster to react quickly and make a play on the ball. Don't make the throws too challenging at first; you want to instill confidence in the youngster before progressing to more challenging throws.

2. **Gradually put the throws a little farther out of her range so that she has to take several steps to catch them.**

   Getting the player to move a little out of her comfort range starts the process of building on her existing skills.

3. **When she starts to catch more balls than she misses, increase the challenge by having her jog in a set direction while you send passes her way.**

4. **When the youngster is again catching the majority of your passes, have her sprint down the field and attempt to catch your passes on the run.**

When working with youngsters on new skills, be patient. Build their confidence in performing a fundamental skill; then slowly add more complex components one at a time. In most cases, you're not going to see huge improvements during the span of a one-hour practice. Over several sessions, though, you'll see positive strides, and you'll be sending more-complete players onto the field on game day.

Exploring different approaches for reaching goals

You can help kids reach their goals in many ways; you just have to find what works best for each player. Some kids require more motivation than others. Some need more feedback and interaction from you. Others require an entirely different approach.

During your practices, pay close attention to the looks on the kids' faces and the way they move on the field. Do the players look excited to participate, and are they moving enthusiastically through the drills? Or is their face all wrinkled up in frustration, and are they lacking spring in their steps? If you're not seeing the reactions you hope for, take a closer look at your drills. Perhaps the drills are too difficult or aren't tailored to the skills you want to focus on. Figure out ways to inject more fun into the drills.

Evaluating the tempo of your practices is important, too. Fast-moving practices that feature little standing-around time tend to be well received by the players, because they simply don't have a chance to be bored and relegated to spectator status.

Moving players to new positions

A lot of times, a child becomes disenchanted with lacrosse because he's not playing the position he had his heart set on when he signed up. You can imagine the heartbreak a child endures if he wanted to experience the thrill of scoring a goal but was stuck on defense at the first practice of the season and hasn't moved since. Sometimes, sliding a player into a new position is all it takes to rekindle his interest. The change of scenery on the field could do wonders for his enthusiasm, and you may just find that the change pays dividends for the team as a whole.

If you're coaching a beginning-level team, you should already be moving the kids around a bit so that they get a chance to experience as many positions as possible. If you're coaching an advanced-level team, it never hurts to tinker with your lineup, not only to keep the players fresh and challenged, but also to evaluate whether different combinations on the field give the team a more potent offense or a more difficult defense to score against.

Keeping Parents in the Game

When it comes to smart coaching moves, keeping parents in the loop all season long deserves a spot near the top of the list. (Chapter 4 covers the importance of conducting a preseason parents' meeting to open the lines of communication.) Setting aside time to talk to parents individually to find out how their child is enjoying the season so far not only shows how much you care, but also is a great way to get the scoop on the impact you're having. These one-on-one chats can be especially comforting to parents who are new to the sport of lacrosse and are unsure how to gauge how their child is performing.

Near the halfway point of the season, notify the parents that you want to set aside a few moments the following week to speak to them individually about their kids and get their input on how the season has gone so far. Making this announcement after a game works well because most youngsters have parents on hand to watch.

These discussions with parents should be brief and conducted out of the earshot of the youngster, to provide the best environment for receiving honest feedback about how the child feels. You can hold these private conversations over the phone or in person during scheduled times before or after a practice.

The following sections discuss some of the topics you want to be sure to cover with parents.

Finding out whether the kids are having fun

You see your players for abbreviated periods — sometimes just for an hour once a week for practice before a Saturday-morning game — so you'll find it hard to gauge a child's real feelings about lacrosse, the events of the season so far, and you.

Having an open, honest discussion with the parents about whether their child is having fun usually results in a candid response. The parents know whether their son can't sleep the night before a game because he's too excited — or too nervous because he's feeling pressure to play well. They know whether their daughter dreads going to practice or enjoys it so much that she wants to be the first one on the field. Whatever insight you can gain is important for evaluating the player's performance, and may help you understand the athlete better, too. Parents are your primary source for the most reliable information, so tap into that source to get a true sense of how the season is going.

Be prepared for honest answers. Even though you may be doing a wonderful coaching job, a child may be having a miserable experience. What some parents divulge to you may sting, but you'd rather have honest feedback and an open conversation than hear that everything is great when it really isn't. If a child isn't enjoying the season, you owe it to him to explore every possible way to reignite his interest and restore the fun.

Whenever you find out about any problems that a child is wrestling with, act quickly to correct them. It isn't fair to the player to allow problems — no matter how big or small — to linger for another couple of practices or games after you become aware of the situation. Maybe her parents can provide a solution for you, or perhaps having a chat with the youngster can tell you everything you need to know to make her situation better.

Addressing other common problems

Following are a few suggestions for addressing common problems:

- ✔ **Doesn't feel connected to the team:** Maybe the youngster got separated from all his buddies when the league formed the teams. Have the kids do their prepractice stretches with partners so they bond with other players.

- ✔ **Too much contact:** Lacrosse can be a rough sport. Some youngsters are going to grow tired of getting knocked around. If so, you can't do much but perhaps suggest another sport that may better suit the child.

- ✔ **Haunted by old mistake:** Embarrassing incidents happen. A child may completely misplay a ball or trip over her own feet while running. Sometimes, the less attention you give it, the less likely she may be to worry about it.

Chapter 14

Taking Your Drills to the Next Level

As your season moves along, you'll encounter more twists and turns than an amusement-park roller coaster, but we're confident that you're up to the task of handling everything that comes your way. One of the most common challenges that youth lacrosse coaches face — and must be prepared for — is adjusting to players' new and improved skills from week to week.

To keep the learning and good times going strong, you must introduce drills that grab kids' attention, get them excited about lacrosse, and give them plenty of chances to develop a variety of offensive and defensive skills. If you turn to the same drills every time you get together with your team, your practices will flop, and the fun will quickly drain out of the season.

In this chapter, we give you all sorts of original drills that you can use to meet your players' needs and propel them to improved levels of play.

Upgrading the Offense

Opponents use a lot of defensive techniques and strategies in an effort to stop your offense from doing what it wants to do: put the ball in the net. Teams that are well versed in all offensive areas of the game, from cradling and passing to catching and shooting, will enjoy playing lacrosse more and will derive more satisfaction from their experience — especially when they see their efforts pay off with quality scoring chances and goals.

This section provides drills you can use to help raise your players' offensive skill level. Many of these drills feature both an offensive and defensive component, so all players will benefit regardless of their roles.

Although the drills in this section focus on the offensive element, be sure to keep a close eye on how players handle their defensive responsibilities, too. You don't want players to develop bad habits or use poor techniques, regardless of the skill you are concentrating on.

Cradling

Whether a youngster is a defender, midfielder, or attacker, being able to move with the ball while going at top speed and making cuts is important for enjoying lacrosse and playing it well. The cradling drills in this section help players master one of the most basic skills of the game.

Dip and Dodge

Sometimes, it's fun to incorporate parents into your drills just to give your practices a different look and feel. This drill is a good one to use for this purpose; it doesn't require much effort on the parents' part, and your players will get a kick out of running through it.

What you need: Approximately ten parents and one ball for each player.

How it works: Position the parents in a line down the length of the field, spacing them 10 yards apart. The players line up at one end of the field, each player with a ball in her stick.

1. **On your command, the first player runs toward the first parent.**

2. **As the player approaches, the parent lifts one arm to waist level.**

3. **The player cuts around the parent quickly, in the opposite direction of the raised arm, and continues at full speed toward the next parent.**

4. **Again, the player moves in the direction opposite whichever arm the next parent opts to raise.**

Coaching pointers: You don't want the kids standing around waiting to run through this drill, so make sure that you keep it moving. When a player reaches the second parent, get the next youngster in line moving. You can easily have several players maneuvering through the line of parents at the same time. Or if you have enough parent volunteers, you can set up two courses, split the kids into two groups, and run both drills at the same time.

You can add a competitive element for older players by timing them to see which one can negotiate the course fastest.

Ground-Ball Scoops

Loose balls on the field represent golden opportunities for your team to go on the offensive — if they're able to scoop up the balls quickly while on the move. This drill helps develop that skill so that your opponents don't claim all the loose balls on game day.

What you need: Two players and a bucket of balls.

How it works: Position one player about 15 yards away, facing you. The other player stands a couple of yards away from you, facing the other player.

1. **Roll a ball to the first player's left or right.**
2. **The player moves toward the ball, scoops it up, and delivers a pass to the player standing next to you.**
3. **As soon as the first player releases the pass, roll another ball that he must scoop up and pass to his teammate.**

Coaching pointers: Be sure to mix up the ways you roll balls to the youngster to scoop up. Besides rolling balls to his left and right, mix in some that force him to charge forward, and put some over his head so that he has to turn and chase them. Players need to execute all these moves during games when a ball is loose on the field.

The older the players are, the more challenging you can make this drill by rolling the balls faster or farther.

Passing and catching

Opponents hate facing teams that can pass and catch the ball well. If your players are good at moving the ball around and down the field, without turning it over by making sloppy or inaccurate passes, they get more chances to put shots on goal. The following drills help mold your players' passing and catching skills.

Face 'Em Fours

When your players are adept at making and receiving passes, they generate more offensive scoring power. This drill enhances hand–eye coordination — a valuable asset in passing and catching the ball.

What you need: Five players and two balls.

How it works: Position four players in a line, spacing them 5 yards apart. Another player stands 10 yards away, facing the foursome, with two balls at her feet.

1. **The single player scoops up the first ball and passes it to one of the other four players.**

2. **As soon as she releases the ball, she scoops up the second ball.**

3. **While the passer is delivering the second ball to another player, the youngster who caught the first ball sends it back to the passer.**

4. **The drill continues with the players trying to keep both balls going at the same time.**

Coaching pointers: This drill puts a real premium on the individual player's ability to catch and release the ball quickly. Make sure she's keeping her stick in the proper position to receive passes. If she allows her stick to drop too low, she wastes valuable time raising it to catch the passes. You want her catching the ball, controlling it, and passing it to a teammate as quickly as possible. Remember, the faster your team can make passes, the more likely it is to keep the opposing team off balance.

Rotate the kids so that they all get a chance to be in different positions in the line, as well as be the designated passer.

3-on-2

Drills that simulate game conditions not only build skills, but also give kids some of that always-valuable confidence. When they encounter similar situations on game day, they can carry over from the practice field the way they executed the skill and enjoy similar success. This drill helps players become proficient in attacking an outnumbered opponent and also bolsters their defensive skills.

What you need: Five players, one goalie, and one ball.

How it works: The goalie takes his position in front of the net. The three offensive players begin about 25 yards from the net; the two defensive players face them, about 15 yards away. On your command, the offensive group attempts to maneuver the ball and score a goal.

Coaching pointers: One of the keys to turning 3-on-2 advantages into goals is to keep constant pressure on the defense. Any time a defense is outnumbered, the more you force it to move and the more field you force it to cover, the more chances you have to put shots in the net. You want the player with the ball driving toward the net, which forces a defender to move to cover him. If no one slides over, he's in good position to shoot; if a defender does cover him, one of his two teammates will be open to receive a pass.

You can turn this drill into a competitive game by awarding 1 point to the offense for each goal scored and 2 points to the defense for a stop. See which unit can reach 10 points first. You can keep the drill moving by allowing only 20 seconds for the offense to get off a shot.

Shooting

Shooting drills are the best part of practice for most of your players, so you want to make sure that the drills are entertaining enough to match the players' enthusiasm about this part of the game. The drills in this section qualify, if we do say so ourselves.

Beat 'Em

The most effective offensive players can deliver accurate shots on goal while being harassed by defenders. This drill helps players become more comfortable releasing shots while being pestered by an opponent.

What you need: Three players, one goalie, and one ball.

How it works: The goalie takes her position in the net. The player who will serve as the passer stands 20 yards from the goal, with a ball in her stick. The player to whom she will pass begins 15 yards from her and 10 yards farther back (see Figure 14-1). A defensive player stands even with the passer, also 15 yards away.

1. **On your command, the offensive player runs toward the defender, cuts around her, and receives the ball from the passer.**

2. **As soon as the ball carrier maneuvers past the defender, the defender turns and pursues her.**

3. **The ball carrier attempts to move in on the goalie and get off a shot, while the defender tries to make the shot more difficult by sticking with the attacker and not allowing a clear opening to shoot at.**

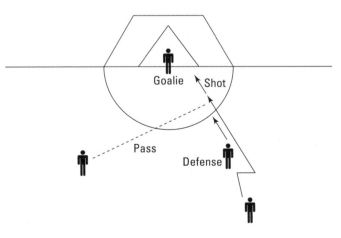

Figure 14-1:
The Beat 'Em drill helps players learn to deal with pesky defenders.

Coaching pointers: This drill encompasses several skills, including making an accurate pass to the cutting attacker. If the pass is off target even just a little bit and forces the intended recipient to slow down or reach back to make the catch, the defender has a chance to recover and can defend more easily. Encourage the defender to hustle at all times, because she doesn't know whether the pass will be on target.

When the offensive player is moving in on the goal, you want him focusing on the net, not looking over his shoulder at the defender or checking his stick to view the ball.

Long-Range Targets

Even though you'd like to think that every time down the field, your team will generate a shot in close on the goalie, that isn't going to happen. So your players must also be able to execute long shots, which can pose problems for goalies when they're made correctly. This drill helps players upgrade this area of their game.

What you need: Three players, one goalie, and one ball.

How it works: The goalie takes his position in the net. Two offensive players begin about 20 yards from the goal, with 15 yards between them (see Figure 14-2). One player cradles the ball in his stick. The lone defender stands 5 yards from the player who doesn't have possession of the ball.

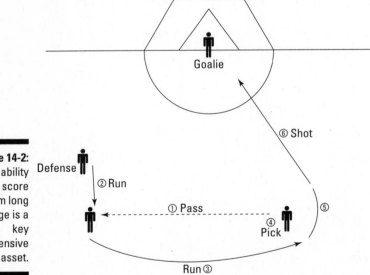

Figure 14-2:
The ability to score from long range is a key offensive asset.

1. The player who has the ball passes it to his teammate (1).

2. After the teammate catches the ball, the defender closes in on him (2).

3. The ball carrier cradles the ball and runs toward his teammate (3), who sets a pick on the defender (4).

4. As the ball carrier circles around his teammate (5), if the pick has been successful, he uses the opening to fire a shot on goal (6).

5. If the defender manages to stay with the player, and a shot isn't available, he passes the ball back to his teammate, who takes a shot on net.

Coaching pointers: After the offensive player has set the pick, if the defender has stayed with the ball carrier, you can allow the attacker to use one-on-one moves to get in a little closer for a shot. Tweaking the drill this way also makes it more challenging for the defender and allows the offensive player to work on his long-range shooting skills, as well as other important offensive techniques.

Facing off

Every time a goal is scored (ideally, by your team!), a face-off occurs. After putting the ball in the net, your team can keep the momentum going by gaining control of the face-off and attacking again. Or if your team has just surrendered a goal, getting possession of the ball and mounting an attack can help keep the opponent from dominating the game. Read on for some face-off drills that can help your players become more effective in this area of the game.

Play Starter

A successful face-off requires teammates to work together. If your players are good at reading and reacting to a face-off, they're more likely to win possession of the ball and go on offense rather than defense. This drill helps your team control those valuable face-offs.

What you need: Six players, two pylons, and one ball.

How it works: Split the six players into two teams of three players. Set a pylon 20 yards behind each face-off player.

The midfielders for both groups take their positions, with the center midfielders in the face-off circle (see Figure 14-3).The midfielder to the face-off player's right provides defensive support by positioning herself along the wing area line on her team's defensive side of the field. The midfielder to the face-off player's left takes a position that relates to where she thinks the ball will be directed.

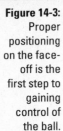
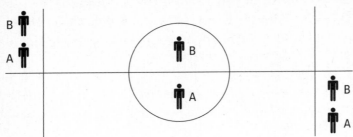

Figure 14-3:
Proper positioning on the face-off is the first step to gaining control of the ball.

1. **On your command, both face-off players vie to control the ball or direct it to a teammate.**

2. **When a team has control of the ball, it attempts to move the ball toward the pylon.**

   A team scores 1 point when a player who is cradling the ball touches the pylon.

3. **The first team to score 5 points wins the drill.**

Coaching pointers: Communication is key for executing face-offs, so give the groups a few seconds to strategize on the type of play they want to work on to gain control of the ball. Having the pylons in play forces the players to think about playing defense, too, because they can't go after the ball without being concerned about what will happen if they overcommit and don't come up with the ball.

Be sure to rotate the kids on each face-off so that they gain experience taking face-offs as well as reacting to them.

King of the Hill

At advanced levels of play, identifying your best face-off players is important, because the more times your team can gain possession of the ball from face-offs, the better their chances of being successful on offense. This drill helps shed light on who your best face-off players are and provides practice for the kids in several other elements of lacrosse.

What you need: Four players, one goalie, and one ball.

How it works: The goalie takes his position in front of the net. Two players stand at midfield for the face-off; the two remaining players stand on each side of the face-off.

1. **On your command, the two face-off players vie for possession of the ball.**

2. **As soon as one face-off player secures possession, the other two players join him on offense.**

3. **The other face-off player takes a defensive role and tries to prevent a goal from being scored as the threesome moves the ball down the field to attack.**

Coaching pointers: Pay close attention to which players are winning most of the face-offs, because at advanced levels of play, these players are the ones you want taking face-offs on game day.

Make sure that the kids are using a variety of face-off techniques. Often, a player will stick with the technique that he's good at, which is counterproductive; your practice sessions should work on those techniques that players aren't as skilled at performing.

Dialing Up the Defense

If you want to spice up your practices and give your players some challenging drills to test their defensive mettle, this section suits your needs. The assortment of drills here can push players who have a good understanding of basic defensive skills to the next level — and beyond. By implementing these drills or tweaking them to fit your team's needs, you'll keep your practices fresh, fun, and productive.

Defending one-on-one

Good defensive play — the kind that smothers opponents and gives them little room to operate — requires each player to handle her own responsibilities when her team doesn't have possession of the ball. The following drills help players raise their defensive level of play.

Defensive Denial

When you are looking to rev up your defensive tenacity, turn to this drill. It features both individual and team defensive components, so players get work facing an opponent's one-on-one moves while teaming up with a partner to shut down an attacker.

What you need: Four players, one goalie, and one ball.

How it works: One player stands at midfield; another player stands 10 yards away from him, with a ball next to him. The other two players stand back in the vicinity of the goal (see Figure 14-4).

1. **The player next to the ball scoops it up and delivers a pass to the player at midfield (1).**

2. **When the player at midfield catches the ball (2), the passer assumes a defensive role.**

3. **The player with the ball attempts to maneuver past the defender (3).**

   When the ball carrier reaches the restraining line, the defender is out of the drill.

4. **The ball carrier continues toward the net and works to get off a shot on goal (4) while being defended by the other two players.**

Coaching pointers: Watch to make sure that the ball carrier is using the proper techniques for protecting the ball so that he doesn't surrender it during any phase of this drill. When the drill becomes the attacker against the two defenders, you want the defenders to communicate on their coverage. If the attacker gets off a quality shot, be sure to address with your defensive players the breakdown that occurred and what they need to do to correct it. (For tips on providing feedback that players will embrace without having their confidence shaken, check out Chapter 6.)

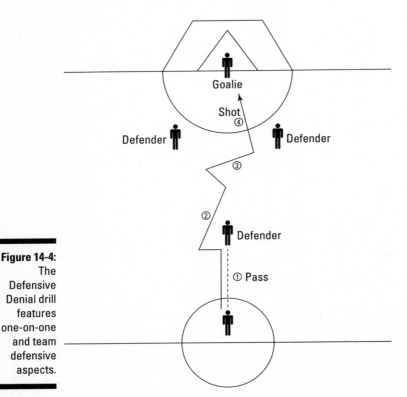

Figure 14-4:
The Defensive Denial drill features one-on-one and team defensive aspects.

Be sure to switch the players around so that all of them get a chance to be the single attacker, as well as to play one-on-one defense and to work with a defensive partner.

Chase and Cover

The ability to react quickly to passes and cover defenders leads to good defense and fewer breakdowns against an attack. This drill helps players learn to make these types of adjustments quickly.

What you need: Four players and one ball.

How it works: Designate three players as passers and one player as a defender. The object of the drill is for the three players to keep the ball away from the defender. Run the drill in two-minute segments, and see how many times the defender is able to gain control of the ball.

Coaching pointers: Be sure to limit the playing area; that way, the offensive players can't simply spread out so far apart that the defender has no chance to cover all the territory. To mix the drill up a bit, you can add another defender to the mix.

One of the great aspects of this drill is that you can run it in different sections all over the field with different groups of players. As always, remember to rotate the kids so that all of them get the chance to be a defender as well as a passer.

Dueling Sticks

Good team defense is vital for keeping the ball out of your net whenever the opponent is attacking, especially when the attack originates from behind your net. This drill works on defending attacks that begin back there.

What you need: Three players and one goalie. A ball.

How it works: One attacking player begins behind the net, with the ball in her stick. The other offensive player starts in front of the net about 10 yards from the goalie, who is in her normal position in front of the net. The defensive player takes a position between the two offensive players. On your command, the two offensive players try to work the ball into position to score, while the defender and the goalie attempt to deny a shot from in close.

Coaching pointers: The defender is at a distinct disadvantage simply because she is outnumbered, which makes this drill challenging. Don't allow the defender to become frustrated; keep encouraging her to work hard, because the more she hustles, the better chance she has of denying a goal.

If you find that the drill is too hard for the majority of the kids, add another defender to even things up.

Manning the net

Stopping fast-paced shots from all angles is a real challenge for goalies at all levels. Run your goalies through the following drills to help them become better at stopping the different types of shots that will be fired their way during games.

Angle Action

During games, goalies face a barrage of shots from many angles, and they often have the added challenge of simply trying to locate the ball while their vision is partially blocked by screeners or other traffic in front of the net. This drill helps goalies become accustomed to dealing with those annoying screens.

What you need: Three players, one goalie, and a bucket of balls.

How it works: Two players set up to the right and left of the goalie, about 15 yards away from the net. A third player sets up in front of the crease area with a bucket of balls (see Figure 14-5).

1. **The player in front of the crease scoops up a ball, fires a pass to one of the two players (1), and slides over a couple of steps so that he is standing between the goalie and the shooter (2).**

2. **The player who caught the pass takes a shot on goal (3).**

3. **Based on the location of the shot, the screener moves to his left or right, or jumps up in the air, to avoid being hit by the ball.**

4. **The goalie must locate the shot and stop it.**

Coaching pointers: One of the keys to dealing with screens is for the goalie to maintain good positioning. You want him to maintain proper footwork and learn to lean to his left or right to see around the screen. When he begins moving his entire body to look around a screen, he takes himself out of position — a mistake that good offensive teams capitalize on quickly.

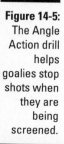

Figure 14-5:
The Angle Action drill helps goalies stop shots when they are being screened.

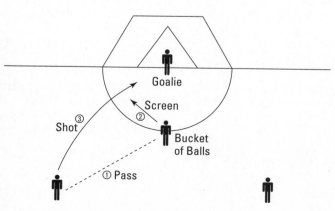

Rebound Bonanza

Loose balls around the front of the net can present problems for defenses, especially if their opponents manage to scoop up the balls first. This drill helps goalies deal with rebounds so that opponents don't have the luxury of taking several shots on goal during a possession.

What you need: Two players, one goalie, and a bucket of balls.

How it works: A player takes a position behind the net, with a bucket of balls. Another player sets up about 15 yards from the goal. The goalie assumes her normal position in the net.

1. **The player behind the net delivers a pass to the player out in front, who catches the ball and takes a shot on net.**

2. **As soon as the first ball goes into the net or is stopped by the goalie, the player behind the net rolls another ball out in front of the net.**

3. **The goalie and shooter go after the ball just as they would for a rebound during a game.**

4. **If the shooter scoops up the ball, she attacks again and tries to score a goal.**

   or

   If the goalie secures the ball, the drill ends momentarily until both players return to the starting position to run through it again.

Coaching pointers: Run this drill at a fast pace to match the intensity of an action-packed game. Be sure to mix up the direction of the rebounds, as well as the distance, so that goalies get a chance to practice going after and getting their hands on all different types of rebounds.

Corner to Corner

Goalies without good reflexes are likely to be about as effective in their jobs as chefs without skillets. This high-intensity drill helps sharpen a key skill.

What you need: Two players, one goalie, and two buckets of balls.

How it works: Position one player behind the net with a bucket of balls and the other player about 10 yards in front of the goalie with another bucket of balls. The goalie assumes his normal position in the net.

1. **The player behind the net passes a ball out to the player in front.**

2. **The player in front catches the ball and moves in on the goalie to take a shot from in close.**

3. **As soon as the shot is released, the player behind the net scoops up a ball and circles around the net from either the left or right to take a shot.**

4. **While this player is on the attack, the player out in front returns to his bucket and scoops up another ball.**

5. **After the player who began behind the net takes a shot, he returns to his starting position to scoop up another ball, and the player out in front launches a shot.**

6. **The drill continues with the same sequence of shots.**

Coaching pointers: Because the goalie faces a barrage of shots during this drill, monitor his footwork closely. Whenever a lot of shots are fired in succession, young goalies tend to get their feet crossed or neglect some of the basic fundamentals. The attackers hold the clear advantage in one-on-one settings, so be sure to applaud your goalie's effort, and make a big deal out of any saves that he makes. Also, encourage the attackers to use a variety of shots, including those that bounce short of the goalie.

You want to build up not only your goalie's skills, but also his confidence. The more confident a goalie is in his skills, the more success he'll have on game day turning away shots.

Putting It All Together: Sample Practice Sessions

One of the first steps to being a successful lacrosse coach is having an array of drills that target different areas of the game and using those drills to enhance players' skills, as well as their understanding and enjoyment of the sport. The drills we introduce in this chapter fill that bill, and you can tweak many of them to suit your team's needs. You can make them more challenging or even scale back the difficulty level a notch or two.

In the following sections, we provide a couple of different practice plans.

Beginner practices

This one-hour sample practice includes a mixture of the introductory drills presented in Chapter 7 and some of those featured in this chapter:

✔ **5 minutes:** Have the kids go through a warm-up and stretching routine. This routine is especially important for older or more-advanced players, who are more likely to be injured when their muscles aren't loosened up properly.

✔ **10 minutes:** Use the Dip and Dodge drill to get the practice off to a fun-filled start, with players working on their cradling skills while weaving around Moms and Dads on the field.

✔ **10 minutes:** Split the team in half. At one end of the field, run the Partner Passes drill (Chapter 7) as a refresher on the fundamentals of passing and catching the ball. At the opposite end of the field, go with the Target Shots drill (Chapter 7). After 5 minutes, rotate the players so that all of them have a chance to participate in both drills.

✔ **15 minutes:** After the refresher on passing and catching the ball with the Partner Passes drill, the 3-on-2 drill gives them the chance to use those passing and shooting skills in a more-competitive setting with defenders challenging them. While this drill is going on at one end of the field, you can have the King of the Hill drill running at the other end of the field so that players can work on their face-off techniques. Be sure to rotate the kids so that all of them get practice in both drills.

✔ **5 minutes:** Use the Ball Chase drill (Chapter 7) to refresh the kids on the proper techniques for scooping up loose balls.

✔ **10 minutes:** Play Starter is a perfect drill to follow up with, as players can transfer the skills they just worked on to this drill. You can run Play Starter in different parts of the field so no one is forced to stand around.

✔ **5 minutes:** Conduct a cool-down session with some light stretching. While the kids are going through these stretches, pump them up by telling them how proud you are of their efforts. They'll leave the field feeling good about themselves and will be eager to return for the next practice or game.

Include in your practices a few basic drills that you can turn to frequently to help ingrain the fundamental techniques of lacrosse.

Don't conduct practices in which every drill you run is new to the players. You'll waste too much time explaining how all the drills work, which cuts into the amount of time kids have to run around on the field working on their skills. Introducing a few new drills at each practice is all right, but make sure that you keep the explanations brief; otherwise, the players' energy and productivity will fizzle.

Intermediate practices

Here is another 1-hour practice, based on the drills covered in this chapter:

- ✔ **5 minutes:** Use your standard warm-up and stretching program to prepare the kids' bodies for practice.

- ✔ **5 minutes:** Use the Ground-Ball Scoops drill to work the kids into the rhythm of practice while focusing on a basic skill.

- ✔ **10 minutes:** Break the team into groups of five for the Face 'Em Fours drill to work on their passing and catching skills.

- ✔ **10 minutes:** The Chase and Cover drill fits nicely into the practice schedule here, because it builds on the preceding drill by adding a defensive component to the passing and catching.

- ✔ **15 minutes:** Split the team in half, with the group at one end of the field running through the Long-Range Targets drill and the other group working on the Defensive Denial drill at the opposite end of the field. The Defensive Denial drill can be run without a goalie, so if you have only one goalie, who is involved with Long-Range Targets, this drill is perfect to run at the same time.

- ✔ **10 minutes:** Break the team in half, and run the Rebound Bonanza drill at one end of the field and the 3-on-2 drill at the other end. Again, if you have only one goalie, the 3-on-2 drill can be run without a goalie.

- ✔ **5 minutes:** End practice with a brief cool-down routine. Remind the kids of any changes in the schedule that they need to be aware of, and thank them for paying attention and doing their best throughout the session.

Chapter 15

Stepping Up the Offense

In This Chapter
▶ Upgrading the offensive skills
▶ Creating quality scoring chances

Weaving around defenders, connecting on long passes with teammates, and scoring goals rank as some of the most significant parts of attacking in lacrosse — and as some of the most popular with kids, too. But many other advanced elements define how effective a team is when it has possession of the ball, and these can also be a lot of fun for the kids to perform. As your players gain more skills in these other areas, they'll get more enjoyment from playing lacrosse, and you'll create a more potent offense.

Here, we go on the offensive, detailing how you can upgrade your team's play by running fast breaks and capitalizing when you have a player advantage. We also present useful information on using picks to create openings and on the best approaches for attacking from behind the net. Read on to rev up your offensive attack and keep those opposing defenses off balance.

Changing Offensive Approaches

As your players gain valuable game-day experience, they become more proficient at moving the ball down the field, attacking opponents, and (we hope) scoring lots of goals. As they progress on the offensive end, of course, many of the teams they go up against will also make great strides defensively. Being able to call on different moves and modes of attack to help generate scoring opportunities for the team is a real asset in the goal-production department, and for keeping pace with the improved play of opposing defenses. Here, we discuss some advanced offensive techniques to help your team create chances to put the ball in the opponent's net on a regular basis.

When you're introducing offensive sets, strategies, and plays, the simpler, the better. You're much better off focusing on a few plays and helping the kids become proficient in those rather than overwhelming them with too much information. If you pile on the plays too quickly, your team won't be completely comfortable — or efficient — at executing any of them.

Running the fast break

Fast breaks are some of the most exciting and action-packed plays in lacrosse — especially when your team is running them instead of defending them! They can materialize at any time during a game, so if your players are good at recognizing and taking advantage of them, they have more potential to develop good scoring opportunities.

The four-on-three is one of the most common fast breaks, and it often poses the most problems for defenses because they have a lot of territory to cover and only three players to defend it. Whenever an opportunity for this fast break occurs, one of the keys is for the three attackers to race down the field, keeping their eyes on the ball and setting up in the defensive zone in a square formation with the ball carrier, who often is a midfielder (see Figure 15-1).

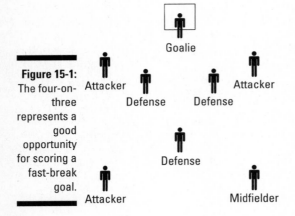

Figure 15-1: The four-on-three represents a good opportunity for scoring a fast-break goal.

Goalie

Attacker   Defense   Defense   Attacker

Defense

Attacker   Midfielder

The ball carrier's first responsibility is to attack the goal area so that defenders are forced to converge on him. If they don't, he'll be in position to take a shot on net, and if they do, he should look to pass the ball to a teammate. Ideally, if one of the two attackers nearest the net is open after cutting toward the goal, he should deliver a pass to those teammates. Here are a few other coaching points to keep in mind in orchestrating fast breaks that produce coveted goals:

✔ **Constant hustle:** Teams that hustle nonstop throughout the game generate more fast breaks than those that don't. Never hesitate to emphasize this fact to your players.

✔ **Quick movement:** The quicker your team passes the ball, the more challenging defense becomes. When offensive players stand still, or the ball carrier slows down or doesn't keep her feet moving, the defense gets valuable time to regroup and set up. When defenses are forced to react constantly to attacks and passes, they run a greater chance of a breakdown that results in a good scoring opportunity for the offense.

✓ **Constant cutting:** Players who use cuts and spin moves to get open will reap the benefits of their hard work by receiving passes and getting chances to take shots on goal.

✓ **Moving to open spaces:** It does little good for a player to cut into an area where a teammate already is (unless he's heading there to set a pick), because that move makes it easier for the defenders to cover both players. Cutting into an open space puts pressure on the defenders to stick with him because he doesn't have support nearby.

Any time your team can push the ball into the attack-goal area outnumbering the opposition, chances are good that a quality scoring chance will develop.

Reading the defense

The better your players are at recognizing what type of defense is being played against them, the greater their chances of depositing the ball in the net. Most teams rely on player-to-player defense. At the more-advanced levels of play, teams resort to zone defenses a little more often. And some teams interchange the two types throughout a game in an effort to keep the opponent off balance. Instilling in your players the confidence that they can conquer any type of defense paves the way to success and fun on game day, and prepares them for their future in lacrosse.

Player-to-player defense

In *player-to-player defense,* each defender is responsible for covering a specific offensive player. (Check out Chapter 12 for more details on this type of defense.) Following are some points about confronting this defense to share with your team:

✓ **Use good attackers.** If you have good attackers who are excellent at dodging and passing, you can create scoring opportunities for your team against the player-to-player defense. (*Dodging* refers to a player maneuvering the ball past a defender to weaken the defense and create an open shot for herself or a teammate. For more on the terms of the game, flip to Chapter 3.)

As soon as the ball handler gets by her defender, other defenders are forced to adjust to account for the unguarded player; if they don't, she has an open shot. If another defender does slide over to offer support, the ball handler can pass to her teammate whom the other defender left unguarded.

> ✔ **Capitalize on weak defenders.** When you recognize that one of the opponent's defenders isn't as quick as some of your attackers, you want the ball in that offensive player's stick so that he can attack and create scoring opportunities for himself or carve out openings for his teammates.

Zone defenses

In a *zone defense,* defensive players are responsible for covering specific areas of the field, based on the location of the ball. This type of defense is used most often when a team is down a player due to a penalty. (For more on penalties, check out Chapter 3.) Keep these coaching tips in mind when going against zones:

> ✔ **Keep good spacing.** Although this offensive concept is an important one to adhere to throughout the game, it's especially key for dealing with zones. The closer together your players are, the easier they are for opponents in a zone to defend. Spread out your players so that the defense has to worry about covering more of the field. The more field area a defense has to cover, the greater the chances that lapses and breakdowns will occur.
>
> ✔ **Use passes across the field.** Passes that go from one side of the field to the other can weaken a zone that is overcommitted to one side of the field.

Using ball movement to your advantage

You can have a roster full of players who are fast and strong, and who deliver on-the-mark passes, but if they don't keep that ball moving when they're on the attack, their offensive productivity will nose-dive. If your players move the ball around a lot, the defense will encounter challenges stopping them.

If your attackers can't maneuver past defenders (see Chapter 11 for techniques for eluding opposing players), you need to rely on other methods to get the job done, such as setting picks (check out "Using picks to create openings," later in this chapter) and passing (see Chapter 9).

During your practice drills or scrimmages, require the unit with the ball to have each player possess it before anyone takes a shot. This requirement puts a premium on passing skills. Also, the kids will be more likely to make quick passes and get that ball moving around, because the sooner everyone gets their stick on the ball, the faster they can fire a shot at the net.

Operating with the player advantage

Whenever your opponent commits a penalty and must play a player short, you want to capitalize, because this gives you a great opportunity to take a high-percentage shot and put a goal on the scoreboard. To help your team register goals while operating with a player advantage, keep these tactics in mind:

- ✔ **Use ball reversal.** You don't want players to get into the habit of simply making passes to the nearest teammate. Have them reverse the ball across the field, too. Sure, long passes are tougher to make, but with practice, your team will become more efficient at making and catching these passes, which in turn will produce a more potent offensive attack.

- ✔ **Be patient.** Patience is a virtue, and that goes for executing your extra-player offense, too. Players don't need to be firing shots just a few seconds into the advantage — unless, of course, they have a great scoring opportunity. Talk to them about being patient and working the ball around the field to produce a quality scoring chance.

- ✔ **Practice plays.** During your practices, work on a couple of plays that your team can call upon when these extra-player situations arise. Knowing these plays will give them confidence that in a game situation, they can execute the plays and score goals against the defense.

 When you introduce a play during practice, first run it without any defenders to give the kids a chance to see how the play is supposed to unfold and where they need to be positioned during its execution. It also helps them become comfortable with their roles before going against defenders.

 You never want players to pass up good open shots just for the sake of running through a set play to its entirety. If the play calls for a specific player to deliver a pass, but she's not being covered and can move toward the net to take an undefended shot, you want her to do so. As players gain experience, they'll learn when they can exploit openings to the advantage of their team.

Generating Scoring Opportunities

Players who have the offensive basics of the game down reasonably well — such as cradling, passing, catching, and shooting — are ready to move to the next level. Helping them get there is up to you. Players who have an array of offensive skills to draw on get more satisfaction out of the game, and they'll probably be more effective on the field. Next, we look at several techniques that will bolster your team's attack and lead to more scoring opportunities.

Using picks to create openings

One of the most effective techniques available for freeing up a teammate from the defender covering him is a pick. Sometimes players are unable to dodge a defender on their own, so a pick can be a helpful alternative.

A *pick* is an offensive maneuver in which one player attempts to block the path of a defender guarding another offensive player, just like what is done in basketball to free a player up from his defender so he can take an open shot. Picks are used in both boys' and girls' lacrosse. When a pick is set, it takes the defender out of good defensive position and often leads to a good scoring chance. Work with your players on the following techniques so that picks can comprise a slice of your offensive attack:

1. **The player setting the pick moves toward the defender she intends to set a pick against, stopping about a foot away from that player.**

2. **She plants her feet slightly beyond shoulder width apart and maintains a firm stance.**

3. **She holds her stick in tight to her body, in a vertical position.**

4. **The player whose defender is being picked runs toward the pick.**

Work with the player to brush shoulders with her teammate who's setting the pick to force the defender to step around the pick to avoid making contact with that player. When executed properly this usually allows the teammate to gain at least a step advantage over the defender.

Due to breakdowns in defensive coverage, the player who set the pick is often open to receive a pass. After executing the pick, she must turn quickly so that she's ready to receive a pass and attack the goal before the opponent has a chance to recover and scramble back into position.

Attacking from behind the net

One of the best signs of a good offense — besides keeping the scoreboard operating busy on game day punching up goals! — is being able to attack from all over the field. When your team is capable of executing different plays from different spots on the field, it keeps the other team off balance, because the opponents can't zero in on stopping anything in particular.

Setting up an attacker behind the opponent's net is one way to go about scoring goals. Following is one type of play your team can run from this position to keep the goalie guessing and create some scoring opportunities:

1. **When your team has the ball behind the opponent's net, two teammates prepare a pick above the crease area.**

   The two players begin the play out in front of the crease, several yards away from each other (see Figure 15-2).

2. **The player on the right runs across the top of the crease area and sets a pick on the defender covering his teammate (see Figure 15-3).**

3. **The player whose defender is picked circles around his teammate with his stick up to receive a pass from his teammate behind the net.**

4. **He quickly unloads a shot on net before the defense has a chance to react to the pick and deny the scoring opportunity.**

Incorporating different plays into your attack keeps the game fresh and fun for the kids, because they won't have to be robotic in their execution.

Figure 15-2:
The setup for running a pick play in front of the opponent's net.

Figure 15-3:
A player
sets a pick
for his
teammate to
circle
around and
receive a
pass.

Entering the attack-goal area

Ball possession is as important to your team as a parachute is to a skydiver.
Every time your players have their sticks on the ball and have moved it down
the field, you want them to be able to make the most of their opportunities.
Whenever your team moves into goal-scoring territory (which we hope will
be often!), keep the following coaching points in mind:

- ✔ **Don't be predictable.** You don't want your players doing the same thing
  every time. A predictable offensive attack makes the defense's job easy,
  because the opponents have a good idea what you plan to do. The more
  you keep the defense off balance, the more goals you're likely to score.

- ✔ **Hone some set plays.** To break down the opposition, rely on a few set plays
  that the kids have become proficient at executing. You want to use the
  plays that your kids are comfortable running — and have the confidence
  to execute — during the opening minute of a game *or* the final seconds
  of a contest in which they are trailing by a goal.

✔ **Use all the players.** Don't rely on only one or two players to take all the shots or to break down the defense with their dodges. When designing plays, make sure that you create a variety so that all your players — not just the most talented ones — have the chance to be the focal point. Besides making all your kids feel like real parts of the team, this tactic is a good strategic move, ensuring that the defense can't focus on stopping one particular player.

✔ **Use screens.** You can't expect to score all your goals from in close each time you take the field. Some goals have to come from the outside, and that's where screens are useful. Scoring long-range goals can not only be a big boost for your team, but also can demoralize the opposing goalie's confidence and shift the game's momentum to your side.

In *screening,* an offensive player positions herself near the crease to block the goalie's view of the shot, similar to what is done in hockey to prevent the goalie from getting a clear view of the incoming shot. Screening isn't the most enjoyable task on the field — after all, the player must put herself in the line of fire between the shooter and the goalie — but it can make a huge difference in offensive productivity.

The screener should position herself about a yard in front of the crease, facing the shooter, and in a direct line between the shooter's stick and the goalie. The screener holds her stick in tight against her body, and when a shot is taken, she jumps to the side (or up in the air, if the shot is low) to avoid being hit by the ball. Then she turns quickly to face the goal to scoop up any rebound or deflection that may have occurred.

Players who are capable of setting screens are just as important as those who possess strong, accurate shots. Take the time to teach this aspect of the game to your players; your offense will reap the benefits.

Fending off body checks

Getting knocked off balance and taken to the ground by an opponent's check (in boys' leagues that allow checking) isn't fun. Facing teams that have good checking skills can make executing on offense seem very difficult. Your job is to help your players learn to avoid the check — or at least fend off a lot of the force of it — so they aren't taken out of the play or don't surrender possession of the ball. Players will derive enormous satisfaction from sidestepping an oncoming defender. Defenders want to alter the attacker's path and steal the ball, so the offensive player's concern is shielding his stick to help keep the ball from getting loose. Here's a way to deal with checks:

1. **The player who's being checked turns his body sideways to protect his stick.**

2. **He moves his top hand up near the throat of his stick. This gives him more control while cradling, which is necessary with hard checks (see Figure 15-4).**

3. **Holding his stick vertically, he takes the contact from the defender and keeps his eyes on the defender, not on the ball in his stick. Holding the stick horizontally makes it easier for defenders to pry the ball loose, so the player should keep the stick vertical.**

4. **As the check is delivered, the ball carrier leans in to the defender. He keeps his feet spread about shoulder width apart, which helps him maintain his balance when contact is made.**

5. **He raises his forearm nearer the defender around chest high. This move helps absorb some of the contact.**

Figure 15-4: Maintaining balance is key when a player is being checked by a defender.

Chapter 16

Tightening the Defense

. . . .

In This Chapter

▶ Shutting down the opposition

▶ Upgrading your goalie's skills

. . . .

*O*ne really neat aspect of a lacrosse season is that no two games are the same. You constantly adapt to changing game conditions, whether in defending an explosive offensive team that scores goals with assembly-line precision or protecting a lead in the closing minutes. The one constant every time your team takes the field, though, is the important role of defense. If you're coaching advanced-level players, or a team with good defensive basics and ready for a skills upgrade, you've come to the right place. Here, we discuss playing defense while your team is down a player, protecting the crease area, and dealing with picks. We devote an entire section to goaltending —from dealing with stick fakes to igniting attacks with good clearing passes.

Playing Strong Defense under Attack

A lacrosse game often hinges on one key play or situation. A game could come down to how well your defenders protect the crease and keep the opponent away from the net in the final minute. Perhaps the game's momentum will shift when your defense keeps the opponent from scoring despite a one- or two-player advantage. Or maybe your squad will defend picks perfectly and frustrate them by denying them good scoring chances. Players who are well versed in all aspects of playing sound defense and who perform defensive skills well while they're under attack will have more success on the field and get more out of their playing experience.

Defending the goal area

What separates great defensive teams from good ones is their ability to deny offenses good scoring opportunities. Sure, good passing teams with talented players will produce their share of openings to take shots — and tally goals — but the more knowledgeable your team is about all aspects of defense, the more success it will have when the opponent sets up at your end of the field.

One of the best defensive techniques your players can use when opponents are charging toward your goal is the stick-on-stick hold, in which a defender closes in tight on an attacker. Here's how it's executed:

1. **Keeping his stick horizontal, the defender moves his hand at the top of his stick down toward his bottom hand (see Figure 16-1).**

2. **He keeps his feet wider than shoulder width apart.**

   If he moves his feet toward the attacker, he exposes himself to a spin move, which can lead to a good scoring opportunity.

3. **He presses the heel of his bottom hand against the opponent's upper arm (see Figure 16-2).**

Figure 16-1:
A defender keeps his stick horizontal to the field in the stick-on-stick hold.

Figure 16-2:
The defender uses the heel of his bottom hand to check the attacker.

Operating in the crease

Although playing strong defense is important all over the field, it's especially important around the crease area. A defensive breakdown in this area, allowing an opposing player to slip free, puts the goalie in a difficult position and often leads to surrendering a goal. Work with your players on the following pointers:

✔ **Avoiding screens:** Goalies fare better stopping the shots that they can actually see coming toward the net, so defenders must be mindful not to block their goalie's vision in the net. They also must keep opposing players from camping out in front of the crease area and blocking the goalie's line of sight.

✔ **Holding the sticks up:** Players should keep their sticks in the air while operating in the crease area. Because the crease and the surrounding area are often congested, holding their sticks vertically allows your players to move quickly and to weave between or around players more easily than if their sticks are horizontal to the field.

✔ **Keeping up the chatter:** Good communication becomes imperative in this area. Besides the goalie letting her defenders know where they need to be positioned, other players near the crease can alert teammates to picks or screens that the opposition is attempting to set.

Defending against the fast break

A big part of attacking in lacrosse involves creating situations in which the offensive players outnumber the defensive players, such as in fast breaks, which can result in some open shots on goal. One of the best indicators of a well-coached team is how it responds in challenging defensive situations so that the opponent can't use fast breaks to produce goals. Whenever the opponent has a fast-break, how the defense fares depends on key areas:

✔ **Deny the high-percentage shots.** Chances are that the opposition will be able to get off a shot; your defenders' job is to make sure that the shot isn't a high-quality one. That means forcing attackers out of the middle of the field and denying passes there, too.

✔ **Use the triangle formation.** One of the most efficient formations to use against a fast break is the triangle. This alignment features one defender about 10 yards in front of the goal (see Figure 16-3) and a defender on either side of him, back closer to the goal:

• The player out front at the top of the triangle is referred to as the *point*. His primary responsibility is to make contact with the opposing player advancing the ball toward the goal. His focus should be on checking the opponent as he approaches to prevent passes to teammates, as well as an open shot.

• The two back defenders, aligned to the right and left of the goal post and 3 to 5 yards in front of the edge of the crease, must react quickly to any passes. If the pass goes into the corner where the right defender is, for example, he slides over to provide coverage, while the defender on the opposite side of the crease shifts to the front of the net to help prevent passes to the center of the field.

Figure 16-3:
The triangle formation can be effective against an opponent's fast break.

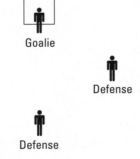

Goalie

Defense   Defense

Defense

Working with the man-down defense

When your team commits a penalty and finds itself down a player, your defense faces a difficult challenge — not only in preventing a goal, but even in stopping a quality shot from being taken. Whenever your defense is a player short, each youngster must cover a little extra territory.

Make sure you focus on this area of the game during your practices. During a scrimmage, for example, randomly sit a player out so that her teammates get a chance to work with the player advantage, as well as defend against it. (Be sure to give the players you're taking out of the scrimmage a drill to work on along the sidelines, so that they aren't forced to stand and watch.)

You can teach your team a basic 2-3 zone alignment (see Figure 16-4) to defend the field when your team finds itself a player short. In this setup, defenders are responsible for covering a specific area of the field rather than an individual player:

- ✔ The two midfielders on the perimeter use poke checks to apply pressure and make it hard for the ball carrier to pass to the middle of the field.

- ✔ The defender in the middle keeps an eye on opponents cutting toward the net to receive passes. She can't afford to stray too far from her position; otherwise, she'll leave a gap that an opponent with good attacking skills can pounce on.

- ✔ The two defenders on the outside of the middle defender cover the action around the goal posts and converge on any opponents who enter the middle area in front of the net.

Figure 16-4: The 2-3 zone alignment works well when your team is down a player.

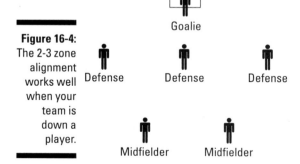

Goalie

Defense   Defense   Defense

Midfielder   Midfielder

Dealing with picks

A pick is simply an offensive player's attempt to block the path of a defender guarding another offensive player. (For more on lacrosse terms, see Chapter 3.) The first step in countering this maneuver is recognizing that it's being set up. As soon as one of your defenders or your goalie sees an opposing player moving to set up a pick, he needs to shout, "Pick!" This shout alerts the defender who is the target of the pick so that he's prepared to deal with it. The defense has two different options for negating a pick:

✔ The player who is being picked fights past the pick and stays with the player he's covering.

✔ If your defenders communicate well, you can have them use the switch. The player who's being picked simply switches his coverage to the other player (see Figure 16-5).

Figure 16-5:
The switch
is an
effective
technique
for dealing
with picks.

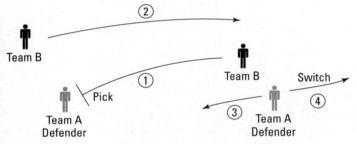

Preventing a team from clearing the ball

Because of the fast-paced nature of lacrosse, possession changes hands (actually, sticks) all over the field at any time. Teams that can make the transition from offense to defense in the blink of an eye can deny the opponent opportunities to clear the ball and formulate an attack. Attempting to prevent an opponent from clearing passes and regaining possession of the ball is known as *riding*. Teams that employ effective riding techniques can be frustrating for opponents to play against, because they make pushing the ball up the field a real challenge. The more passes your team can force the opponent to make, the greater the chance of a turnover.

When executing the riding technique, the defender approaches the opponent at an angle (see Figure 16-6). While keeping his bottom hand on his stick, he runs alongside the opponent and swings his stick up across the opponent's chest (see Figure 16-7). Be sure to keep the stick under control so as to avoid a slashing penalty. Using good body position that turns a player around is more important than risking a penalty by trying to take the ball away.

Whenever possible, your players should ride an opponent toward the sideline, which becomes a sort of extra defender as it limits movement options.

Figure 16-6:
Players
angle
toward the
attacker
when
executing
the riding
technique.

Figure 16-7:
The
defender
swings his
stick up
when riding
an
opponent.

Guarding the Goal

Playing good defense is a team effort, but much of the responsibility falls to the goalie, who puts the exclamation point on a defensive effort by stopping a shot. In this section, we discuss how your goalie can make shots more difficult to convert to goals and help your players push the ball down the field and generate scoring opportunities of their own against the opposing goalie.

Using the upper body against stick fakes

When attackers charge in on goal, looking to score, they often resort to using stick fakes to lure the goalie out of position so that more of the net is exposed. Being successful in the nets requires recognizing when stick fakes are being used — and, of course, not falling for them. Following are some coaching pointers for dealing with stick fakes:

✔ **Be patient.** When an opposing player attacks the net, the goalie naturally is eager to react to the player's moves and make a stop — sometimes, a bit too eager. When a goalie reacts too quickly to moves, he takes himself out of position and leaves a larger section of the net open for shots. Coach your goalies to wait until a shooter releases the ball from his stick before committing to moving and making the save.

✔ **Maintain good positioning.** During practices, work with your goalies to remain square to the shooter at all times. If they focus on remaining square, they will be less likely to lunge at the attacker or to allow themselves to be pulled in the direction of the fake.

Using the legs to stop shots

Low shots are challenging for young goalies to deal with, because those shots may bounce or skip along the ground. Also, they force the goalie to move her stick quickly from around chest high (see Chapter 10 for a rundown of the basic position goaltenders should use) to ground level. Goalies must rely on good leg movement to execute the underhand block — the best technique for dealing with low shots. Here's how to do this block:

1. **When the goalie's right hand is on top of the stick at the throat, she rotates it so that the pocket is closer to the field than the handle and she pushes her left elbow out to the side (see Figure 16-8).**

2. **Keeping the pocket of the stick square to the ball, she pushes the stick downward with her right hand.**

3. **She steps toward the ball and moves the head of the stick slightly forward to meet the shot.**

4. **If the shot is low, she keeps her feet close together behind her stick. This stance is extra protection in case the ball gets past the stick.**

The goalie should always step toward the shooter's stick with her closer foot. She should focus on being square to the shooter's stick, not body, because the attacker can move the ball to one side to create a different angle for the shot.

Figure 16-8:
Goalies can use the underhand block to stop shots below waist level.

Retrieving loose balls

Loose balls that reside outside the crease area — usually, the result of rebounds or deflected shots — represent opportunities for the opposition to take shots from in close, if the goalie doesn't get there first. To deny attacking players possession of these coveted loose balls, the goalie must act quickly, using the proper technique to get his stick on them.

1. **He moves toward the loose ball and lowers the head of his stick so that it skims the top of the field.**

2. He bends down low and keeps his eyes focused on the ball as he makes contact with it with his stick.

3. He brings the ball up so that he's in position to deliver a pass to an open teammate if there's a fast-break opportunity.

Sometimes, a goalie wanders out of the crease to secure a loose ball, only to have an opposing player beat him to it and get a wide-open net to shoot the ball into. After getting beaten this way a few times, the goalie may be reluctant to venture out of the crease to go after loose balls, but encourage him to remain aggressive and pursue any that are within his range. Goalies become better at these types of plays with experience.

Executing passes to begin attacks

Your attack can originate from many areas of the field, including in front of your net. A goalie who is good at clearing the ball with short, medium, or long passes can help your team advance the ball down the field quickly and mount an attack that keeps the opponent off balance.

Clearing refers to moving the ball out of the defensive end of the field and out of trouble. Here's how a clearing pass is delivered:

1. A right-handed goalie puts her left hand on the butt end of the stick and her right hand just below the middle of the stick.

2. She brings the stick over her right shoulder so that it's close to parallel to the field (see Figure 16-9).

3. She steps toward her intended target with her left foot.

4. She uses her bottom hand to pull her stick down toward her stomach.

5. She pushes her top hand forward and snaps her wrist toward the intended recipient.

6. She follows through, bringing her stick across to her left hip.

Following are some pointers on clearing that your goalies can use:

✔ **Focus on the sides.** Clearing passes should be directed to teammates on either side of the field. The goalie should avoid sending passes to the middle of the field, simply because if an opponent intercepts the pass, she's in dangerous scoring territory with the ball on her stick.

✔ **Avoid rainbow throws.** Ideally, a clearing pass should be a straight line with just a little arc, rather a big rainbow that stays in the air a long time. The longer the ball is in the air, the more time the opposition has to react to it, and the less likely the pass will reach the intended target.

- ✔ **Capitalize on the view.** Goalies are in the best position to see where the opposition's positioning is weakest, because they can survey the entire field. When a goalie sees a teammate breaking free down the sideline, if he recognizes the situation and executes a clearing pass to that teammate quickly, there is a good chance of catching the opponent off balance and out of position — a great way to create a quality scoring opportunity.

- ✔ **Recover and reorganize.** As goalies gain experience, they become much better at evaluating how the opposing players are positioned and when it's appropriate to attack with a long pass, and when teammates down-field are too well covered and a less risky pass is called for.

- ✔ **Don't turn the ball over.** If the defender is applying aggressive pressure on the goalie, she must take a few seconds to gain her composure before delivering a clearing pass. You never want your goalie to feel pressured into making a bad pass that gives the ball right back. Have her survey the field and take her time determining where the ball should go.

Figure 16-9:
A clearing pass is a good offensive weapon for goalies.

Part V:
The Extra Points

The 5th Wave By Rich Tennant

"Let's see — I'll need some children's aspirin for my players and some sedatives for their parents."

In this part . . .

The foods and fluids your players consume before they get to the field directly affect how they perform on it. This part serves up some pre- and post-game nutritional tips, and looks at some ways you can help reduce the chance that the season will be derailed by an injury. If you're forced to deal with a problem parent, coach, or player, you can find some solutions for those headaches in this part. And if you're interested in coaching at a more advanced level, you can find details on coaching a travel lacrosse team, too.

Chapter 17

Staying Healthy and Injury Free

*Y*ou know that coaching a youth lacrosse team involves all sorts of responsibilities. Coaching also involves dealing with injuries and explaining how proper nutrition and hydration affect performance. In this chapter, you find everything you need to know about reducing the risk of injuries on the field. We go over how to treat the minor injuries that pop up (such as cuts and sprains) and how to recognize the major injuries that require immediate medical attention. We also provide detailed information on nutrition and hydration: the foods and fluids kids should be consuming to enhance their performance, as well as the ones they should steer clear of.

Promoting a Healthy Diet

You can teach kids how to deliver a pass to a teammate on the move, but if they aren't eating the right foods before arriving at the field, their performance will be compromised. Although you can't control what your team eats before practices and games, you can affect it to a certain degree by what you teach them about good nutrition and how it affects performance. Spend some time discussing the importance of good nutritional habits.

Discussing nutrition with your players (and even with their parents) can make a difference in what they consume before practices and games, and it may even affect their eating habits on a regular basis. TV commercials push candy bars, chips, and sugar-coated cereals, but nutrition is in the basic food groups. Children can gain healthier eating habits if you explain what a difference it can make in their ability to play lacrosse. Two primary ingredients fuel a child's muscles and get used up the longer the activity goes on:

- ✔ **Fluids:** Kids lose fluids through perspiration, which is why water is so vital to keep their body temperatures from rising during exercise. The longer children exercise without replacing lost fluids, and the more extreme the temperatures and conditions happen to be that day, the less effective their performances will be, and the worse they will feel overall.

- ✔ **Glucose:** *Glucose* is a carbohydrate sugar and an important muscle fuel. It's carried to the working muscles through the bloodstream and stored in the muscles as glycogen. A child steadily depletes his glycogen stores throughout a lacrosse contest. The more carbohydrate fuel a child loses during competition, the less energy he has to perform at his peak.

Talking to kids about how today's food choices can affect their health years from now won't be very effective, because young minds really can't relate to the long term. But if you frame your discussion in terms of how their meal this morning affects their performance in the game this afternoon, you're much more likely to grab their attention. Keeping your discussion focused on the short term has a much greater chance of influencing kids' eating habits.

Fueling up before the game

When your players show up at games with empty stomachs — or after devouring burgers, fries, and sodas — their energy levels are low, and they have trouble performing and concentrating. A nutritious pregame meal clears the way for children to execute at their optimum level. Youngsters should eat a healthy meal (or at least some healthy snacks) comprised of plenty of carbohydrates to have the muscle energy to play and perform at a high level.

The pregame meal should be rich in carbohydrates, which convert to energy faster and more efficiently than other nutrients. Pastas, breads, cereals, and whole grains, along with fruits or vegetables work well. Good pregame snacks include bagels, yogurt, dried fruit, fresh fruit, energy bars, fruit granola bars, and whole-grain crackers with peanut butter or cheese.

Encourage your players to stay away from candy, cookies, and doughnuts because the high sugar content will leave them feeling sluggish once the sugar leaves their bloodstream. Fatty food like bacon should be avoided because it takes longer to digest, and foods high in salt content are also a big no-no because they can result in the child retaining fluids and even feeling bloated.

Players should consume their pregame meal about two hours before the game. They should avoid eating within an hour of game time, because their bodies will spend the first half digesting the food, detracting from their performance.

If your players feel sluggish in the second half or don't seem to perform as well as in the first half, you may be able to trace the problem to their diet. If so, experiment during practices by changing the players' eating habits to find what works best for them. Have them consume healthy snacks before a practice, for example, and see whether they notice any difference in their energy levels later in the practice. If they typically get tired toward the end of your practices but feel more energetic after consuming some of those healthy snacks, they can use that knowledge and eat like that before games, too.

If your team has a morning game, and the kids simply aren't able to get up early enough to have a proper pregame meal, make sure that they focus on eating a nutritionally sound dinner the night before. This meal should be a big serving of pasta with some vegetables, chicken, or fish. Even the night before a game, kids should steer clear of candy, ice cream, and other sweets, which can rob them of much-needed energy on game day.

Filling up after the game

What you say to your players following a game affects their confidence and self-esteem, as well as how they view their lacrosse skills. Similarly, what the players eat following a contest affects their bodies and how they feel. Rewarding kids for a game well played with a tasty snack is a lot of fun and a nice gesture for their hard work, but regularly giving them junk food sends the wrong message about the importance of proper nutritional habits. Following are some postgame tips to keep in mind:

✔ **Concentrate on carbohydrates.** Carbohydrate-rich foods that also have some protein value are the most beneficial foods for youngsters to eat after a day of running up and down the field. Ideally, the postgame meal or snack should resemble the pregame meal, the only difference being that the portions are a little bit smaller. Turkey sandwiches, fresh fruit, and crackers with cheese are great postgame foods.

✔ **Feed them fast.** The sooner your players get food into their stomachs after a game, the better. Plenty of research indicates that youngsters get the greatest benefits by consuming foods packed with carbohydrates within 30 minutes after a game or practice.

✔ **Occasional junk food is OK.** You know the saying "Everything in moderation." The same goes for those foods that aren't the most nutritious but that kids love, such as pizza and ice cream. Indulging your team with these tasty treats occasionally is perfectly OK. But if you give junk food regularly, your messages about nutrition will go to waste.

Drinking Up: Keeping Players Hydrated

The importance of children consuming lots of fluids, and the right kinds of fluids, simply can't be stated enough. When kids are running up and down the field trying to generate scoring opportunities, and exerting lots of energy attempting to keep the other team away from the goal, their body temperatures climb. Children who don't consume adequate amounts of water during games — especially those contested in hot and humid conditions — are at increased risk of becoming dehydrated and suffering muscle cramps, heat exhaustion, or heat stroke.

Muscle cramps generally affect the quadriceps, hamstrings, or calves. When enough fluids aren't consumed, the muscles that are being used a lot can go into spasms and tighten up on the youngster. Coaches can massage the tight muscles to help them loosen up, as well as have the player do some light stretching of the affected area. Applying heat, along with massage, helps promote blood flow to resolve the problem.

Heat exhaustion is caused by dehydration, and symptoms include profuse sweating, nausea, headache, chills, dizziness, and extreme thirst. Immediately have the child moved to a cool, shaded area, and have him consume cool fluids. You should also apply ice to his neck and back to help cool his body. Seek medical attention.

Heat stroke is much more severe: The child's life is in danger because he stops sweating, which pushes his body temperature to dangerously high levels. Call emergency medical personnel immediately. Warning signs are red or flushed skin, rapid pulse, rapid breathing, vomiting, seizures, unconsciousness, and cardiac arrest. While waiting for medical personnel to arrive, cool the player's body with wet towels or pour cool water over him. Ice packs should be applied to the neck, back, abdomen, armpits, and between the legs. Provide cool fluids if the player is conscious. If he's unconscious and vomiting, roll him onto his side to keep his throat clear.

The younger the children, the less they sweat, because their sweat glands aren't completely developed at this stage in their life. As a result, their bodies soak up more heat when they play games in high temperatures and humidity.

What players should drink

Players should consume adequate water before, during, and after games. Flavored sports drinks are also good sources for fluids, as the electrolyte content prompts fluid intake and fluid retention and distribution in the body.

Do your best to keep the kids from drinking caffeinated beverages. These types of drinks are no-nos because they act as diuretics — exactly the opposite of what you're trying to accomplish in keeping the kids hydrated. Also keep kids away from carbonated drinks; carbonation discourages drinking by making a child feel fuller.

Energy drinks should also not be consumed by children. These typically provide about as much caffeine as an average cup of instant coffee, twice as much as in a can of soda pop. Plus, the amount of sugar is usually higher than what is found in other beverages, which can slow the body's absorption of water, making them unhealthy to use during or after activity. Because caffeine is a stimulant, it increases heart rate, blood pressure and body temperature, and if too much is consumed, it can cause changes in the heart's rhythm.

How much players should drink

How much water should your players be drinking? The amount varies, because game conditions dictate whether they need increased water consumption to remain sufficiently hydrated. Also, with so many different body types, kids sweat at different rates and need different levels of fluids to keep themselves hydrated.

Although the condition is rare, you should be aware of *water intoxication,* also known as *hyperhydration* or *water poisoning.* It occurs when large amounts of water are consumed in a short period of time, causing a potentially fatal disturbance in brain function. Symptoms include confusion, inattentiveness, blurred vision, poor coordination, nausea, vomiting, rapid breathing, and drowsiness. Healthy youngsters are at little risk of overconsuming water, however, and should never refrain from drinking it to rehydrate during physical activity. The best preventive measure for kids participating in activities that promote heavy sweating, such as lacrosse, is to consume fluids to help maintain electrolyte balance. This means drinking plenty of the right kinds of fluids the day before the game, as well as on game day. Remind players that all the sweat that comes out of their bodies must be replaced by fluids, which is why it is important to consume them throughout the game. When a person's water and electrolyte intake matches what the body has sweated out, water intoxication isn't likely to occur.

When players should drink

Generally speaking, you want kids consuming water whenever possible. They should drink a glass of water with their pregame meal, consume water during the pregame warm-up, and sip water whenever they come out of the game.

After expending a lot of energy, your players need to consume lots of fluids to replenish what they lost. Giving them water after a game helps their livers and kidneys push out waste, a key element in helping their bodies recover.

Don't worry that drinking water will compromise players' performance. Most kids drink based on need, with thirst being the mechanism that tells them to drink. If you schedule plenty of water breaks, you won't have to worry about kids sitting on the sidelines chugging too much water and not being able to perform on the field.

Never withhold water as a form of punishment for any player who is misbehaving or who fails to adhere to your team rules. Proper hydration is just too important to a child's health and well being. No matter how serious the issue is or how disappointed you are in the youngster's actions, never resort to cutting off fluids. (For details on dealing with problem players, turn to Chapter 18.)

Hydration tips

Here are some additional tips to help keep those young bodies hydrated and performing at their most efficient levels:

- **Talk about hydration in simple terms.** If you're coaching younger children, even though they hear you telling them to take drinks of water, chances are that they still aren't consuming as much as they should be. During a break in practice or a timeout during a game, try telling the players to take a specific number of sips of water. This type of instruction helps ensure that the kids get enough fluids into their bodies.

- **Encourage drinking.** On game day, many kids are so into the game and excited about what is going on out on the field that they forget about consuming water, so you have to encourage them to drink. During time-outs and at halftime, when you're providing encouragement and discussing game strategy, remind the players to drink water. Kids should be sipping from their water bottles while you talk to them.

- **Get the parents involved.** Parents can help you ensure that your players are properly hydrated. On the car ride over to the game, for example, the parents can have their child drink some water. Spreading the water intake out helps ensure that a child's body remains hydrated and that he doesn't become bloated by trying to drink too much in one sitting.

- **Always have extra water available.** Be sure to bring extra water so that it's readily available to refill any water bottle that runs dry. You can even designate a couple of different parents each week to be responsible for bringing extra water, because you should never have a shortage of water at any practice or game.

Schedule plenty of water breaks throughout the practice. Any time a youngster needs water, encourage him to get a drink. You should never withhold water from a child for any reason.

An Ounce of Prevention: Conditioning Your Team

Conditioning your players is just as important as teaching them different aspects of shooting and defending, particularly at the more-advanced levels of lacrosse. Consider this: If your team is talented on the attack and great at defending, but is gasping for air several minutes into the game, its effectiveness nose-dives, and the opponent can take advantage at both ends of the field. Even lesser-skilled players who are well conditioned are big assets to the team; they can cause havoc for the opposition by chasing down loose balls in the second half of a game when other players are too tired to retrieve them.

Because lacrosse involves lots of running mixed with short, high-intensity bursts — such as when players are attacking or forced to defend an attacker — the best-conditioned players are those who have a combination of aerobic and anaerobic fitness so that they can perform at their top levels all game long.

You may already be familiar with these terms, but just in case, here is a brief refresher:

- ✓ **Aerobic:** *Aerobic* fitness refers to the level at which youngsters can take in and use oxygen. The stronger a youngster's heart and lungs are, the longer she's able to run up and down the field without tiring.

- ✓ **Anaerobic:** *Anaerobic* fitness pertains to how long a youngster can perform at high intensity, such as sprinting after a loose ball or darting past a defender and down the field.

Players who are tired and fatigued are at greater risk of injury than those who have more energy in their tank. Also, players often become sloppier in their technique when they don't have the energy to move their feet and get into the proper position. During games, keep a close eye on those kids who are tiring and could use a breather on the bench.

It's a good idea to have a signal kids can use — such as raising a fist — to let you know that they are tired and need a break. You don't want a player shouting out to you from the field that he's tired; the opponent will hear this information and exploit it by attacking the tired player.

The most productive practices incorporate a variety of the skills needed to play lacrosse without overwhelming kids in the process. The same goes for conditioning them. When you can incorporate conditioning into your practices without the kids even realizing that it's taking place, they will reap more benefits. Although having kids run mind-numbing laps around the lacrosse field will get them in better shape, it'll also bore them and may even drive them away from the sport. Also, you're wasting valuable practice time if you just have the players run without doing anything else at the same time. Instead, use drills that emphasize constant movement and eliminate standing around. Your players will be more conditioned — and more effective, too! (Check out Chapter 7 for some great practice drills.)

Getting players' hearts pumping

Devoting a few minutes at the start of practices to getting the kids' bodies warmed up paves the way to a more productive session and reduces the risk of injuries. The younger your players are, the less elaborate your warm-ups need to be. You can simply have the kids perform some basic jumping jacks and light running to get them ready for the action on the field. If you're overseeing an older and more-advanced lacrosse team, you'll want your warm-up to be much more specific to meet the players' needs.

At the more-competitive levels of lacrosse, including the travel-team level (for details on coaching a lacrosse travel team, flip to Chapter 19), you sometimes know in advance which players will be on your team. If so, you can meet with them before the season to discuss conditioning. You can encourage them to begin running to help build up their cardiovascular endurance, which will enable them to perform at higher levels for longer periods on game day. If they have access to weights, you can also encourage them to do some lifting — always under adult supervision. You can even ask a professional trainer from a local gym or a strength-and-conditioning coach from a nearby collegiate team to share insights on this aspect of the game with your players.

Cooling down in practices and games

Warm-ups play an important role in getting kids' bodies prepped for participation, and though they are easily overlooked, cool-downs following practices and games are equally important for maintaining the long-term health of your team. The cool-down helps reduce muscle soreness, aids circulation, and helps clear waste products from the muscles. After practices or games, have your players perform some light stretches — perhaps some of the same stretches that you used for the pregame warm-up.

Have your players get into the habit of going through the cool-down process every time they participate in a practice or game. The cool-down doesn't have to be quite as focused as the warm-up session, because the purpose is to wind down from an activity rather than build up to one. Completing a cool-down takes only a couple of minutes, and the kids will reap benefits.

Following a game, you can turn the cool-down period into a fun activity for the kids by talking to them about some of the interesting or humorous aspects of the game while they go through their stretches. Joke with them about anything unusual or funny that may have happened in the game. Or take a more serious approach with the older players, and highlight some of the positives that unfolded. You can point out how well they executed a fast-break opportunity or how well they defended the opposition's attack, for example.

A Pound of Cure: Recognizing and Treating Injuries

Eliminating the threat of injuries during practices and games is impossible, although how you handle them when they do pop up has a significant impact on how the children view their future lacrosse participation. Thankfully, most of the injuries you'll likely encounter will be minor in nature. Bumps, bruises, scrapes and the occasional twisted ankle will be the types of injuries that you will see most often. The quicker you respond to them and provide the necessary treatment the less likely a child will be traumatized by the injury and be ready to return to action.

Bringing your first-aid kit

A first-aid kit is like a health insurance policy: You need to have one but hope you never need to use it. Injuries are part of lacrosse, so you must come to practice prepared to deal with injuries. Some leagues issue a first-aid kit to each coach; others leave it up to the coach to bring supplies to the field.

If the league doesn't provide first-aid kits, talk to the program director about the importance of having them; perhaps she can correct the oversight. In the meantime, never conduct a practice or go to a game without your kit. Check out Chapter 17 for the run down of the items that should be in the kit.

You should stock your kit with the following items:

- ✔ **Antiseptic spray or wipes:** Use these items to clean out cuts and abrasions.
- ✔ **Athletic tape:** Tape can hold ice bags in place when you need to reduce swelling around an injury.
- ✔ **Bandages in different sizes:** Use waterproof bandages to cover cuts and scrapes.
- ✔ **Bee-sting kit:** You can pick up one of these kits at your local pharmacy and have it on hand in case one of your players gets stung.
- ✔ **CPR mouth barrier:** You need one of these items in the event that a child needs mouth-to-mouth resuscitation.
- ✔ **Emergency tooth-preserving system:** Use one of these kits for a tooth that gets knocked out. You can pick it up at a local pharmacy or ask your dentist where you can purchase one.
- ✔ **Freezer-type storage bags:** Plastic storage bags are great for holding ice packs.
- ✔ **Hot and cold packs:** For applying to injured areas of the body.
- ✔ **Insect repellant:** Use repellant to combat those pesky bugs that can take a bite out of the fun.
- ✔ **Latex gloves:** You need to wear gloves while dealing with bloody cuts and wounds. If any parents mention to you that their child has allergies to latex, be sure to stock your kit with gloves made of a different material.
- ✔ **Nail clippers:** A pair of clippers comes in handy for repairing torn nails.
- ✔ **Prescriptions:** You need to be aware of any medical conditions that youngsters on your team have. If a child has asthma, for example, make sure that his parents give you a spare bronchodilator to keep in your first-aid kit in case the child forgets his and the situation calls for it.
- ✔ **Scissors:** You need scissors to cut bandages and athletic tape.
- ✔ **Sterile eyewash and prepackaged sterile eye pads:** You need these items when any type of debris becomes stuck in a child's eye.
- ✔ **Tweezers:** Use tweezers to remove any debris that becomes lodged in a child's skin.

Keeping accurate records

Whenever a child suffers an injury that you provide any type of treatment for, be sure to write down the nature of the injury, how it happened, and exactly how you handled it — including whether you applied a bandage or ice and any other steps you took. Record this information in your practice planner or in a separate log book. Do so the same day, while the event is still fresh in your mind.

Regardless of how minor the injury is, be sure to inform the child's parents about what happened and how you treated it. Never withhold information from them for any reason.

Unfortunately, we live in a litigious society, so having an accurate account of everything that transpired is vital in case you need to recount what happened — in a court of law, for example. Having detailed notes of everything that happened protects you from unwarranted accusations.

Detailed practice plans, with dates, are evidence that you taught your players specific skills safely and properly, so they also protect you against unfounded lawsuits. Don't discard these records after the season is over. Keep these accounts, along with your dated practice plans and notes, for several years.

Tending to Common Lacrosse Injuries

Most injuries that your players suffer involve bumps, bruises, cuts, and twisted ankles. These injuries may seem minor to you, but they may seem pretty major to a child who suddenly sees blood on her leg or is unable to put any weight on her ankle when she tries to walk. By acting quickly and administering the proper treatment for routine injuries while comforting the youngster, you can usually help her bounce back and return to action fairly quickly.

Never give aspirin or any other types of over-the-counter medications to children unless you have written permission to do so from the parent or guardian. Also, if you will be providing any type of prescription medicine to children, always make sure that you have the instructions and consent from the parent in writing.

Cuts and scrapes

Cuts and scrapes can produce major tears among young players, but luckily, they are minor injuries that you can treat quickly and effectively with the materials in your first-aid kit. Just be sure to keep the following pointers in mind:

- ✔ **Wear latex gloves.** Any time one of your players suffers a cut, the first thing you should do is grab a pair of latex gloves or use some other type of blood barrier to limit your contact with the blood.

✔ **Apply direct pressure.** You can stop bleeding by applying direct pressure to the wound with a clean dressing. If you have trouble stopping the bleeding, elevate the child's injured area above his heart while maintaining the pressure.

✔ **Clean it.** After you stop the bleeding, clean the wound. You can use pre-moistened towelettes or over-the-counter alcohol swabs and antibiotic creams to clean minor cuts and scrapes.

✔ **Cover it.** Use a bandage or piece of sterile gauze to cover the cut, and secure it tightly in place with athletic tape, particularly if the child is interested in continuing to play.

✔ **Discard the trash.** Place your gloves and any other materials that may have blood on them in a sealed bag, and put the bag in the trash so that no one else risks coming into contact with these materials. Check with your league to see if the facility that you practice and play at has special containers that are used to discard these types of materials.

Although fearing HIV/AIDS is certainly understandable, it should never be a factor in providing help to an injured player on your team. You're at risk only if you allow the blood of an HIV-positive person to come into contact with an open wound that you have. If one of your players has AIDS or is HIV-positive, the parents certainly should make you aware of this fact during your preseason parents' meeting, which we discuss in Chapter 4. Whether you're aware of the player's HIV status or not, however, the fact that you're wearing latex gloves provides the protection you need to treat the injured child.

Twists, sprains, and strains

Because lacrosse is a contact sport that requires players to run at full speed and make all sorts of sudden stops and cuts, collisions involving different parts of the body take place all over the field.

If you are coaching in a boys' league that allows checking (for more details on checking, head to Chapter 10), injuries may be even more prevalent.

Some of the movements that players execute — and some of the collisions that accompany them — can result in muscle strains and sprains, as well as bruises. Because lacrosse involves all areas of the body, from the ankles and knees for running to the wrists and shoulders for shooting, you have to be prepared to tend injuries to all body parts.

When a player strains a muscle or twists an ankle, keep in mind the RICE method for treatment:

- ✔ **Rest:** Immediately get the child to the sideline so that she can rest the injury. If the child has twisted her ankle, for example, have an assistant coach or a parent from the stands help you carry the child off the field so that she doesn't put any additional pressure on the injured area.

- ✔ **Ice:** Apply ice to the injured area. The ice helps reduce the swelling and pain. Don't apply the ice directly to the skin; wrap the ice bag in a towel and then place it on the injured area.

- ✔ **Compress:** Compress the injured area by using athletic tape or any other type of material to hold the ice in place.

- ✔ **Elevate:** Have the child elevate the injury above his heart to prevent blood from pooling in the injured area.

After any swelling, discoloration, or pain subsides, you can allow the youngster to return to competition.

If any of these symptoms are present for more than a couple of days, however, the player should be examined by a physician before you allow her back on the field. You never want a child to return to the field when her injury hasn't healed completely, because that puts her at greater risk of reinjuring the area and missing even more action.

Other injuries

As players become bigger and stronger at the more-advanced and competitive levels of lacrosse, and are capable of running faster and checking harder, other types of injuries may occur. In the following sections, we discuss some of these injuries and how you should respond if they occur.

Broken bone

When a child is in a lot of pain following contact — either from colliding with another player or from landing on the playing field hard or at an awkward angle — a bone may be broken.

Whenever you sense that a child may have broken a bone, proceed cautiously. Your first step is immobilizing the injured area with a splint. A broken finger can be propped up with a splint, wrapped gently with tape to hold it in place until a doctor can examine the injury. When you are dealing with a more severe break, such as an arm or leg, get medical attention to care for it properly.

A broken bone sticking through a child's skin is the worst-case scenario, requiring you to call medical personnel to provide treatment. Never try to push the bone back in. Keep your hands off it, and cover the area with sterile gauze until help arrives.

Bruises

Bruising results from an impact against the body, such as a ball hitting a player's thigh, as blood from the capillaries is released into the tissues under the skin that leaves a mark that can be black, blue, or even yellowish in color. The bruise eventually fades as the blood is absorbed by the tissues and carried away. The best treatment for bruises is to apply ice to the injured area, which stops the blood flow and limits the size of the bruise. If the bruise swells, or does not go away within a week, have the child visit a doctor for further evaluation.

Concussion

A *concussion* is a jarring injury to the head, face, or jaw resulting in a disturbance of the brain. Take seriously any type of injury involving a child's head, and don't allow him to resume playing until he has been examined by a medical professional.

If a youngster reports any of the following symptoms, seek medical attention for her:

- Headache or pressure in the head
- Nausea or vomiting
- Balance problems or dizziness
- Double or blurry vision

- Sensitivity to light or sound
- Feeling sluggish, hazy, foggy, or groggy
- Concentration or memory problems
- Confusion

A child doesn't have to lose consciousness to suffer a concussion. Any time you see a child bump heads with another player, or hit his head on the field hard after being tripped or losing his balance, remove him from the activity, and observe him carefully. Be on the lookout for irritable mood swings, memory loss, and vision problems — telltale signs that a concussion has occurred.

A youngster who suffers a mild concussion typically needs at least a week to recover before resuming normal activities. A severe concussion usually sidelines a youngster for at least a month; in this case, the player needs a doctor's OK before returning to the lacrosse field.

Eye injury

All injuries can be pretty frightening to a child, especially those that involve problems with their vision. Check out the following eye injuries that can occur during practices and games:

- **Foreign object in the eye:** Any foreign body lodged in the eye, such as a fleck of dirt, needs attention. Usually, this kind of injury is simply a nuisance, but if the irritation doesn't go away, it needs to be evaluated by an eye specialist. Symptoms are tearing, pain, and redness.

  You can remove most objects easily with a cotton swab and saline wash. If the surface of the youngster's eye isn't seriously injured, and her vision isn't impaired, she can return to competition as soon as the object is removed.

- **Injury to the eyeball:** A direct injury to the eyeball is a medical emergency. Symptoms are extreme pain, loss of vision, hazy vision, double vision, change in vision colors, or obvious lacerations or abrasions of the eye. If the vision loss is the result of a direct impact to the eye, apply a dry, sterile eye patch or piece of gauze to the eye, along with a bag of crushed ice; then immediately get the youngster to an emergency facility for treatment.

- **Poked in eye:** Even though lacrosse players wear protective eye gear, sometimes they still get poked in the eye. If that happens to one of your players, examine the eye. If the player isn't in significant pain, and you see minimal redness and no discharge or bleeding, simply clean the area out with cool water, and allow him to rest for a while before returning to play. If you notice any type of discharge or blood coming from the eye, get the child to a doctor immediately.

- **Orbital fracture:** A fracture of the bony frame around the eye is serious and requires expert medical treatment. Symptoms are severe pain, with possible double vision or other vision problems. These symptoms may be accompanied by cuts, abrasions, bleeding, and black-and-blue marks. If any youngster suffers significant injury to the area around the eye, she should be transported to a facility where she can be x-rayed to determine whether a fracture has occurred.

Shin splints

Shin splints are common in lacrosse because lots of running is involved. The primary cause of the injury is related to the weight pounding down on the shin. Other factors include muscle weakness, poor flexibility, improper warm-up and cool-down exercises, and improper footwear. This injury typically is easy to identify: pain in the shin. Shin splints develop in four stages:

1. **Pain after activity**

2. **Pain before and after activity without affecting performance**

3. **Pain before, during, and after activity, adversely affecting performance**

4. **Constant pain that prohibits activity**

The early stages of shin splints are relatively mild, but later stages can get much more severe. If the injury isn't managed properly, it can lead to a stress fracture. If a player develops shin splints, use ice to reduce pain and swelling and forbid weight-bearing activities to allow the affected area time to heal.

Wind knocked out

A youngster who has the wind knocked out of her for the first time may panic when she has trouble breathing. Comfort her and have her take short, quick breaths, panting like a puppy until she can resume breathing normally again.

Tooth knocked out

If a child has a tooth knocked out, retrieve the tooth, place it in a sterile gauze pad with some saline solution, and get the child to a dentist immediately.

Nosebleed

Whenever a group of youngsters are involved in a contact sport like lacrosse, they run the risk of nosebleeds — particularly in girls' games, because in most programs, girls don't wear full protective helmets like boys do. A lot of children cringe at the sight of blood — their own or someone else's — so act quickly to control the damage. Grab a clean piece of gauze, and put it over the nose while gently squeezing the youngster's nostrils together. The gauze catches any excess blood coming out of the nose and makes the situation less dramatic for the child. Also, tilt the child's head slightly forward.

If the bleeding hasn't stopped after a couple of minutes, the injury may be more serious, and the youngster should be taken to a doctor immediately.

Handling an emergency situation

Unfortunately, serious injuries sometimes occur, and you must be prepared to deal with them. Just as you spend time practicing cradling, passing, and defending attacks with your players, you must go over with your assistants how you will respond in an emergency. How you respond — and how quickly — can save a youngster's life. Following are some tips to keep in mind:

✔ **Know your location.** Be aware of the name of the facility where you're playing, as well as the address. In the event that you have to call 911, being able to provide accurate information right away helps ensure that emergency personnel arrive at the proper location as quickly as possible.

✔ **Have each child's emergency information on hand.** Those important forms we discuss in Chapter 4 are crucial in the event that medical personnel need to know whether the child is allergic to any type of medication. Always carry those forms in your first-aid kit, and have them easily accessible in the event of an emergency.

✔ **Provide only treatment that you are capable of performing.** While awaiting the arrival of medical personnel, provide only the first-aid care that you're trained to perform.

✔ **Calm the child.** If the youngster is conscious, comfort him by talking to him in a calm, relaxed voice. Let him know that he's going to be OK and that medical help is on the way. If you display signs of being worried or upset, the child will pick up on them — and likely will become even more afraid than he already is.

✔ **Alert parents, if they're not in attendance.** If the child's parents aren't in attendance, one of your assistant coaches should be responsible for calling them to let them know what's going on. Your foremost responsibility at a time like this is the child, so if you've already designated someone else to make that initial call to the parents, you don't have to waste unnecessary time when all your attention needs to be focused on the youngster.

You must be prepared to assess any injury, including loss of consciousness. The acronym *COACH* is a handy reminder. Follow these steps:

✔ **C:** Determine whether the child is *conscious.*

✔ **O:** Is the child breathing and getting *oxygen?*

✔ **A:** *Ask* the youngster where she is hurt.

✔ **C:** *Control* the area that's painful.

✔ **H:** What type of *help* is required? Decide whether you need to call for immediate medical assistance and have the child taken to the hospital.

When you're approaching an injured child, keep the COACH sequence in mind. Look at his lip color, feel his chest, or put your cheek next to his nose to see whether he's breathing. If he isn't breathing, and you don't see or feel a pulse in his neck or wrist, you must immediately initiate cardiopulmonary resuscitation (CPR) and have someone call for emergency medical assistance.

We strongly recommended that anyone who coaches youth lacrosse (or any other youth sport) be certified in CPR. All youth lacrosse coaches should receive CPR and first-aid training from the American Red Cross (www.red cross.org) or another nationally recognized organization. At every practice and game, you're responsible for the safety and well being of every single player. Take the time to take the class. You'll be glad you did.

Proceed cautiously when dealing with any injury, particularly one that involves the head, neck, or spine. Never attempt to move a player with such an injury; doing can cause further damage. Call for emergency medical assistance anytime you're dealing with a serious injury. If a child sustains an injury to the head or neck, calm her down and restrain her in the position in which you found her while emergency medical assistance is responding.

Calling for calm after an injury

Because of the physical nature of lacrosse, players may suffer injuries during games. Much as adult motorists slow down at the scene of an accident to see what happened, children are naturally curious and will want to see how their teammate is doing or get a closer look at what happened to an opposing player. When a player goes down with an injury, keep the rest of the players away from him. You don't want the entire team crowding around the injured child; if he sees everyone hovering with concerned looks, he may panic. Make sure you go over with your players in advance how you want them to behave when one of their teammates or a player on the opposing team is injured. You want them to return to their bench area so that you and anyone else who is helping out with the team can concentrate on providing care to the child and call for medical personnel if the situation is serious. You don't want your players to be a distraction or to get in the way unnecessarily while treatment is being provided.

Chapter 18

Challenges Every Lacrosse Coach Will Face

. . . .

In This Chapter

▶ Communicating with problematic parents

▶ Handling cantankerous coaches

▶ Managing player issues

. . . .

Some of the most obvious tasks that you'll devote attention to this season are teaching your players fundamental offensive and defensive skills, putting together fun-filled practices, and making game day memorable for all the right reasons. Other areas requiring your attention include handling all sorts of problems that can pop up from time to time — problems involving parents, opposing coaches, your own assistants, and your players themselves.

This chapter lays out everything you need to know to deal with these issues. We give you tips on doling out discipline to your players who disobey team rules and share insights on solving those tricky problems with your assistant coaches when you don't see eye to eye. We also dig in to how to keep parents' behavior in check and what to do when it crosses the line, as well as how to contend with opposing coaches whose methods aren't appropriate for the youth lacrosse level.

We hope you don't encounter any of these unpleasant situations, but if you do, use the remedies in this chapter so that the problems don't detract from your players' lacrosse experience.

Dealing with Problem Parents

As crazy as it may sound, childish behavior at youth lacrosse games doesn't always involve the kids. Any time you bring a group of parents together — all of whom have different backgrounds, motivations, and hopes for their children — problems are likely to flare up on occasion. Most of these problems will be minor in nature and easily rectified; others may take on a more serious tone.

Take the time to conduct a preseason parents' meeting (see Chapter 4), in which you lay some key groundwork to prevent problems from escalating. During the meeting, detail your expectations of parent behavior during games; clearly explain what constitutes appropriate and inappropriate behavior for both parents and children. Then hold everyone, including yourself, accountable for adhering to this code of behavior.

Laying out your expectations for parental behavior before the first face-off of the season is important, but it's by no means a guarantee that every parent is going to be a model of good behavior all season long. Be prepared to step forward at the first indication of trouble. Any time you allow a problem to linger, it has the potential to blossom into something much worse.

The following sections look at some of the most common types of problem parents that you may deal with this season, and discuss the best ways to deal with them quickly and effectively.

Win-at-all-costs parents

Parents shell out a lot of money to buy their kids lacrosse sticks, helmets, and gloves, not to mention all the time they spend shuttling them to midweek practices and weekend games. Naturally, with so much invested in the season, they want to see their kids excel and reap the benefits of participating. But some parents may expect their children — and you — to perform at levels that are entirely unrealistic.

These parents will be satisfied only if their child wins a shiny first-place trophy that they can display on their mantel at home. This type of expectation — totally unfair, unrealistic, and unhealthy for the kids — creates a lot of unnecessary stress. The additional pressure also infringes on the other kids' enjoyment of the game and threatens to spoil the season for everyone.

Win-at-all-costs parents place such an emphasis on winning games that losses are viewed as catastrophic. This unhealthy outlook, along what these parents are teaching at home about how important winning is, goes against everything you're trying to teach the kids about doing their best and having fun.

What makes them tick

Here are a couple of other points to be aware of when dealing with these types of parents:

> ✔ **They do whatever it takes to win.** These parents want victories for the team and accolades for their child, and they may resort to any measures to win. They may shout at referees whenever calls go against their child or his team; try intimidation tactics to influence the referee's calls (even if the ref is a teenager officiating a beginning-level game for minimum wage);

and loudly criticize the opposing coach and team, especially if the other team happens to be winning or doing a really good job of defending their child and not allowing him to show off his skills.

✔ **They see a target on your back.** Rest assured that your coaching style will be on these parents' radar screen for second-guessing and criticism whenever the outcome of a game doesn't turn out in your team's favor. Everything from how you chose to attack the defense to the types of face-off techniques your players used during the game will be put under a microscope and dissected.

Regardless of the age level of the youngsters, these parents are likely to confront you about the importance of playing the more-athletic kids more often and benching the less-skilled players, all to help ensure that the team wins more games and their child receives more playing time. They critique your game strategy following losses, question your lineup, analyze your substitution patterns, and offer their unsolicited advice regarding your offensive tactics and defensive philosophy.

What to do about them

These tips can help you deal with win-at-all-costs parents:

✔ **Take control.** Take the approach that when your players step onto the field, that field is their classroom. You simply can't allow outside influences to disrupt your messages about striving to do your best, adhering to the rules, being a good sport, and accepting wins and losses with dignity. How parents choose to rear their children, and what they say to their children at home, is out of your control. But when your practice begins or a game gets under way, you assume full control, and what you say goes at all times.

✔ **Hold a pregame parents' meeting.** To help stem the competitive tide and prevent it from enveloping the other parents, give a brief, friendly talk to all the parents before your next game. Spending a couple of minutes talking to the entire group, reminding the parents that their children play in a recreational youth lacrosse league, and pointing out that winning isn't the most important factor may help put parents in the proper frame of mind. If the league has staff members who monitor the behavior of fans, tell your parents that their actions are being observed and that you'd hate to see their children embarrassed if parents are asked to leave the facility because they couldn't control themselves during the game.

✔ **Talk to parents privately.** If you find that the group chat doesn't help, arrange to speak privately with any parent who's still causing disruptions. Share your concerns that her comments are a real detriment not only to her child's development, but also to the rest of the team. Be sure to reiterate that you're trying to help all the kids learn skills and that although winning the game is one of the objectives that you're striving to achieve (at more advanced levels of play), it's not the sole objective.

✔ **Discuss alternatives — and consequences.** Let a win-at-all-costs parent know that if he isn't happy with your coaching philosophy, he should consider coaching himself next season or look into signing his child up for a more competitive team. In the meantime, you need his cooperation. Tell him that you don't want him to be absent from this exciting time in his child's life, but if the improper behavior continues to detract from the values you're teaching, your only recourse will be to speak to the league director.

Don't be confrontational in this discussion, but be firm in your stance, because you have the welfare of an entire group of kids to look out for. You may also want the recreation supervisor or league director to be present during the discussion to lend additional support.

Parents who use the team as a babysitting service

Many children's activity-filled schedules have their parents pulling their hair out, driving them to practices and games at all hours of the day. Driving all over town can be exhausting work, which is why some parents may view your practices — and sometimes even games — as a convenient babysitting service.

Single parenting plays an ever-increasing role in family life today, of course, so Mom or Dad simply may not have the luxury of hanging out at the lacrosse field if they have other responsibilities, such as getting another sibling to a different practice on the other side of town. But ideally, you want parents to be part of the practice regimen whenever possible and to be there on game day, providing positive support and encouragement for the entire team.

After you run a handful of practices and coach a few games, you get a pretty good sense of which parents are taking advantage of you by using you as an unpaid babysitting service. During your interactions with the kids, begin gauging what type of family life they have at home, and use your conversations with parents before practices and games to get a feel for what types of people they are. All this information can help you relate to your players more effectively.

One of the best ways to get parents to stick around for practice is to include them in some of your drills, as we discuss in Chapter 6. When those parents who typically don't hang around see all the fun the other parents are having with their children, they may start hanging around themselves, wanting to be part of the action.

Let parents know that their presence, even during a routine practice during the middle of the week, can do a great deal for a child's confidence while maintaining her interest in the sport. You can even mention a drill you've done in practice that their child has taken a real liking to and suggest that they work on it with her at home. Practicing at home will help the child continue to improve that particular area of her game and get her parents more involved in her development, which is good news for everyone.

Lacrosse is a sport that many parents are not entirely familiar with, so their roles may be a bit unclear to them. Even if you outline their responsibilities for them at your preseason parents meeting your message may not have sunk in or it got lost in the shuffle of practices and games. A quick, casual conversation with parents when they arrive to pick their children up after practice may be all you need to make a difference. Let them know that you think their children could really benefit from having them take a more active interest in their lacrosse. A child who finally gets a handle on a skill that he's been struggling to master derives a lot more satisfaction if he can glance over to the sidelines and get a smile or a nod of approval from Mom or Dad.

Parents who question their child's playing time

Some parents pay more attention to their child's playing time than they do to their retirement accounts, and with good reason. Parents don't sign their child up for lacrosse, write a check to cover the registration fee, and purchase all sorts of equipment just to see her sitting on the bench. Unfortunately, depending on the number of kids who have been assigned to your team, your hands may be tied, and you must rotate players in and out of games. Based on the size of your team, kids may get a chance to play in only half the game.

At advanced levels of play, in which skill level dictates game-day minutes, many parents relate playing time to their own parenting skills. The more skilled their child is at attacking or defending — and the more playing time he receives because of those skills — the better parenting job they assume that they're doing. In their eyes, the child's playing time becomes a status symbol; they think that it reflects favorably on them as they sit in the stands with the other parents.

Frustration with their child's playing time is a fairly common complaint among parents. Luckily, it's also fairly easy to handle. Here are some points to keep in mind:

- ✔ **Lean on the program policy.** Most leagues have a clear policy regarding playing time. At beginning levels, equal playing time is important so that everyone gets a fair chance to run around on the field and experience different aspects of the game. Before the season starts, take time to explain to parents how you will distribute those coveted game-day minutes (see Chapter 4).

Some parents may still think their child deserves more minutes because of his tremendous lacrosse skills. If you find yourself in one of these conversations, let the parents know that you enjoy coaching their son and that you'd love to give him more playing time, but you have to abide by the rules of the league, as well as be fair to all your players. After all, rules are rules.

✔ **Revisit your preseason chat.** Offer a friendly reminder of what you stated during your preseason meeting (covered in Chapter 4): that kids will receive an equal amount of playing time as long as they're regular participants at practice. Remind parents that kids who don't attend practice can't simply show up on game day and expect the same treatment as those players who do attend every practice.

✔ **Monitor the minutes.** For a couple of very good reasons, you should track the minutes your kids get on the field on game day: It's the right way to ensure that each child is getting her fair share, and it's exactly the proof you can turn to if disgruntled parents question why their child isn't playing as much as some of her teammates. Written documentation of the great lengths you go to make the season fair for everyone is usually enough to make your point. If you have assistant coaches, you can appoint one of them to track each player's minutes to ensure fairness. (Check out Chapter 4 for details on how to choose your assistant coaches.)

Disruptive parents

Coaching a youth lacrosse team has many wonderful aspects, and kids also enjoy many benefits from their participation. Unfortunately, any time parents step across the line of good behavior, their actions can smother the fun and embarrass their child in the process. Why some parents act irresponsibly and behave poorly while watching a youth lacrosse game is a mystery much of the time, likely involving factors that are out of your control. What *is* in your control is your ability to keep negative parental behavior from ruining your players' experience on the field.

Whenever a parent makes an inappropriate comment or is too demonstrative in his actions, address the problem as soon as possible. Ignoring a misbehaving parent, or being reluctant to address the situation, sends an awful message to everyone — parents and children alike — that this type of behavior is acceptable. Parents must know that inappropriate words and actions won't be tolerated in any form. Dealing with these types of problems swiftly also lets the other team parents know that if they step (or act) out of line, you'll deal with them accordingly. Parents who are there to be supportive and enjoy their children's lacrosse experience will appreciate your commitment to ensuring that everyone has a rewarding time and that you won't allow inappropriate behavior to spoil the day.

How do you handle a parent who has just shouted an embarrassing comment? What do you do when parents yell across the field at a coach who appears to be running up the score on your team? What do you do when tensions seem to be rising among parents who are unhappy with how the game is unfolding? In the following sections, we provide some strategies to help you deal with such situations. Because you're only human, such disruptions are bound to rattle you at times, so we also advise you what *not* to do.

What to do

Following are some approaches you can use to help keep everyone's tempers in check and the game moving along without any unnecessary disruptions for the kids:

- ✔ **Remind parents of the rules in a friendly tone.** Quite often, parents don't even realize that they've crossed the line. You can be firm — yet friendly — in reminding them to keep their emotions in check and their comments to themselves. Usually, this reminder is enough to remedy the situation.

- ✔ **Be familiar with your league's parent policy.** As we discuss in Chapter 2, knowing your league's rules thoroughly is extremely important. Youth lacrosse leagues around the country are instituting parent sportsmanship programs — both voluntary and mandatory — to help give parents a clear understanding of their roles and responsibilities.

   If your league doesn't have a sportsmanship program for parents, you may want to recommend one to your league director. Such a program is sure to make life easier for all the coaches in the league, encouraging parents to work with coaches in their children's best interests.

- ✔ **Set an example of civility.** You can defuse a tense situation with an upset parent by maintaining a calm, friendly demeanor. Setting a civil tone right from the start is a critical building block in a productive discussion. Granted, being civil may be difficult at times, particularly when the parent is accusing you of being the worst lacrosse coach she's ever come across. Take a deep breath and never allow yourself to be lured into an argument. You've got to defuse tense situations rather than fuel them.

- ✔ **Be prepared to listen.** If you're not willing to listen to what parents have to say, how can you expect them to listen to you? Focus as much on listening as on trying to get your point across, and a parent is likely to work with you and not against you.

- ✔ **Watch your (body) language.** Just as your tone and body language influence your interactions with the kids, they affect your dealings with parents. Suppose that a parent asks you why his child got to play in only half the game, and before responding, you put your hands on your hips. That parent will perceive you as being upset before you even respond to the question. Mixed body-language signals or a negative tone can set up an unproductive, unhealthy conversation that can spiral out of control.

✔ **Remove parents from the field only as a last resort.** Having a parent removed from the playing area is an extreme step to take. But sometimes ejection is the only way to ensure the safety and well being of the young participants on the field, as well as of the other spectators. Being thrown out is certainly an embarrassment for the parent who's being removed, as well as for the child whose fun game of lacrosse is being interrupted.

Keep in mind that when parents request a meeting with you, in most cases they are doing so out of genuine love and concern for their child's well being, and you should respect that concern. Make it clear to the parents that you want the best for their child, just as they do. Listen intently to whatever concerns the parents may have; then talk through the issue with them to come up with a solution. A good idea is to end the chat on a positive note by acknowledging the child's attributes and pointing out what a pleasure she is to coach.

What not to do

Sometimes, as frustration levels mount regarding specific issues, you may be tempted to do just about anything to rid yourself of the problem. We advise you to steer clear of the following actions:

✔ **Fire back at the parents.** Parents may agree to meet with you about their behavior and then use the meeting as an opportunity to bombard you with accusations and complaints about how you are running the team. Those comments may be upsetting, but don't turn the meeting into a tennis match of insults, with negative words being fired back and forth. Getting lured into this type of heated discussion accomplishes nothing and serves no useful purpose. If the situation is unavoidable, calmly listen to the complaints and then state your case in a reasonable manner without antagonizing the parent in the process.

✔ **Embarrass the parents.** Parenting young lacrosse players isn't easy, so as the coach, you must accept the fact that some parents have difficulty getting a grip on their emotions. When they see their child knocked down or tripped by an opposing player, and the referee doesn't call a penalty, they may have difficulty keeping their displeasure to themselves. When you hear a comment shouted from the stands, try looking over your shoulder at the offending parent. That brief eye contact lets her know that what she just said is unacceptable and that she needs to tone down her behavior.

✔ **Take out your frustration on the child.** No matter how poorly parents behave or what mean-spirited words come out of their mouths, never take out your frustration on their child. Remember, the youngsters on your team have no control of how their parents behave on game day, so don't slice their playing time or take any other drastic measures in an effort to rein in the emotional outbursts. Push your feelings about the parents to the side and continue coaching these children as enthusiastically as you do the other players.

✔ **Have postgame discussions in the parking lot.** Mature discussions typically don't occur in the parking lot after games, when emotions often run high. Explain to the parents that you're happy to meet with them to discuss any concerns they may have, but at a time that's convenient for all of you and in a place that's private — not in front of their child, the rest of the team, and the parents of opposing players.

Perpetually late parents

Late arrivals are a real nuisance when you've settled into a seat at the movie theater and are forced to stand up ten minutes later as people work their way down the aisle in the dark to find some seats, jostling your popcorn and soda in the process. Late arrivals are just as aggravating when you're trying to run a lacrosse practice. When kids appear midway through a practice, the entire flow of the session is thrown off, and a player who shows up in the middle of a game can create chaos with your substitution patterns.

Besides the inconvenience factor, keep in mind that kids who arrive late have missed the valuable prepractice or pregame warm-up (see Chapter 17 for more information) and will be at increased risk of injury if you send them out onto the field right away.

Late arrivals must be addressed as soon as they occur, because if you let them go and allow them to continue, the consequences can be even more problematic. If you have a few kids who aren't on time for a game, for example, and you don't have enough players to put on the field, you may be forced to forfeit.

Talking to tardy players

Following are a few tips that you can use to help get the kids to your practices and games on time:

✔ **Talk to the team as a whole.** As soon as late arrivals are beginning to create problems, talk to the entire team to reinforce your expectations on attendance. Make the chat a quick one, but stress that being part of a team is a commitment — one that needs to be kept at midweek practices and championship games alike. Make it clear that you're at the field on time for all practices and games, and that you expect and deserve the same consideration from every one of your players.

✔ **Make roll call a big deal.** Even though you can easily see which kids are at the practice, employ a fun roll call during the team's warm-up. You can call out funny nicknames for players, for example, or use an amusing voice that gets a chuckle from the kids. Even if you have only a dozen kids on your team, and a roll call isn't necessary from the standpoint of knowing who's there and who hasn't arrived yet, roll call can still be a fun moment that the kids enjoy being part of and won't want to miss.

✔ **Play fun games before practice.** If you throw in fun little games before practice begins, you may be pleasantly surprised by the number of kids who suddenly show up at practice well ahead of time. Ideally, they're pestering their parents to get them to practice early so that they don't miss out on this activity with their teammates.

✔ **Award equal playing time for on-time arrival.** Game-day minutes are valuable, so you should hand them out equally to players who are consistently on time for practices and who participate in the entire session. For players who are continually late, you should cut playing time accordingly. Giving equal playing time to a child who always turns up late simply isn't fair to his teammates who show up on time week after week.

What makes this issue tricky is that a child may have to rely on her parents to get her to the practice on time. As we discuss in Chapter 4, you should address the importance of showing up on time at your preseason parents' meeting. Explain how crucial punctuality is, both for the season to run smoothly and for the children to learn and develop skills (not to mention for your sanity!).

Talking to tardy parents

Any time you speak to a child about lateness, be sure to follow up with his parent. Keeping the parents in the loop reinforces how important being on time is to you. Many parents simply don't realize what a big disruption their child's lateness causes for the rest of the team. Ideally, a brief conversation reminding parents of the importance of having everyone at the field on time is all you need to prevent the problem from occurring during the remainder of the season.

Following are a few things you may want to mention to parents to ensure that the discussion goes smoothly and that all parties are happy at the conclusion:

✔ **Lateness is a nuisance for the entire team.** Explain to parents that late arrivals are a disruption for the entire team. Stress that you really need the child to be on time at every practice, for both the team's sake and his own development. The more practice time he misses, the fewer touches he gets with the ball. Over the course of the season, getting less practice will affect several areas of his game, including moving with the ball, passing to teammates, and shooting. It also makes building a cohesive unit more difficult, because his teammates aren't getting as many repetitions working with him.

✔ **Toss out some possible solutions.** Work with the parents to find a solution, which could be as simple as having a teammate's parent who lives nearby pick up the youngster and bring her to practice. (Check with the other parent before mentioning this possible alternative, of course.)

✔ **Practice attendance translates to playing time.** Remind parents that playing time in games is distributed based on practice attendance and that you'd hate to see their child penalized, but you have to be fair to the kids who are on time.

✔ **Timely attendance builds skills.** Because each of your practices builds on what you covered in the previous sessions, kids who are late miss out on valuable minutes. When a child is late and misses your instructions or a drill that emphasizes what you've addressed, his development is compromised, and his practice in that particular skill is limited.

Handling Problem Coaches

Volunteer lacrosse coaches show up at the field with all sorts of backgrounds and experiences with the sport. You will meet a lot of great people who care deeply about kids and want to ensure that all the players on the field have a fun and rewarding experience. Unfortunately, you may also encounter those who just don't get it when it comes to kids and lacrosse. Although you're more likely to see rude, out-of-control, and offensive behavior among coaches in the older age groups, it also happens at the beginning levels when games become competitive.

The following sections look at some of the most common problems you may encounter with coaches — both opposing coaches and those on your own sideline.

Opposing coaches who encourage unsafe play

Protecting your players and ensuring that both teams use only safe techniques on game days should be your top concern. Sure, in a contact sport like lacrosse, injuries happen. You can't always avoid the normal bumps and bruises that occur during the course of a season, particularly if you are coaching in a boys' league that allows checking. But if you find your team going against a squad that's being encouraged to use unsafe methods that put your players' well being at risk, you have to take immediate action. Here are some steps you should take:

- ✔ **Speak with the officials.** Any time you have a concern about inappropriate play on the field, speak with the referee, expressing concern that your players are being put at unnecessary risk. Be clear that you're concerned about the welfare of all the kids, not about how she's calling the game. Never be reluctant to bring up any issue that directly affects player safety. One of the referee's most important responsibilities is to protect the players, so by working with her — not against her — you can help ensure a safe day on the lacrosse field for all the youngsters.

- ✔ **Never confront the opposing coaches directly.** Use the referee as your intermediary to resolve the situation. Heading over to confront the opposing coach will just escalate the problems and cause more conflict. A direct confrontation could also antagonize the coach, who may feel that you've put his coaching techniques in question in front of all the fans. He may view your action as a ploy to affect his team's play, particularly if he's winning the game.

- ✔ **Put a halt to the game.** If the rough play doesn't cease after you've explained your concerns to the referee, and the kids' safety continues to be in jeopardy, your only recourse is to remove your team from the field. We hope you never encounter this situation, and in all likelihood, you never will. But if you do, keep in mind that finishing a lacrosse game simply to get it in the books, at the risk of injury to a child, is never worth it.

- ✔ **Meet with the league director.** If a league director monitors games at the facility where your team plays and is on the premises, speak with her about your concerns before pulling your players off the field. If she's not available, meet with her as soon as possible to explain your concerns about the game and why you felt that terminating the contest was in the best interest of your team.

Opposing coaches who display poor sportsmanship

It would be great for all the players in the league if every coach were a model of good behavior who shared only positive comments and instructions with his team. If you're lucky, you'll find yourself in that type of league, but the reality is that you'll find an occasional coach pacing up and down the side-line, wearing out his lungs, and screaming at players to run faster and defend better. These coaches may shower negative comments on referees and dispute any call that doesn't favor their team.

What's the best way to handle opposing coaches who are sabotaging the experience for everyone involved? Here are a few tips to keep in mind when the game heats up:

- ✔ **Keep a level head.** Opposing coaches who display unsportsmanlike behavior challenge your patience, test your poise, and can really get under your skin. You have to discover for yourself what works — and stick to it, no matter how discouraging the situation gets — for remaining a constant model of good behavior for your team. Your solution may be as simple as taking a deep breath and counting to 10; or turning your back and talking to your players on the bench. Find what works for you.

- ✔ **Use the situation as a teaching moment.** Point out to your team members the type of boorish behavior that's taking place on the other sideline. Remind them that they have to rise above that type of conduct, and demonstrate that they can be much better behaved.

- ✔ **Meet with the league director.** Make her aware which coach is setting a poor example for the kids, and outline the behavior that is disrupting the experience for everyone else.

- ✔ **Gather your team for a chat.** When the opposing coach is causing distractions with his behavior, get your kids together, and tell them to ignore the shouting and to focus on playing their own game. Keep talking to them in a positive manner; keep their attention focused on the game and on using their skills. Don't allow their attention to wander to the opposing coach's obnoxious behavior.

Dissenting assistants on your team

Assistant coaches play important roles on your team. They're extra sets of eyes and ears during games, and they can help provide instruction and keep drills moving during practices. But as I discuss in Chapter 4, exercising great caution in selecting people for these key positions is extremely important. What are some of the problems that you can run into with your assistant coaches? You may have an assistant who:

✔ **Wants his child to receive more playing time:** This person may have had ulterior motives from the start and volunteered to help you out simply as a way to get her child on the field more often or to play a specific position she had her eye on for her daughter. At the first sign of trouble have a private chat with the assistant and let her know that in order to continue in her role she'll have to abide by your rules and keep her focus on helping *all* of the kids.

✔ **Causes distractions during games:** Even the most laid-back, mild-mannered parents can evolve into sideline screamers as soon as the game begins. This type of behavior detracts from the kids' enjoyment and interferes with your coaching. Swift action is a must in these situations so that the assistant's behavior doesn't disrupt the entire game. Talk to them right away to rein in their emotional outbursts.

✔ **Isn't an effective teacher of skills:** You can't afford to have assistants who can't reinforce the proper way to perform a skill. Also, having unqualified assistants isn't fair to the kids. Even worse, assistants who teach kids unsafe techniques can create unnecessary risk of injury — not only to your players, but also to opposing players. You may have some great, well-meaning parents who raised their hands and volunteered to help you out, but if their knowledge of lacrosse is limited, or if they're unable to pick up from you how to teach and work with kids in a positive manner, all sorts of problems could occur. You can release the parent from his duties; or if he genuinely wants to help kids work with him on the proper way to teach skills so that he can make a positive impact during your practices.

✔ **Reveals a coaching philosophy that is opposite of yours:** During your preseason meeting with the parents (see Chapter 4), you should stress that winning is going to take a back seat to skill development, safety, and fun. Although all the parents may have nodded in agreement with your words back then, you may discover after the games begin that the parents who are now your assistants no longer share those views. Basically, they go against everything you want to stress to the kids and undermine the positive impact you are trying to make on each youngster. Have a chat with the assistant and give him a refresher on your philosophy and how you want him interacting with the players. If this discussion doesn't alleviate the problem, thank him for his time and relieve him of his duties.

Your assistant coaches are an extension of you — which makes everything they say and do on your behalf extremely important to the overall success of the season. Especially during your first few practices of the season, monitor them closely to see how they interact with the kids, oversee drills, and teach skills.

If an assistant isn't getting the job done or isn't adhering to the philosophies you're looking to instill in your team, you need to have a one-on-one talk with him right away to reinforce what you want to accomplish this season. Usually, this chat is enough to get the assistant back on the right track. If problems continue, let him know that you think it's in the best interest of the team for him to step down from his assistant duties. The position is simply too important for you to let a problem linger any longer than necessary, because it will detract from the kids' lacrosse experience. Be sure to thank the assistant for his time and effort, and encourage him to continue being a part of his child's season as a positive sideline supporter.

Dealing with Discipline Problems on Your Own Team

Teaching kids cradling, attacking, shooting, and defending are just some of the many aspects of lacrosse that test your coaching skills. Making sure that youngsters listen to your instructions, respect your authority, and abide by the team rules you set forth can pose a whole new set of challenges that you may not have been completely aware of — or prepared for — when you stepped forward to volunteer this season.

Because you're likely to be dealing with at least a dozen kids, chances are that at some point during the season, you'll have to discipline a child who steps over the line. Don't jump to the conclusion that children misbehave simply as a means to cause trouble. Sometimes, children act out in a disruptive manner because they're frustrated by their lack of progress, they feel that their contributions are going unnoticed, or they don't feel that they're really part of the team.

Giving players three strikes

You can rely on the three-strikes technique when dealing with discipline problems among your players. This method is effective because it gives the children a little room for error and gives you the chance to restructure their behavior.

Be sure to inform the parents of the procedure you will be following before any problems materialize so that everyone fully understands how punishment will be handed out.

Here's how the three-strikes technique works.

Strike one

The first time one of your players displays unacceptable behavior, issue a verbal warning. Let her know that you're not pleased with what she said or did, and that if she says or does it again, you'll hand out punishment.

Behavior that merits a strike-one warning includes swearing during a game or displaying unsportsmanlike conduct, such as refusing to shake the hand of an opposing player following a game. In most cases, when a child knows that a stricter measure will be enforced if she repeats the behavior, she isn't likely to do it again.

You're dealing with all different types of kids, of course, and for whatever reasons, some of them may ignore your warning or simply may not take it seriously. So be aware that your first warning may not produce the desired effect. Be willing to go to the next discipline level so that players don't trample your authority.

Strike two

If a player continues to disobey your instructions — if he's still swearing during games, for example — you have to go beyond the strike-one verbal warning to resolve the problem before it becomes an even bigger distraction to the team. Stepping up the punishment, such as taking away a portion of his playing time in the next game, sends a clear message that he has no room for negotiation and that if he doesn't stop this behavior immediately, he's not going to get back on the field. Let the player know in clear and specific terms that if he misbehaves again, he will jeopardize his future with the team.

After a strike-two warning, meet with the parents, and let them know what took place with their child. Explain to them that you want their child to be part of this team and that he won't have to face repercussions the rest of the season if he starts behaving in an appropriate manner. Relay exactly what you said to the child so that the parents can follow through at home. This reinforcement makes the child aware of the seriousness of his behavior and the need to take immediate action so he can continue playing on the team.

Let the parents know that their child will be sitting on the bench for an extended period as punishment for his behavior. If you happen to be coaching in a more competitive league, and the offending child is a starter, not allowing him to start is usually all you need to do to turn his behavior around.

Strike three

Most players steer clear of this unpleasant territory. In this three-tiered approach to passing out punishment, with coveted playing time at stake, most youngsters behave after the first or second verbal warning. But in the rare event that a child continues to behave in an unacceptable fashion, you may have no choice but to remove her from the team. You have a responsibility to all the players and can't allow one child's behavior to disrupt the experience for everyone else.

Ideally, you never want to be in a position to force a child away from lacrosse. Before you resort to this measure, a good idea is to meet with the league director to explain what has happened so far.

If the child does end up being kicked off the team, you can go so far as to allow her to return if she's willing to apologize to you and the team, and promises to be a model of good behavior from then on. Kids can turn over a new leaf. Maybe a few days away from the team will make her realize how much she misses playing lacrosse. When she knows that the door is cracked open for her return if she apologizes for her indiscretions, the potential exists for everything to work out in the end.

Trying other techniques

Following are a few other tips for handling behavior problems among your players:

- **Avoid using laps as punishment.** When a child disobeys your orders, you may be tempted to send him on a lap around the field as punishment, but refrain from going that route. Conditioning drills should never be used as a form of punishment. Because conditioning plays a very important role in lacrosse, especially at the more advanced levels of play, you don't want children associating conditioning and running with punishment. You want them to have a positive outlook on conditioning — not a negative one that can slow their development and take away some of their effectiveness.

- **Stick to your word.** When you outline your team rules, and describe the discipline that you'll deliver for breaking them, be sure to follow through whenever disciplinary action is warranted. Backing up your talk with action maintains your authority and respect with the team. You don't want to lose credibility, or your players' trust or respect, by failing to follow through when a team violation occurs.

- **Enforce the rules evenly.** One of the most disastrous moves you can make in disciplining children is playing favorites, allowing some kids to get away with certain behavior while punishing others for the same infraction. A youngster's ability to shoot the ball more accurately than her teammates or defend better doesn't mean that you should create another level of rules for her. Doing so divides the team and causes resentment among players, which is a surefire way to destroy team unity.

✔ **Apply punishment fairly.** Your job is to coach lacrosse, not to dole out punishment at every turn. Keep a level perspective while enforcing team policies. If a child forgets his water bottle at practice, don't view that infraction as being equal to swearing during a practice or game. During the course of a season, minor lapses are going to occur; don't go out of your way to turn them into major problems.

✔ **Ditch the doghouse.** When a misbehaving child's discipline is completed, both you and she have to push the problem to the side and move forward. Clinging to animosity or ill feelings won't do either of you any good. Show the child that you are willing to forget her past behavior by treating her exactly as you have all season. Keeping a child in the doghouse simply isn't fair when you've already punished her for her transgression. Instead, focus on making sure that she feels like a valued member of the team again. Recognize her when she does something well, which will help reassure her that the past problems have been forgotten.

✔ **Control your emotions.** Shouting or losing your temper distorts the discipline you're trying to enforce and set a poor example for the team.

✔ **Never discipline players for mistakes on the field.** Disciplining a child for an error on the field is never appropriate, even if it results in a winning goal for the opposition in the final seconds of a tied game. Breakdowns on defense, turnovers, and errant passes are always going to occur and should never result in any type of punishment.

On the other hand, if a player intentionally tries to injure an opponent or teammate — by tripping him, for example — immediately remove that player from the game. This type of behavior may warrant further disciplinary action on your part, depending on the severity of the action, the intent, and other factors that led up to the tripping incident.

The nonlistener

No matter how interesting your instructions, or how much great information you have to share with the kids, some are going to pay little attention to what you have to say about how to play the game. Some may think they already know how to perform all the skills, and others may just have no interest in learning from you and will tune you out and do their own thing. This inattentiveness can be especially troublesome if they employ techniques that, despite your continued instruction on how to perform them the right way, pose injury risks for other players.

If you see that a child isn't listening to your instructions, sit him down in practice and have him watch how the rest of the team follows your directions. After a few minutes, ask him whether he's ready to return to play and listen to what you have to say. Your nonlistener is likely to be much more receptive to your instructions after spending any length of time by your side while his teammates are on the field.

If the child isn't performing a skill correctly, and you suspect that she wasn't paying attention, ask the child why she isn't doing it like you demonstrated. Maybe she didn't understand your instructions and out of frustration tried doing it the way she thinks it should be done.

Playing time is as valuable to you as a hand full of aces is to a poker player. When dealing with problems with your players taking away playing time — or just the mere threat of it — is a great equalizer for a lot of problems. It also has the power to change attitudes and improve attention spans. No one enjoys having his fanny stuck on the bench while his friends and teammates are out on the field during Game Day. Taking away playing time from a child who misbehaves is no different than a parent taking away TV, computer games, or treats from a child at home who misbehaves.

The nonstop talker

You may find that some kids on your team talk more than a radio deejay, and that can cause some problems from time to time. When you have players on the team who are more interested in talking than listening to what you have to say it can create a lot of unwanted distractions. This is particularly true if the team is only hearing bits and pieces of your instructions, because your effectiveness as a coach is being compromised, along with the development of the rest of your squad. Read on to see which techniques work best for curbing the vocal cords of those kids whose mouths seem to run non-stop.

As soon as you get a sense that too much talking is going on, toss out a reminder to the team that when you're speaking all the team members must remain quiet so that everyone can hear what you are saying. If that fails and the talking continues, you may have to call the player out in front of everyone. For example, say something like "Evan, please don't talk while I'm addressing the team. It's important that everyone hears what I'm going over. If you have a comment or question, please hold it until I'm done or raise your hand."

Either of those approaches usually quiets the problem, but if you continue to experience disruptions, it's time for a one-on-one chat. Pull the player aside and be firm in your stance that he must abide by your rules or face the consequences — and then spell those rules out clearly so he knows the penalties for any continued misbehavior. If you have to reprimand him again to be quiet, let him know that he's going to lose significant amounts of playing time. Usually this threat is enough to get his attention — and close his mouth.

Any time you have a personal chat with a youngster regarding his behavior, and what the results will be if it continues in a negative fashion, be sure to alert his parents, as well. Keeping Mom and Dad updated on what is going on helps prevent further problems down the road if you are forced to discipline the child.

Failures to communicate: Coaching kids who don't (or won't) listen

No matter how interesting your instructions are or how much great information you have to share, some kids pay little attention to what you have to say. Some think they already know how to perform all the skills; others have no interest in learning from you, so they tune you out and do their own thing. Here are some tips on coping with inattentive players:

✔ If you see that a child isn't listening to your instructions, sit him down during practice, and have him watch how the rest of the team follows your directions. After a few minutes, ask him whether he's ready to return to play and listen to what you have to say. Your nonlistener is likely to be much more receptive to your instructions after spending any length of time by your side while his teammates are on the field.

✔ If the child isn't performing a skill correctly, and you suspect that she wasn't paying attention, ask the child why she isn't doing it the way you demonstrated. Maybe she didn't understand your instructions and, out of frustration, tried performing the skill the way she thought it should be done.

✔ As soon as you get a sense that too much talking is going on, remind the players that when you're speaking, they must remain quiet so that everyone can hear what you are saying. If that reminder fails, and the talking continues, you may have to call a player out in front of everyone. Say something like this: "Evan, please don't talk while I'm addressing the team. It's important that everyone hears what I'm going over. If you have a comment or question, please hold it until I'm done or raise your hand."

✔ If you continue to experience disruptions, pull the player aside for a one-on-one chat. Be firm in your stance that she must abide by your rules or face the consequences — and then spell those rules out clearly so that she knows the penalties for continued misbehavior. Let her know that she's going to lose significant amounts of playing time if you have to reprimand her again. Usually, this threat is enough to get a child's attention — and close her mouth.

Chapter 19

Coaching a Lacrosse Travel Team

Many kids love the challenge of developing new lacrosse skills and, as they progress, putting those skills to use in more-competitive programs. The same goes for some coaches, who crave teaching advanced strategies and techniques to players in highly competitive environments. At this point, coaching travel teams enters the picture.

If you think you're ready to take over a travel lacrosse team, this chapter is for you. Here, you find everything you need to know to make your transition to the travel-team sideline a smoother one. You get details on the do's and don'ts of running a tryout, tips for putting together your team, insight on dealing with problems that can arise on the road, and pointers for making the season a rewarding one.

Getting Familiar with Travel Teams

The travel-team environment is vastly different from what you may have been used to in local recreation programs. The games tend to be highly competitive, and your team will be facing opponents from different communities — in some cases, even from different states. As long as you maintain your focus on providing for the best interests of all the kids, the travel-team experience can be richly rewarding for everyone involved.

Travel teams are good opportunities for youngsters who are interested in focusing on lacrosse as their main sport and who want to play against top-level competition on a regular basis. These teams give kids the chance to play in highly competitive tournaments against other talented teams. They also require a much greater time commitment from both players and parents than recreational lacrosse programs do.

A typical week on a travel team usually involves several practices, and weekends are often swallowed up by traveling and competing in tournaments. Seasons typically run much longer than in recreational programs and usually entail a larger financial commitment from parents to cover all the costs associated with travel.

Generally speaking, travel teams are best for older kids with advanced skills. Because of the increased level of play, the added pressure that typically accompanies these teams, and the fuller schedule of practices and games, most experts say that kids younger than 12 should not be involved with travel teams. Instead, they should be introduced to a variety of sports and activities that allow them to develop a wide range of skills — including balance, coordination, and agility — before specializing in one sport.

This guideline is a general one, of course. Children mature at vastly different rates, both emotionally and physically, and some 11-year-olds may be better equipped to handle the travel-team experience than a 13-year-old would be.

Assembling Your Travel Team

Coaching youth lacrosse can be challenging, and taking the reins of a travel team presents even more situations that will test your coaching prowess. Besides running tryouts and analyzing players' abilities, you have the unpleasant task of breaking the bad news to those players who didn't make the team. In this section, we explore how to handle all these areas.

Planning the tryout

Orchestrating a well-run lacrosse tryout speaks volumes about your coaching ability and makes choosing the players much easier. The following pointers can help you plan your tryout efficiently so that you can select the players who most deserve to play on the team.

Limit the tryout to 1 hour for kids ages 12 and younger. For older kids, you can bump it up to 1½ to 2 hours. If you need to hold a couple of sessions to evaluate all the kids effectively, that's fine. You're much better off holding a pair of 1-hour sessions than a single 2-hour session.

Start on a positive note

Take a couple of minutes at the start of the tryout to introduce yourself and outline how you plan to run the session. Letting players know ahead of time what is in store for them will ease their stress and eliminate surprises along the way. Also, it allows them to focus on performing to the best of their ability — which is good news for you, because you'll get an accurate gauge of their skills and talent level.

Warm up the players

You must keep the safety and well being of the players in mind at all times, which means approaching the tryout the same way you would a regular practice with your team. Begin by having the players go through a proper warm-up. (For more on warming up, see Chapter 17.) If you rely on the players to warm up on their own, some of them may not do a very effective job, thereby opening the door to unwanted injuries.

Avoid choosing players to lead the stretches. Even if you're familiar with some of the players and know that they'd do a great job leading the warm-ups, that tactic sends the wrong message to everyone else. The other kids may think that you're already playing favorites and that these kids are tapped for positions on the team before they even try out.

Provide a few pointers

You don't want to get too caught up in coaching, simply because that takes away from the purpose of the tryout: evaluating the players' skills. But sprinkling your tryout with some coaching pointers isn't a bad idea. After all, providing some coaching tips will give you a chance to observe how the kids react to instruction, feedback, and even constructive criticism. You'll be coaching some of these players for several months, so it's helpful to gain some insight into how receptive they are to your feedback.

Make drills gamelike

Running timed sprints down the field isn't a good evaluation tool; neither is determining how quickly a youngster can maneuver with the ball through a series of cones. If one player completes the course in 22 seconds, and another youngster takes 20 seconds, what have you really learned about the talent level of these two individuals? Not a whole lot, especially if the player who ran through the cones faster had his head down the entire time — a tactic that won't bode well when he's on the field in a game and needs to know where his teammates are, as well as any defenders who are converging on him.

The best way to assess talent and determine whether players are ready for competition at the travel-team level is to put them in situations that closely mirror game conditions. That way, you see how they respond to pressure and what types of decisions they make while playing both offense and defense.

Maximize the action

Observing players in small-sided games — two-on-two or three-on-three — provides a wealth of information on their abilities. Putting them in situations that allow them plenty of touches of the ball will help you determine how they make the transition from offense to defense, how they recognize various situations, and how they plan to move and defend. Taking in all this information and noticing these tendencies are vital for getting a true evaluation of a youngster's abilities in lacrosse.

This information will also be extremely valuable for the players you do end up choosing, because you can use it to help determine which positions they are best suited for.

Limit the stations

If you elect to use several stations during your tryout — such as a shooting station to evaluate a goalie's performance and other players' shooting skills — limit the number of stations you have going at the same time. (A station is simply an area of the field that is devoted to a specific skill that the players work on during practice.) Having too many stations running simultaneously prevents you from monitoring all the players effectively. The more assistants that you have helping out, the more stations you can run. If you've only got one assistant, it does little good to have half a dozen stations running at one time because it's impossible to monitor all the kids and how they are performing skills.

Also, if some kids see that you are not at their station watching them, they (understandably) may not be quite as focused on giving their best effort, which detracts from the effectiveness of the entire tryout process.

Thank the players and parents

At the conclusion of the tryout, be sure to thank the players for following instructions and doing their best. Also thank the parents for their willingness to get the kids to the field on time and for adjusting their busy schedules to accommodate the tryout. Saying "Thank you" is a nice touch that further demonstrates how much you truly care.

Selecting players

Planning a well-structured tryout is the first step in putting together your travel team. Now, while the kids are running, passing, defending, giving it their all, and collecting grass stains, you've got to keep close tabs on all of them to determine which ones deserve the chance to play for you this season.

Evaluating skills is important, but be sure that you and your assistants take a look at these sometimes-overlooked areas during the selection process:

- **Teamwork:** Assessing how players work with their teammates is crucial. A great passer is an asset to the team if she looks for open teammates; she's a major liability if she's reluctant to give up possession of the ball. A highly skilled player must be a team player to fit into the framework of your squad.

- **Demeanor:** Does the player get noticeably upset when a teammate fails to deliver an accurate pass to him that could have resulted in a scoring opportunity? Does he get visibly frustrated when his pass isn't handled efficiently and the opposing team gains possession of the ball? You want players who are supportive, rather than negative, toward their teammates.

- **Competitive spirit:** Don't neglect the mental aspect. Keep a close watch on each player to see what type of competitor she is. When she loses the ball to a defender, does she focus on regaining possession, or does she tend to become frustrated and pout? Is she a good sport who plays within the rules, or does she resort to unfavorable tactics at times?

These traits aren't automatic qualifiers or disqualifiers, because you have to evaluate each child individually. But if you elect to choose a child who behaved inappropriately at times during the tryout, you are responsible for working with that youngster and teaching him the importance of behaving in a respectful manner.

Having extra sets of eyes overseeing the tryout can be a big help, particularly if you have a large turnout. If you have several adults helping you, make sure that they get a chance to see all the kids perform; otherwise, their evaluations won't be as accurate and comprehensive as they could be. To make the process more effective, make a list of the skills you want your evaluators to monitor, such as speed, quickness, shooting, passing, receiving, and defending.

If you're taking the place of a coach who handled the team last season, ask her advice, because she has valuable information about the types of kids who play and compete best at this level.

Breaking the good — and bad — news to players

Informing a child that he made the team and seeing that smile on his face are great perks of coaching a travel lacrosse team. Unfortunately, those perks are balanced by the need to give bad news to the kids who *didn't* make the team. You and the players alike will experience a wide range of emotions when it comes to this part of the travel-team process. You'll have happiness and heartbreak, smiles and sadness, and deliriousness and disappointment.

Here are some do's and don'ts when it comes to informing kids whether they will be wearing a travel-team jersey for you this season:

- ✔ **Don't drag the process out.** Make your decisions in a timely manner. Think about going on an interview for a job you really coveted and how nerve-wracking it was, waiting to hear whether you got the position. The kids who try out for your lacrosse team feel the same way. Naturally, they're going to be anxious to hear whether they made the cut, so be as prompt as possible in your decision-making process.

- ✔ **Notify everyone.** Sure, your life would be much easier if all you had to do was deliver the good news to the kids who made the team. But in fairness to all the youngsters who sweated and poured out their hearts in every drill you put them through, you've got to personally let every player know whether or not she made the team.

- ✔ **Discuss your playing-time policy.** When informing kids that they made the team, be sure to clearly explain to them (and their parents) that playing time during the season will be determined by ability. Some parents may be under the impression that because they're taking on additional costs, their child will be starting every game. Make sure that everyone understands that travel teams are vastly different from recreational leagues, and that although all players will receive plenty of work in practice, playing time in games will be handed out to those who possess the most skills and who can put the team in position to perform at its best.

- ✔ **Break bad news gently.** Yes, a child will be disappointed when she finds out that she didn't make the team. But what you say — and how you say it — can determine how long that disappointment lingers and whether she uses it as motivation to work on her skills. (See the nearby sidebar, "Cushioning the blow of bad news.")

Cushioning the blow of bad news

Telling a child that he didn't make the team is like telling him that he won't have any presents to open on his birthday. This news can crush a child's confidence and self-esteem, and you've got to do everything you can to soften the blow of this setback. You don't want it to squash a player's enthusiasm for the sport or derail his interest in playing.

Make it clear that your choice is not a judgment of the child as a person. Let the youngster and his parents know what areas of his game you were impressed with, as well as the areas that he should do a little more work on. A good idea is to offer specific suggestions on how he can improve the weaker areas of his game.

Also make sure that you encourage him to try out again next season. He simply may need one more season of recreational play to hone his skills before he makes the jump to this more-competitive level of play. You don't want the child to regret that he tried out.

Handling Problems away from Home

Coaching a travel lacrosse team involves much more than just figuring out who should handle the offensive and defensive roles or who should start in goal in the upcoming weekend tournament. Several issues often arise away from the field, and you must deal with all of them, because they directly affect everyone's experience. This section takes a look at some of the most common problems that pop up on the road.

Safety issues

Being in charge of a large group of youngsters for an out-of-town tournament that requires an overnight stay is an enormous responsibility. Just think about it: You've got to ensure the safety of every child on the lacrosse field, on the road to and from the event, and at the location where the team is staying overnight. You're going to be accountable at all times. You're also a chaperone, so you need to monitor and know the whereabouts of all your players all the time. Keep the following tips in mind to ensure all the kids' safety:

- ✔ **Pair 'em up:** Partner the kids up and make sure they understand they are responsible for knowing the whereabouts of their partner at all times during the trip.

- ✔ **Make carpool assignments:** By making specific assignments of who is driving which kids you'll have written documentation of where the kids are at all times.

- ✔ **Enforce curfews:** It's simply not safe to have kids roaming around the motel without adult supervision, so set reasonable curfews based on their ages and hold them to it. Make it clear that any players who break curfew will not be allowed to play in the upcoming game.

Behavior issues

What unfolds on the field is certainly a major responsibility of yours, but what takes place away from it should also have your full attention. When you take a team of kids (and parents) to a weekend tournament, certain issues have the potential to crop up at some point, including the following.

Curfews

Children naturally enjoy staying in motels and swimming in the pool, but if they're going to perform at their best on the field, you must enforce curfews. The ages of the players and the starting time of their game the following day should dictate the time of the curfew.

Let both the kids and their parents know in advance what time the curfew will be. This notice helps eliminate the chance that misunderstandings will occur.

Excessive parental partying

For many busy families these days, weekend lacrosse tournaments are the only vacations they have time for, so parents want to enjoy themselves. That's perfectly fine as long as their good times don't escalate into problems, such as excessive drinking or noise in the motel during the evening.

Before departing for any tournament that will require an overnight stay, let the parents know that you want them to have a good time and enjoy themselves, but remind them that the tournament is a youth lacrosse event. Parents need to model good behavior and set a good example at all times.

If partying parents pose a problem, the following are some pointers to keep in mind:

- ✔ **Address it right away.** You don't want situations to escalate out of control, or carry over from one night to the next if it's an extended stay for your team. The quicker you act, the sooner the problem can be resolved.

- ✔ **Offer reminders.** Take time to remind the parents that this is a youth sports event and to act accordingly. Parents may not have realized they were behaving inappropriately, and your reminder is often all it takes to put things in perspective.

Extracurricular activities

Competing in tournaments in different locations provides opportunities for sightseeing and for participating in activities away from the lacrosse field. But the last thing you want is for your players to be so exhausted from sightseeing that they can't give you their best efforts.

Before departing for the event, go over the tournament schedule with the players and their parents, and let them know well in advance whether they'll have any time for extracurricular activities. Clearly, if the team happens to be playing four games in a two-day period, parents won't be able to arrange extra activities for their kids.

If your team gets a break in the tournament schedule, you need to decide whether you want to organize a team activity or to allow the parents and kids to do their own things.

Keep in mind the added expense of extra activities; you don't want to put a financial strain on some parents or force them to participate in events that they may not be able to afford. You also don't want one child to be left out of an activity if the rest of the team is going. Spending an off day at a nearby amusement park, for example, isn't a great idea if ticket prices are out of range for some parents.

Enjoying the Season

Sometimes, youngsters need a little time to adjust to the travel-team schedule. After all, they have more practices and games to play in during the week than they're accustomed to; they have suitcases to pack and new locales to play in for out-of-town tournaments; and they have increased competition for playing time, because some of their teammates are bigger, stronger, and more skilled in some areas of the game than they are.

The following sections cover how you can help ensure that your players aren't overwhelmed by the experience and that they have a memorable lacrosse experience — for all the right reasons.

Warding off burnout

Some lacrosse travel-team seasons can stretch on for several months, which increases the chance that players will suffer burnout. Burnout typically involves a combination of physical and emotional exhaustion. Even though kids love playing lacrosse, if they are subjected to a heavier practice schedule than they are accustomed to, as well as an increased number of games, they are susceptible to burnout.

Here are some tips to keep your team energized and avoid being tripped up by burnout:

- ✔ **Rely on variety.** With the extra practice load, providing kids a wide range of drills throughout the week is more important than ever. The more variety you spice up your practices with, the less likely your players are to become drained from participating.

- ✔ **Emphasize fun.** Pressure to win can be a heavy burden on a team; eventually, it can sap your kids' energy and cripple their enthusiasm. You want your players to do their best to win games, of course, but you don't want them to forget to have fun. Remind them that lacrosse is a fun sport to play and that you want them to enjoy their participation. Make it clear to them that doing their best, and having fun doing so, outweighs winning.

✔ **Modify the practice schedule.** If your team has a heavy tournament schedule on the horizon or will be playing several games in a short time span, ease back on the practice schedule leading up to those games. This cutback will help keep the kids' energy and enthusiasm at optimum levels. Cutting back on practice can also help prevent problems, because after burnout settles in, the only real solution is plenty of rest and time away from the sport.

Keeping everyone interested in the game

Even though you distribute the biggest chunks of playing time to the most talented players at the travel-team level, remember that every child — whether she's the team's leading scorer or the least talented member of the group — plays an important role. You're responsible for making sure that your players are fully aware of that fact.

When players are on the bench during games, you want them to be actively involved in cheering their teammates on and supporting them. Also encourage them to monitor the action closely. Having the players keep an eye on the game not only holds their attention, but also enables them to spot weaknesses of the opposing team that your team could exploit. Encouraging players to take an active role in all areas of the game, whether they are on the field or not, enhances their experience and further instills the message that they are valuable members of the team.

Part VI:
The Part of Tens

The 5th Wave   By Rich Tennant

"Cameron's approach to coaching youth lacrosse
is a combination of Vince Lombardi, Dr. Phil,
and Harry Potter."

In this part . . .

If you're looking for some clever ways to prepare your players for a lacrosse game, or to help your goaltender turn in a strong performance in the nets, you've come to the right place. You also get the scoop on qualities that all good lacrosse players possess and how you can instill those traits in the kids under your care.

Chapter 20

Ten Qualities All Good Lacrosse Players Possess

In This Chapter

▶ Mastering the basics

▶ Motivating and setting a shining example

▶ Focusing on the feet

*L*acrosse requires a broad range of skills to play — let alone to play well. Some kids naturally have a lot of the qualities that make a talented and well-rounded player; others need to work a little bit harder to develop those traits. As the coach, you can help instill these coveted qualities in your players to help them get the most out of their season playing for you.

Fanatical About the Fundamentals

One of the really neat things about lacrosse (besides the cool equipment) is that those players who aren't the biggest, strongest, or fastest can excel on the field when they thoroughly understand the fundamental skills and how to use them against opposing players. Although natural athletic ability is always a bonus, it's not a necessity for being a productive player at the offensive and defensive ends of the field. Players who have mastered the fundamentals are valuable to any team at any level of play, because they

✔ Understand how to pass the ball accurately while being defended.

✔ Have mastered catching and can snag passes on the run or in traffic.

✔ Know how to scoop up loose balls and are proficient at doing so.

One of the best approaches for instilling a love of the basics in players is to continually stress their importance at every practice. The more your players understand how passionate you are about these areas of the game, the more of a liking they'll take to them — and it'll pay off in their performance. So, during your practices be sure to make a big deal out of the little things players do well.

Loves the Game

Kids who are passionate about lacrosse tend to perform more efficiently, and at higher levels, than those whose feelings for the sport are just so-so. You can help fuel your players' desire for the game by making practices fun-filled experiences, and by reminding them that simply doing their best and putting forth their maximum effort is what participating in lacrosse is all about. The right coaching approach can lead a child to become enamored with lacrosse; the wrong approach can spur him to look for another sport to participate in.

Devoted to Defense

All kids love running up and down the field with the ball and attacking on offense, but what they do on defense often makes the biggest difference. Because your team will spend roughly half of every game on defense, those players who commit to excelling in this area of the game will be valuable assets. By praising your players' defensive tenacity and willingness to play as enthusiastically without the ball as with it, you'll help mold those coveted all-around players, whom all coaches love for their ability to affect the game.

Cares Deeply About the Team

Scoring goals and hearing the applause from all the moms, dads, and grandparents ranks high on most players' list. But the kids who care about making the team better, even when they're not the ones actually putting the ball in the net, are truly the most valuable. How do you spot them? They're the ones who get genuinely excited when a teammate scores — maybe even more so than if they had scored themselves. Some kids are naturally inclined to care more about the team than about themselves. During your practices monitor your compliments to make sure you aren't zeroing in on just the ones scoring the goals. Recognize the efforts of the players who made the passes that generated the scoring opportunity. When kids see that you applaud with as much enthusiasm the passes that lead to goals as you do the actual goals, they'll be much more likely to buy into your team-oriented approach.

Master Motivator

Players can get their motivation for doing their best during practices and games from many sources. Although coaches and parents are the most obvious motivators, teammates can also handle this role — and excel at it, too. Some players have a natural gift for pushing their teammates to play with more enthusiasm, to concentrate harder, and to strive for higher levels.

Although you need to understand the role that you play in motivating players, and how to best go about it (check out Chapter 2 for more details), when you discover players who are good at motivating their teammates, take full advantage of that skill. As you'll see, many times kids respond much better to teammates encouraging them and pushing them than they do to adults.

Never allow players to use intimidation tactics, cursing, or any demeaning words while trying to push their teammates to higher levels of performance.

Fantastic with Footwork

In dancing, balancing on a tightrope, and playing lacrosse, the importance of good footwork simply can't be overstated. The better the footwork, the greater the chance of success at both ends of the field. Lacrosse requires a great deal of hand-eye coordination for passing and catching balls, but players must rely on their feet to get into position to make those passes and catches.

On defense, a player's ability to maneuver her feet takes on an even more prominent role, because the better she is at moving in all directions — with no notice — the better she can shut down opposing players. During your practice drills (check out Chapters 7 and 14 for a wide selection of drills), be sure to watch your players' footwork so that they don't develop bad habits that will minimize their offensive and defensive effectiveness on game day.

A Good Sport

Sure, as a lacrosse coach, you love having players who possess powerful shots that opposing goalies find impossible to stop, or who are so fleet of foot that defenders struggle to keep up with them. Yet one of the most important characteristics — and often, one that doesn't get the attention it deserves — is being a good sport.

The essence of competing in lacrosse is to do your best and display good sportsmanship at all times, win or lose. That can be tough when the team lost a close game or certain calls didn't go your way, but losses are part of the game. Make sure that your players understand that they can't win all the time, because they can't control the outcome of games. The sooner they understand that, the better. What they *can* control is how they behave during and after games, which is a direct reflection on you, as both a coach and a person.

A Good Listener

No matter how good a coach you are, if you can't get the players to soak up your knowledge, your team won't be nearly as effective as it could be. The best lacrosse players recognize that the quickest route to learning and improving is listening to the coaches. Good listening skills affect other aspects of the game, too. At more-advanced levels of play, you may make strategy adjustments at halftime. If some players aren't listening, chances are good that the team won't perform as well as it could have, because everyone wasn't on the same page. Kids have short attention spans. Stick to simple points and don't resort to long-winded speeches. Remember, the less chance you allow the kids' minds to wander, the more they'll learn from you.

Understands the Rules

If you take a vacation in a foreign country, your trip will be more enjoyable if you understand the language. The same principle applies to lacrosse. The better players understand the rules — many of which may seem fairly bizarre — the more fun they'll have playing the game and the more effective they'll be on the field. (For a rundown on the rules of lacrosse, check out Chapter 3.)

Leads by Example

The best teammates are the ones kids can look up to — and strive to emulate — because of their positive work ethic, attitude, and overall approach to the game. These players help set a positive tone during practice by working hard and having fun doing so, which naturally encourages other teammates to follow in their footsteps. Continually talk to players about the importance of working hard and doing their best at all times. Remind them that they don't have to be the most talented in order to make a difference in games. It's the kids who chase down loose balls that can swing games in their team's favor, and that's accomplished simply by hustling at all times. Applaud these traits in your players, and they'll be more likely to embrace them.

Chapter 21

Ten Ways to Prepare Players for a Lacrosse Game

Many aspects go into preparing a lacrosse team to take the field, and you can go about the job in many ways. The better you are at getting the kids ready for game day, the more likely they are to perform up to their abilities — and to have a lot of fun at the same time.

From what to say in pregame practices to how you interact with your players before taking the field, this chapter has you covered. Use the information presented here to prepare your players for an exciting, fun-filled day of lacrosse.

Scout the Opposition

If you're coaching an advanced-level lacrosse team, one of the best ways to prepare your team for the upcoming game is to check out the opponent ahead of time. By attending one of the opposing team's games, you can gain a good perspective about how the players attack when they have the ball on offense, which players take the majority of the shots, and how they tend to perform on defense. You can share this valuable information with your players to let them know which opponents they need to pay extra attention to in certain aspects of the game.

Visualize Success

Visualization is a great tool to help your players get in the proper mindset to play well. The night before a game, for example, encourage players to visualize making accurate passes and scooping up loose balls, as well as performing other skills that they'll rely on during the game. If a player has a positive image in his head, that image will increase his chance of performing the skill during the game just the way he imagined it.

Accentuate the Positive at Practice

You can help boost a team's confidence and send it into the next game poised to play well simply by choreographing the final minutes of your pregame practice. This coaching trick is a great one to rely on, and here's how it works: In your last practice leading up to a game, run a drill that allows the team to perform its strongest skill or run a play that it always does well. This drill instills in kids a positive memory that they'll take away from the field with them — one that will reside in their memory banks on game day.

Express Your Enthusiasm

Youngsters involved in lacrosse want to play well to make their coaches, parents, and other family members proud of them. You can help increase their chances of turning in a strong performance by letting them know before the game begins that you are eager to watch them in action. Just a few seconds of praise are often enough to fuel a game-long boost in your players' confidence and self-esteem. You can talk to individual players about particular skills they worked on in practice during the week and improved on, such as scooping up loose balls or defending against an attacking player.

Accept Mistakes

The best lacrosse players in the collegiate and professional ranks drop passes, overrun loose balls, and send passes sailing over teammates' heads. These events are known as *mistakes,* and they happen to everybody at every level of play.

Although mistakes aren't fun to make, your players must understand that they happen from time to time. Players can't allow mistakes to infringe on their experience or affect the remainder of the game. If a player makes an errant pass that is intercepted by the opposition, for example, he can't change his style of play and be afraid to make other passes.

Before the game, encourage players to push mistakes out of their mind the moment they happen and to direct all their attention to the next play.

Sidestep the Pressure Phrases

Just like an attacking player sidestepping the check of an oncoming defender, you must avoid using pressure phrases in your interactions with the team. Setting a performance goal for the team — such as scoring eight goals in a game or committing only five turnovers — may seem to be motivational, but it can have the reverse effect of setting the kids up for disappointment. They could play really well that day but leave the field frustrated because they failed to reach your goal.

Your players can only give you their best efforts; they can't control the outcome of games.

Share Your Own Experiences

You can use your childhood experiences playing lacrosse, or any other organized sport, to help your players learn and grow. If you can share a humorous experience with your team, that story lets them know that crazy things happen to everyone on the lacrosse field and that they have to accept the unexpected. If your players can learn to laugh about the quirks of the game, they'll be able to forget mistakes faster and can continue having fun playing the game.

Relating some of your childhood sports memories can also serve other purposes. Telling your players how you overcame some adversity, for example, lets them know that they can achieve success too.

Focus on the Fun Factor

Telling players to have fun during their lacrosse game is simple, straightforward, and to the point. It's also one of the most important points you can stress to young players. Don't worry about overstating the fun factor, because you really can't do it enough. Participating in organized lacrosse — at any age or ability level — must be fun, because playing the game is all about fun. Instilling enjoyment in your players paves the way for a great day of lacrosse.

Minimize Instructions

Kids are like sponges; they can soak up a lot of information. But if you get carried away with your instructions, whether during your pregame talk or during the last practice before a game, chances are that they won't retain as much as you had hoped. Keep your instructions to a minimum. That way, your main points are more likely to stick with the players, who are less likely to become overwhelmed and confused.

Take a Few Deep Breaths

Sometimes, adults get nervous filing their tax returns, meeting the future in-laws for the first time, or asking an attractive co-worker out for dinner. We get nervous because we really care about what happens (especially when it comes to not getting shot down on that date request!).

By the same token, some of your players are likely to experience butterflies in their stomachs before games. Nervousness is perfectly normal — and a good indicator that they really care about the game and performing well in it.

Let them know that even professional athletes experience jitters before games. To ensure that nerves don't handcuff their ability to perform, have them take a few deep breaths, inhaling and exhaling slowly, which helps calm the body and relax the muscles.

Chapter 22

Twelve Tips to Help Goaltenders Excel in the Nets

Goaltender is arguably the most difficult lacrosse position for kids to learn, and you can easily see why: A ball keeps whipping at high speed toward the net the goalie is protecting, with shots coming from all sorts of angles. Compounding the difficulty of stopping these shots (which can arrive everywhere from low to the ground to shoulder high and above), other players are moving back and forth in front of the net, obstructing the goalie's vision.

For a rundown of the fundamentals of playing goaltender, check out Chapter 10. For some really good tips — if we do say so ourselves — to help your young goalies excel at this position, read on.

Moving Past Mistakes

Being forgetful isn't good when it comes to your anniversary or where you left your car keys, but it's a great trait for lacrosse goalies to adopt, and you can help. When goaltenders surrender goals, they're going to be disappointed — understandably — but some kids take disappointment a lot harder than others do.

During your practices, remind your goalies that they *will* give up goals during games, because shutouts are rare and difficult to pull off. Emphasize the fact that how they bounce back from lost goals makes the real difference in their level of play. Work with them to shove the score out of their minds and focus on the next shot or play. Let them know that if they spend time thinking about the goal just scored, they won't be able to devote their full attention to the current play, which increases the likelihood of giving up a goal that they might have been able to stop otherwise.

Exercising the Vocal Cords

Lacrosse is a team sport that requires constant communication, especially at the defensive end of the field, to minimize scoring threats from the opposition. Because the goalie has the best view of the field and can spot plays unfolding more easily than his teammates, who may have their backs turned defending other players, he must let them know when they need to apply pressure on a player, defend a cutter, or get out and cover a player who is roaming free. They are also the field general and can't be afraid to direct their teammates on where they need to be based on the location of the ball or the positioning of the opponent.

Goalies can make their jobs much easier, and be more successful in the process, if they let their teammates know what needs to be done to tighten defensive play.

Staying Alert

Maintaining complete concentration during an entire lacrosse game can be pretty tough for a goaltender to pull off, especially if much of the play takes place at the opposite end of the field. Also, other factors may vie for a goalie's attention, such as Grandma on the sidelines taking pictures or a younger sibling trying to catch her eye.

To help keep a goalie's attention from wandering off course, teach her tricks she can use to maintain focus and stay sharp so that when the opposition is attacking at her end of the field, she'll be ready to make saves. When her team is on the attack, for example, she can keep track of the number of passes her teammates make or how many shots they generate on goal. The goalie can also help point out tendencies he notices in the opposing goalie — such as he always drops his stick low to the ground when a player winds up to take a shot — that can benefit his teammates and lead to more goals. Tracking the action keeps the goalie's mind active and into the game, and leaves less room for straying to nongame thoughts such as what she's going to do after the game or what she's having for dinner.

Talking to Yourself

Having conversations with yourself can seem a bit abnormal, but for a lacrosse goalie, one-sided chats can be as useful as quick reactions in stopping shots. Being a successful goalie requires having not just good skills, but also the confidence that when a shot is on the way, he'll be able to turn it away. Encourage your goalie to remind himself that he's good at what he does, which is why you've positioned him in front of the net.

Here are some other phrases you should encourage goalies to recite to themselves:

- "I love being challenged and making great saves."
- "I will stop the next shot to help my team."
- "I'm an excellent goalie."
- "I've had a great week of practice and know I'm going to play really well today."

Taking Some Deep Breaths

A little pre-game nervousness is fine, but too much of it can hinder reflexes and cut down on effectiveness. The best lacrosse goalies are those who are relaxed when the game begins. Sure, great reflexes and natural athletic ability help, but relaxed goalies tend to fare better and have more success denying shots than those who are uptight.

Teach your goalie to take a few long, deep breaths, sucking air all the way into her lungs and then slowly exhaling. Deep breathing before the game begins is the perfect antidote to unwanted nerves and helps relax the goalie's body so she can perform to the best of her ability.

Building Reflexes

Good reflexes come in handy for stopping shots and frustrating opponents. Executing fundamental techniques is crucial to success in the nets (refer to Chapter 10), but a goalie who knows that he has sharp reflexes knows that he can challenge shooters and change the momentum of the game with a big save — such as snatching an in-close shot out of the air in the blink of an eye. Every practice should include a goalie drill that targets building reflexes. Check out Chapters 7 and 14 for some drills that meet those needs.

Visualizing Positive Play

"If you see it, you can achieve it" may sound like a corny motivational phrase or a sticker slapped on a car's bumper, but in terms of making a youth lacrosse goalie effective, this phrase really does pack some punch. Work with your goalies to get them into the habit of visualizing stopping all sorts of shots. The night before a game, while they're lying in bed relaxed, encourage them to spend five minutes picturing themselves making good saves. This positive imagery can transfer over to game day and help them trust their ability. Before your practices start, have the goalies spend a moment visualizing having success stopping shots too, to help them get into the routine of carrying over those thoughts and images to their actual play on the field.

Maintain Good Conditioning

Just because a goalie doesn't do anywhere near the amount of running as an attacker, or any of his other teammates, that doesn't mean that conditioning takes a backseat when playing in front of the net. A goalie is required to move from side to side, and make lots of sudden moves, all of which can tire him out and lead to slower reaction times when dealing with opponents' shots. Goalies must take pride in their conditioning, because the stronger they are and the better shape they're in, the more success they'll enjoy denying goals.

Focus on Becoming a Well-Rounded Player

Being a lacrosse goalie that opponents cringe facing means being skillful in different aspects of the game. Stopping shots is the top priority for any goalie, but there's more to it. Goalies who are excellent passers can spark fast-break attacks that keep the opposition off balance. Goalies should be encouraged to work on their passing skills, during practice and at home with family or friends if they are interested in improving in this area. During your practice drills don't just have your goalies stop shots and simply toss the ball to the side. Incorporate passing components so this area isn't neglected. A goalie who can make accurate passes to help his team get out of the defensive zone makes life easier on himself because that translates into fewer shots he'll have to face — and more the opposing goalie may see instead.

Being Observant Before the Game

Goalies can learn a lot about an opponent by observing them — before the game begins. At the advanced levels of lacrosse, you want your goalies to spend a little time evaluating the opposition. He can spend a couple of minutes watching the opponent warm-up, where he may notice certain tendencies in how players shoot the ball, or where they aim the majority of their shots. For example, maybe certain attackers always shoot low to the left corner. Having this knowledge could make the difference between making a save and giving up a goal when he is faced defending a shot from this player during the game. You don't want him to spend a lot of time observing, but a few minutes can be useful in succeeding in certain situations. Sending players out onto the field who are confident in their abilities is important, but even more so for your goaltender since she is the last line of defense for preventing opponents from celebrating goals. During your team's pre-game warm-up it's a good idea to hover around the net and sprinkle positive comments toward her about how well she's positioning herself on shots or how sharp her reflexes look today. This can build confidence and fuel top performances.

Molding Well-Rounded Players

Being a lacrosse goalie whom opponents cringe playing against requires being well-rounded in many different aspects of the game. Sure, stopping shots is the top priority for any goalie, but that is only one dimension of the position. Goalies who are excellent passers can spark fast-break attacks that keep the opposition off balance. During your practice drills don't just have your goalies stop shots and simply toss the ball to the side. Incorporate passing components too, so this area of the game isn't neglected. A goalie who can make accurate passes to help his team get out of the defensive zone helps himself because it means fewer shots he'll have to face.

Divulging Tendencies

A lot goes into making a save on a shot: footwork, positioning, hand-eye coordination, and even a little insight from you. At the advanced levels of lacrosse, spend some time evaluating the opposition. While you or an assistant watch their pre-game warm-up, you may notice certain tendencies that your goalie could benefit from knowing. Maybe certain attackers always shoot low to the left corner. This knowledge can make the difference between making a save and giving up a goal if your goalie is faced defending a shot from this player during the game. You don't want to overwhelm the goalie with too much information, but a few tidbits can sometimes be useful.

Index